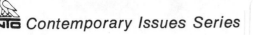 Contemporary Issues Series

D0360631

JUSTICE
RE
W

c overview
e problem
of judicial
reform

by
M. Rohrer

Contributors and Consultants

Credit for this work should be given to Mark Arnold, Bob Baker, and Jack MacMillan of Boston College, Joel Perwin and Laurence Tribe of Harvard University, and William Snyder of the University of Illinois, Chicago Circle.

To Mother and Father.

Contents

Part One   **Introduction to the Jury System**   **1**

1   Trial by Jury   **3**

Part Two   **Deficiencies of the Jury System**   **25**

2   The Role of the Jury   **27**

3   Court Backlogs   **37**

4   Pretrial Publicity   **59**

5   Justice, the Poor, and Minority Groups   **123**

6   Military Justice   **149**

7   Capital Punishment   **167**

Part Three   **Alternatives to the Jury System**   **177**

8   Plea Bargaining   **179**

9   Juvenile Courts   **195**

10   First Amendment Rights   **207**

11   No-Fault Insurance   **245**

12   Arbitration, Mediation, and No-Fault Alternatives   **257**

Part Four   **Assessment**   **267**

13   Retrospect and Prospects   **269**

Notes   **275**

Preface

Law and order remains an issue in this country primarily because all levels of government have failed to make the effort necessary to uncover the real sources of the problem and to provide the resources necessary to solve it. As another election year approaches, and the issue of crime in the streets looms once more on the horizon, it is essential that every attempt be made to present the public with a clear understanding of why the problem exists and to offer some clear solutions which address the true causes. This book is such an effort.

To attempt an analysis of the overall crime problem and the shortcomings in our means of dealing with it is far too broad and complicated a task for a single book. This work will focus primarily on the nation's much maligned court system, which has been accused by some of coddling criminals, releasing them on technicalities and generally treating them too leniently and by others of aiding in the suppression of dissent, of repressing minorities and denying civil liberties. Sadly, both charges bear a great deal of truth. Our courts are overcrowded, understaffed, unable to deal effectively with the mass of cases before them. The need for improvement has grown so severe that many drastic changes are being seriously proposed. Civil liberties may be endangered in some instances, but the problem is so serious that many would be willing to risk the consequences of abridging them still further. Yet, surprisingly enough, new attitudes toward First Amendment rights are emerging from curious sources for various reasons, among them the precarious combination of libertarianism and repression which instantly followed the first publications of the "secret" Pentagon document entitled *History of Decision-Making Process on Vietnam Policy*.

Nevertheless, the single constitutional right most frequently violated is that of trial by jury. In the conflict between law and order and civil libertarianism, there are those on both sides who see reasons for abolishing the tradition of jury trial. Both sides see the overcrowding of courts as a major problem, as it makes the courts less effective in convicting criminals and more prone to sacrificing civil liberties. They in turn view time-consuming jury trials as a primary reason for such delay and overcrowding. Or, they may see the jury system as an unnecessary source of prejudice, or an intolerably expensive legal luxury. There are substantial reasons for all of these beliefs.

The jury system has its defenders, too, and this book will examine their arguments, finding in some instances that the expansion, rather than restriction, of jury trials may be a solution to some problems. In most instances it will be demonstrated that the root of our legal crisis has been simple neglect. The apparent conflict between keeping order in society and protecting the rights of the individual exists only because we insist on keeping our courts in a crippled state, unable to perform both tasks simultaneously. If we would merely devote sufficient resources to upgrading the system we could have courts with the time and ability to deal efficiently with their burdens without having to take shortcuts at the expense of justice and accuracy. Hopefully, this book will demonstrate where and how such efforts are possible. Specifically, it will show not only that there remains a place in our system for the right to trial by a jury of one's peers but also that such a right is essential and, in some instances, should be extended.

Part I provides a history of the jury system, cataloging its precedents in European nations and tracing the origins of our American system.

Part II focuses on the problems that have pervaded the system in the last third of the twentieth century. Chapter 2 considers the reasons why the jury system exists and finds that there are still strong arguments for maintaining it, then provides a detailed description of how the jury trial functions in our legal system.

Of course the fact that the system functions effectively and has certain advantages can justify its use only if those advantages are not outweighed by its deficiencies. Chapter 3 examines the severe impact overcrowding and delay have had throughout our court system and considers the extent to which the jury can be held responsible. It is concluded that the jury has little to do with these problems, and other, more appropriate solutions are proposed.

Chapter 4 examines the dangers involved in pretrial publicity and the influence it may have on a jury's ability to assess with fairness and accuracy a defendant's guilt or innocence. After examining the impact of such publicity in a number of famous cases, the chapter turns to an evaluation of the current means of protecting defendants from such advance treatment by the media. It is suggested that despite some shortcomings, these methods are as effective as any yet proposed.

Chapter 5 provides a detailed analysis of the problems faced by the poor and members of political and racial minorities when they are confronted with our system of justice. Our present legal structure systematically, though often unintentionally, discriminates against the poor and minorities while the public—sometimes out of approval—follows a policy of benign neglect toward their problems.

Chapter 6 considers a more obscure area of our legal system, the code and practice of military justice. Too often that system bears a greater resemblance to the Roman military codes from which it was drawn than to our present-day ideal. Tragically, those who enlist to defend the nation's freedom are required to sacrifice their own liberties to the arbitrary and often unjust whims of their commanders. This chapter examines the entire court-martial system and evaluates the use of the civilian jury in military trials as a possible solution to the injustice now prevalent in such cases.

Chapter 7 describes the most awesome power given to the jury: the power to decide whether a man will live or die. Whether capital punishment is unjustified murder or a necessary deterrent to capital crime is the issue. In fact, the evidence available seems to indicate that capital punishment serves no practical purpose. Thirty states may now be sanctioning the unjustifiable execution of hundreds of men and women.

It thus appears that the modern jury trial faces some severe criticisms, and it may be that it is simply too expensive a luxury to persist in the future. Part III seeks to examine the implications of this conclusion for both criminal and civil courts. While Part II concentrates on some of the deficiencies that have become apparent in the modern jury system and on possible alterations in the powers of the jury, Part III will consider overall structural alterations in the system.

The structural changes proposed for criminal courts involve using the jury in types of cases other than those they now hear. Chapters 8 and 9 will consider the possibility of using jury trials as alternatives to plea-bargaining practices in criminal courts and "judicial discretion" in juvenile courts. Holding jury trials in both of these categories may be the only feasible alternative to these injustices.

Chapter 10 considers civil liberties and First Amendment rights and proposes that the interpretation of free speech be significantly broadened. It suggests a new standard upon which the jury should base its findings of guilt or innocence. The issue of whether a bench trial is a better alternative in such cases is also discussed. Finally a general theory of relevant issues arising from free-speech conflicts is examined.

Chapters 11 and 12 deal with automobile insurance cases, selected because they constitute the vast majority of civil cases and their conclusions are generally valid with respect to other civil disputes. Two alternatives to jury trial in these cases are discussed: no-fault insurance and arbitration and mediation by independent examiners. These cases, like all others, are decided in the hopelessly overcrowded civil courts. The proposed alternatives may be essential for the sake of justice yet at the same time may be impossible to implement because of the lack of court space. As in the previous chapters, any discussion of alternate systems to the jury must be considered in the context of this problem.

Part IV concludes the book by considering the federal government's increasing attempts to punish wrongdoers and arbitrate private disputes. This power to intervene in the affairs of men, and especially to determine whether they shall live or die, is one which must be carefully controlled. In our representative system of government a watchful citizenry, fully informed of how and why this power is used and able to check its implementation when necessary, is absolutely essential.

The law exists to provide "liberty and justice for all." It is critical that we keep this fact in mind: the cry for law and order must never be allowed to obscure the priority of justice. We should not take the simplistic view of the problem and permit our desire for order to sanction injustice. But we have reversed our priorities, and there is a substantial danger that we will continue to do so.

This book, then, attempts to provide the facts necessary to see through political rhetoric and to understand our current legal crisis.

D. M. R.
Boston, Mass.
July 5, 1971

Introduction

[T]he trial by jury ever has been, and I trust ever will be, looked upon as the glory of the English law. And if it has so great an advantage over others in regulating civil property, much must that advantage be heightened when it is applied to criminal cases! . . .

[I]t is the most transcendent privilege which any subject can enjoy, or wish for, that he cannot be affected either in his property, his liberty, or his person, but by the unanimous consent of twelve of his neighbors and equals.

Blackstone, *Commentaries*, Vol. III, p. 379.

The right to trial by jury . . . may have value and importance. Even so, [it is] not of the very essence of a scheme of ordered liberty. To abolish [it] is not to violate a "principle of justice so rooted in the traditions and conscience of our people as to be ranked as fundamental." . . . Few would be so narrow or provincial as to maintain that a fair and enlightened system of justice would be impossible without [it].

J. Cardozo, *Palko* v. *Connecticut*, 302 U.S. 319, 325.

The merits of the jury system have been the subject of debate ever since the inception of that institution. Not only are scholars and laymen alike far from unanimous in agreeing that trial by jury is the *sine qua non* of a fair and accurate judicial process; there are those who seriously doubt that the system is worthwhile at all. Nevertheless the jury system is deeply imbedded in our legal tradition. The right to trial by jury in criminal cases and suits at common law tried in the federal courts is guaranteed by the Sixth and Seventh Amendments to the Constitution. And the Supreme Court has held that the due process clause of the Fourteenth Amendment requires the state courts to afford trial by jury in serious criminal cases. Because the jury system is sustained by both tradition and constitutional imperative, its vitality as an institution seems assured. Lingering doubts and growing criticism notwithstanding, it is most likely that the jury system will be with us for a long time to come.

Despite the permanence of the jury system, debate as to its merits cannot be considered merely academic. There may be substantial opportunity for reform within the system to improve its operation. In addition, there are numerous aspects of the judicial process in which the role of the jury is uncertain. Its efficacy in deciding so-called "political" cases and cases involving freedom of speech or the press has been widely discussed. There have been proposals to extend the right of jury trial to military courts-martial and to juvenile court proceedings. The role of the jury in sentencing, especially in capital cases, has also been the subject of controversy. It would be useful to approach such issues not with an irrefutable presumption that trial by jury is always good and should be extended wherever possible, but with a healthy skepticism as to whether the lay jury is the panacea it is often touted to be.

The jury system was originally designed to protect citizens from the application of harsh laws by judges controlled by an oppressive government. In its early days this system acquired an impressive record of providing such protection. In England, when poaching and petty larceny were punishable by death, juries refused to convict. And witchcraft trials in America ended when juries would no longer pass sentence. That one cannot be punished but by a jury of his peers has thus long been thought to to be an important safeguard of individual liberty.

There are other ways in which the jury system contributes to the democratic form of government. Service on a jury provides a citizen with an opportunity to participate in government, to witness its operation first-hand. The jury is also a guarantor of integrity in the judicial branch. Presumably it would be more difficult to bribe or corrupt twelve jurors than a single, permanent judge.

Whether the jury's significance as a guardian of liberty and a cog in the wheel of democracy is as great today as it once was is at least open to question. The experience of jury duty may generate more disenchantment than civic pride, and participation in government does not achieve its purpose if it leaves a sour taste in the mouth of the participant. Those called for jury duty usually must serve a month, with consequent inconvenience and loss of wages which are rarely offset by the meager salary paid to jurors. The experience itself can be most unpleasant. Much of one's time is spent in uncomfortable quarters waiting to be selected, and many persons called for jury duty are never chosen to actually sit on a jury. When one is selected for a jury, the chances of the case being even interesting are not high. And jurors can come away with a terrible sense of frustration after having listened attentively to a long case, looking forward to discharging their responsibility, only to have the judge direct a verdict at the close of the evidence, or, worse yet, enter judgment notwithstanding the verdict after the jury has deliberated and reached agreement. Not surprisingly, people exposed to the experience of serving on a jury feel more that their time has been wasted than that they have performed an important civic duty.

The importance of a jury system as a bulwark against corruption is also doubtful. There is no way of determining the extent of bribery of judges, although what indicators there are do not suggest that it is widespread. The theory that it is harder to "reach" twelve jurors than one judge is sound, but where unanimity is required, it is necessary to find only one corruptible juror in twelve in order to prevent a conviction in a criminal case or the imposition of liability in a civil action.

Most importantly, the role of the jury as a safeguard against oppressive government has lost much of its significance, at least in this country. Where there is representative government, with myriad protections built into it, the danger of oppression is not nearly so grave as it once was. Moreover, the judiciary in the United States has become largely independent of the other branches of government, particularly at the federal level, and has on many occasions stood in the way of government encroachment on individual rights. And if there is a threat today of government oppression, it is not of such a character that juries are likely to stand in its way. There are those who believe that the government has embarked on a campaign to suppress certain dissident groups. Assuming this to be true, it is doubtful that the typical jury would provide resistance to such suppression. Juries are drawn from the masses, the great majority of whom do not identify or even sympathize with Black Panthers or Weathermen. More often than not the cries of "political trial" and "oppression" can be expected to fall on deaf ears in the jury box.

An additional reason why the jury is not an effective deterrent to unfair prosecution or to unreasonable imposition of liability is that jurors are continually told that their function is to find the facts and not to act as legislators. When initially sworn in, each juror takes an oath to follow the law as it is given to him by the court. The judge instructs the jurors that it is not their function to ignore the law, or to disregard laws they do not like. If they want the laws changed they must do it through their legislative representatives; if a law is thought to be unconstitutional, an aggrieved party may seek to have it overturned by a reviewing court. Similar instructions are given at the close of a case before the jury begins its deliberations, and the jurors are again reminded of their oaths to follow the law. In fact, there is no effective way to enforce the jury's duty to follow the law. A verdict will be upset only by some tangible phenomenon, such as bribery or other improper communication with a juror. The mental processes of the jurors will not be looked into, even if a juror subsequently admits that he and his fellow jurors had decided to ignore all or part of the court's instructions. Jurors do not know this, however, and are usually impressed with their oaths and their obligation to follow the law according to the court's prescriptions. Thus, whereas it is practically possible for a jury to rise up and refuse to convict when it believes a law is unjust or a prosecution unfair, this rarely happens anymore.

While the advantages of the jury system have diminished over time, the disadvantages have become increasingly acute. When juries were composed of persons who had witnessed the event from which a controversy arose, or who were familiar with the facts surrounding a case, they were probably in the best position to resolve the matter at issue. But in the vast majority of trials today, juries begin wholly ignorant of the cases they hear; in those instances where the dispute or offense has been publicized, jurors are instructed to consider only the evidence presented in court. Thus the sole function of the jury is to hear and evaluate evidence, and to reach a verdict by resolving disputed facts and applying the law as it is given to them by the court.

It is relevant to ask whether lay juries are competent to perform that function. There was a time when jury trials were relatively simple. Determining whether a defendant has committed a theft, or whether a party is in breach of a contract, would not be difficult if the trial were brief and the evidence not complicated. There continue to be many simple cases tried before juries, but there are also many which are extremely complex and which inevitably baffle a jury of laymen.

The first problem is understanding the testimony. In cases involving securities transactions, patent disputes, medical malpractice, and so on, the lawyers and witnesses may use terminology that is beyond the comprehension of the jurors. Witnesses can be asked to explain the meanings of unfamiliar terms, of course, but there remains a very real risk that some or all of the jurors will fail to grasp the explanations at all, or will not remember them later. Maps, charts, and diagrams are sometimes shown to the jury which could be understood only after careful study by an expert in the particular field. After a witness has testified concerning such exhibits, they disappear until the jury retires to deliberate, at which time the jurors are supposed to remember what the exhibits were intended to prove.

Added to the problem of understanding the evidence is the difficulty of remembering it. Although some trials last only a few days, it is not uncommon for others to last two or three weeks, or even months. For a person unequipped by training or experience, remembering even uncomplicated evidence is virtually impossible. This would be true even if the evidence were presented in a strictly logical order, with each issue treated in its entirety one at a time. Such is usually not the case, however, since each witness may have testimony pertinent to a number of issues, all of which will be taken before the next witness is called. Some courts permit jurors to take notes during a trial. Note-taking is a partial solution to the memory problem, but its use is limited since most jurors are not likely to be skilled note-takers; it is often difficult for one to read back one's notes long after they were made. Moreover, there is always a risk that testimony will be missed while a note of the immediately preceding testimony is being made.

The absurdity of expecting a jury to remember the evidence in a long and complex trial is particularly apparent when contrasted with the procedure a judge may follow if a case is tried without a jury. If the judge is unable to render a verdict after the lawyers have made their final arguments, he may take the case under advisement and direct the parties to file post-trial briefs. He can then sift through the issues, refer to a transcript of the testimony when necessary, check legal authorities applicable to each issue, and generally deliberate free from the time pressures inherently felt by a sequestered jury (and juries are always sequestered during their deliberations).

In addition to finding the facts, juries must apply the law to the facts in order to reach a verdict. To do this correctly they must understand the instructions given them by the court. Sometimes these instructions would be incomprehensible even to an attorney hearing them delivered orally for the first time. Courts often use painstakingly precise legal terminology in phrasing their instructions in order to avoid committing any error that would be reversible on appeal. In using legal terminology, however, the judge virtually assures that the jury will not know what he is talking about. Using layman's language would help but not totally cure the problem. It is often necessary to make subtle distinctions among legal concepts, or to explain that certain evidence is to be considered with respect to only one specified issue or to only one of many defendants. Understanding such subtleties requires a sophistication that one not educated in the law cannot possibly be expected to have.

Competent evaluation of evidence and correct application of the law require more than just understanding and recall; they also require an ability to set aside one's personal biases and analyze a case objectively. While no one is perfect in this regard, an experienced judge is surely less impressionable and sympathetic than a jury is likely to be. Jurors commonly decide cases not on their merits but on the basis of their reactions to the lawyers for each side. A charismatic and impressive lawyer can be much more valuable in a jury trial than a meritorious presentation of the case. Much as they try to obey precautionary instructions, juries find it difficult not to be influenced by factors which under the law they are required to overlook. For example, if an objection to certain testimony is sustained by the court, the jury is told to disregard it. Although they may conscientiously try to do so, jurors cannot eliminate such information from their minds if it appears to have some bearing on the case. This is especially true if the jury does not understand the basis for the court's ruling. Such rulings are not usually explained to the jury, and it may sympathize with one side if the opposition continually objects to questions and the objections are sustained.

Juries also tend to bring to the jury box natural prejudices against certain kinds of parties. Large corporations, insurance companies, and wealthy defendants can expect little sympathy from a jury. Another natural target is the United States Government; little wonder, then, that the Federal Tort Claims Act, by which Congress has consented to suits against the United States, expressly provides that trials in such cases shall *not* be by jury.

If juries are so incompetent to evaluate evidence and apply the law, it is puzzling that the jury system has survived as long as it has. One reason is that most of the objections to it are based on conjecture. Speculation will not compel change so readily as actual knowledge, and we have no way of knowing with any degree of certainty whether or not the jury system functions well. In the first place, there is no objective standard by which jury verdicts can be judged. The reason why trials are held at all is that there is no definite independent means for determining which side is right or wrong. Secondly, there has been relatively little exposure of what actually occurs in the jury room, let alone what goes on in the mind of each individual juror as he listens to the evidence or participates in deliberations. On one occasion a project was undertaken secretly to observe jury deliberations for study purposes; this violation of the sanctity of jury privacy generated such a wave of indignant protest that it has not been repeated.

Now and then interviews with jurors reveal interesting accounts of how verdicts were reached. There are reported instances of verdicts reached by the flip of a coin, or the drawing of ballots out of a hat. Apparently there have been cases in which two criminal defendants were tried together on the same evidence, and the juries resolved disagreement over their guilt or innocence by compromise—one defendant was found guilty and the other not guilty. Many times juries have calculated the amount of damages to be awarded in a civil suit by having each juror write down an amount he believed to be appropriate and then taking an average. Such instances are isolated; yet what we do know about the competence of jurors and the difficulty of the task they face makes it reasonable to assume that a disturbingly large portion of cases are decided irrationally. If the jury system is not to be replaced, it may at least be possible to institute some reforms which would improve its operation.

One obvious approach would be to alter the selection process in order to upgrade the average intelligence of jurors. It is common practice to exempt from jury duty professional people, such as doctors, lawyers, clergymen, executives, and teachers. Excluding people with presumably above-average intelligence necessarily limits the intellectual makeup of juries. However, there are sound reasons why such persons are exempted from jury duty: it is generally felt that their service to the community is too important to be sacrificed for this purpose. Lawyers are exempt because of the risk that they would substitute their own views of the law for those of the judges. And it may be argued that persons with professional stature might have undue influence on other jurors. It has also been a practice in widely publicized cases to exclude from juries those who have become familiar with the facts and the parties by reading about them in the newspapers. Of course, limiting the jury makeup in such a case to those who have not been exposed to news coverage means that jurors are selected by the lowest common denominator.

It would be possible to impose certain standards, such as minimum educational achievement. But the drawback of imposing relatively high standards is that juries will not be representative of the community. The dilemma of intelligence versus representativeness is evident in the recommendation of the Judicial Conference of the United States (26 F.R.D. 421):

> In order that . . . jurors . . . may be truly representative of the community, the sources from which they are selected should include all economic and social groups of the community. The jury list should represent as high a degree of intelligence, morality, integrity, and common sense as possible.

Representativeness may be irrelevant to a jury's functions of finding facts and applying the law, except in cases that require application of a community standard, such as "reasonable care" in a negligence action, or "acceptable limits of candor" in an obscenity prosecution. Nevertheless, the notion that a jury must be composed of one's peers rather than of an intellectual elite persists, and it effectively limits the possibility of significantly raising the average intelligence level of juries.

There may be means of improving the administration of the jury system in order to increase the probability of rational verdicts. Note-taking by jurors has already been mentioned. Consideration should also be given to encouraging jurors to speak up during the course of a trial when something is said that they do not understand. Such questions could be asked during the testimony of a witness, the argument of counsel, or the court's charge to the jury.

Another device which is provided for by law but which is not used extensively in many courts is the special verdict. Under the more common general verdict system the jury hears the evidence, is instructed on the law, and returns a verdict of guilty or not guilty, liable or not liable. With the special verdict procedure the court submits to the jury a list of specific factual questions which the jury must answer. Taking the answers as findings of fact, the court then applies the law and enters judgment accordingly. The most obvious advantage of the special verdict is that it is possible to know what the jury has done. There may be many separate factual issues in a case, with distinct legal principles to be applied to each. With a general verdict it is not known how the jury decided each factual issue, or whether it even considered all of them; nor can it be determined how the jury applied the law to each issue. The special verdict is therefore not only revealing; it also compels the jury to focus on all the relevant aspects and disregard irrelevant ones. Finally, the special verdict largely eliminates the need for complicated instructions on the law. Some instruction does remain necessary, but complex legal principles may be omitted because it is the judge who applies the law to the jury's findings of fact.

In evaluating the jury system and possible ways of changing it, one should bear in mind that alternative systems are subject to some of the same criticisms, and perhaps some additional ones. It should not be inferred from what has been said that anything would be better than trial by jury, or that if it is retained the jury system must be subjected to substantial revision. The point is simply that the jury system should not unthinkingly be accepted as an institution essential to the fair administration of justice. Nothing could more seriously impair progressive improvement in our judicial system than to permit any institution to be enshrined by tradition. Surely the merits and faults of the jury system should be carefully studied before it is extended into areas where it is not now prevalent, such as the military or the juvenile courts. In other words, before one concludes that a given rule or procedure is bad merely because it precludes or undermines trial by jury, one should ponder the question of whether the jury system itself is really such a good thing.

William E. Snyder
Chicago, Illinois

I Introduction to the Jury System

1 Trial by Jury

One day long ago, when the earth raged with the anomie of infancy, a human being, living perhaps in an apelike body but with the soul and brain of man, studied the chaos around him and perceived that out of this he could make order. It was at this instant that justice was born, for justice is little more than one's own scheme of order, one's own settlement of conflict, and at this instant as well, more than any other in history, the appendages and trappings of justice were born.

It is but a small leap from the perception that one can impose a solution for conflict to the realization that similar solutions can be consistently imposed upon similar conflicts. It is the purpose of law, in its fullest and crudest province, to construct and apply consistent solutions to problems. It hardly matters, in this sense, whether a solution employs courtroom adjudication, or trial by combat, or oaths to God, or terrifying ordeals; each method is law, each is someone's justice.

From the construction of a legal system which seeks to generalize solutions to problems comes the inevitable necessity to identify the nature of the conflicts to be resolved, to determine precisely what happened, in order to apportion losses and responsibilities fairly. It is to the jury that we assign this task. Thus, when the first apelike creature decided to fashion order from chaos, he signaled the inexorable progress which created the jury system well over a million years later. Since that time, to isolate the dimensions and highlights of that progress has been the task of many treatises, as it is of this chapter.

In the course of its development the jury has been four things. In its most primitive and simple state, the jury consisted simply of a class or body of persons, indefinite in number and unsworn but empowered to decide, either upon personal knowledge or upon the "evidence" laid before them, the outcome of the trial—to correlate the undefined mixture of the facts of a controversy with the law to be applied to them. This amorphous body developed into a selected group of persons, limited in number and obliged by oath, who determined facts and the law on their personal knowledge alone. Later, it developed into a mixed functionary body, and decided partly on personal knowledge and partly on the evidence laid before it, the facts in a controversy. The jury may be defined as consisting of a specified number of individuals selected from the community and sworn to decide any disputed matter of fact by judging evidence lawfully submitted to them. This body is quite distinct from the court.1

This brief definition of the modern jury is vitally important in considering its development. The twelve individuals are selected from the body of the community; they are sworn; they decide only matters of fact; they judge the evidence submitted to them. And they are quite distinct from the court.

We shall begin our search for the origin and development of the jury system with the classical systems of Greece and Rome; then we shall consider the ancient Germanic tribes, the early Britons and Anglo-Saxons, Scandinavian practices, the Norman influence, the Plantagenet legal "explosion," and finally the American development. Somewhere in these two thousand years the modern jury system was born, molded, and formed.

THE GREEK AND THE ROMAN SYSTEMS

The ancient Greek states were governed as political communities and their legal and political systems were often constructed to identify the "sense" of the community as a whole. In Attica, and later under the hegemony of Athens, there developed legal tribunals known as *dikasts*. Six thousand citizens over thirty years of age were annually selected by lot from the entire community, six hundred from each of the ten tribes. Five thousand of these citizens were arranged in ten panels, or *decuries* of five hundred each. The remaining one thousand were held in reserve to fill vacancies created by death or absences. All six thousand took a prescribed oath.2

Not only was the Greek *dikast* designed to generate a general sense, it tried to confront a problem of legal adjudication which exists even today, the problem of a jury's susceptibility to corruption and intimidation. The *dikasteries*, under the system provided by Pericles (467-428 B.C.), were constructed to make corruption impossible. *Decuries* were assigned by lot to cases to be tried, and only just before the trials began. This practice, along with the massive number of people trying a case and a system of secret suffrage, made the trial a solemn process and immune to influence.3

The *dikastery* was the "first institution known to history which presents characteristic features of jury trial."4 Chosen from the community at large, and including the wealthy as well as the poor and illiterate, it adjudicated the cases in dispute. But in function, as well as numbers, the *dikasts* were far from the juries we know today. In Athens, the *dikasts* judged the laws as well as the facts.

Because the law-fact dichotomy is so crucial in the development of juries, we will define it more specifically. Law, in its widest sense, is a rule of action; technically, it is "a general rule of human action, taking cognizance only of external acts, enforced by a determinate human authority paramount within a state."5 A fact is anything that has been done, or something that comes to pass, an act, a deed, an effect produced or achieved, an event. The sole function of the modern jury is to determine fact, while the court applies the technical rules of law to the facts as established.6

In ancient Greece it was relatively simple for one body to apply both law and fact because the laws were not numerous and they were couched in succinct and familiar terms. In large measure, a finding of fact *was* the law, while today the application of complex legal principles may well relieve guilt or liability which the facts alone would mandate. For example, a man who clearly libels another according to the facts may be privileged to do so in a number of ways. These privileges are *legal* constructs, and are applied despite the *fact* that a libel has been committed.

In Athens there were very few such legal constructs. Indeed, it was the increased complexity and attending professionalization of the legal system that demanded a structural separation of fact from law. The *dikasts*, then, were not juries in that they applied both the law and fact. If anything, they were the court itself, the entire legal entity, subject only to the slight and general direction of the presiding magistrate and under no legal obligation to follow any instruction. They did, however, embody a crucial element of the modern jury: they were not professionals of the court who served justice as a lifetime occupation. They sat for one year only and were chosen from the community as a whole by lot. In this respect, they strikingly foreshadowed the juries of today.

The development of the Roman *judex*, which has been translated to mean both "judge" and "juryman" (neither of which accurately reflects its meaning), took place in three stages. The first began with the adoption of the Twelve Tables, around 450 B.C., and ended with the passage of the *leges Juliae*, around 30 B.C., which were enforced under Julius as well as Augustus Caesar.7 In Rome, the administration of justice between man and man was an attribute of sovereignty—that is, a matter for governmental adjudication, not popular decision—and hence was exercised originally by the kings and then by the consuls, who only later delegated authority to the *praetors*.8 The first stage of development also involved the *actio sacramenti*, which was a mock combat or feigned quarrel between the parties to an action. It was followed by the intervention of a magistrate, who referred the disputed question to a private person, called the *judex* or *arbitrator*, who simply decided which litigant was correct in his claim. The *actio*, then, was simply a means by which the state could force disputants to submit their controversy to arbitration.

The second stage began with the adoption of the formulary system, which replaced the symbolic frictions employed in the *actio*. The *formula* was a legal document, drawn up by the *praetor* after hearing the claims of both parties and containing instructions to the *judex* on the points at issue and the mode of deciding the case according to the facts which should be proved. Thus there was a definite and structural separation of law from fact in Roman courts. Both procedures were performed by the magistrate and were called the *in jure* proceeding (that which comes before judgment). Thus the *in jure* proceeding became a series of directions founded upon the legal aspects of the case. The *in judicio* (as to the verdict) proceeding, performed by the *judex*, became a careful investigation of the facts of the case. In this way the formulary system "brought into prominence one of the most essential features of the jury system."9

The formulary system flourished, as did the essentially democratic institutions of the republican era. With the decay of the republic in A.D. 300 and the development of imperialism, the judicial arm of government was radically altered. It was consonant with republicanism that private, nonprofessional citizens shared in the administration of justice, but the revolution of Diocletian and Constantine resulted in bringing the administration of justice entirely under the control of the emperor and his officers. The entire system of *jus* and *judicium* was overthrown. The new procedures not only grew out of the autocractic tendency of the new government but were in part rendered necessary by the decay of public spirit among the citizens, who avoided all public duties.10

In the old system, the magistrate frequently assumed entire control of a case, and hence he dispensed with the services of the *judex*. Diocletian abolished the formulary system and ordered the exclusive use of the magistrate for proceedings *in jus* and *in jure*.

For over three hundred years, however, the *judex* proceeding institutionalized many elements that have been incorporated in modern juries. The *judex* was a private citizen, selected for a specific case, who determined the facts of a controversy and applied them to the legal principles described by the magistrate (the arm of the court). The system was strikingly similar to the definition of the modern jury with which we began.

The anology between our present-day jurors and the *judices* in criminal case is in some ways even stronger than in the civil controversies in which the *judex* operated. In criminal trials it was the province of the *judices* to determine guilt and innocence. They were also empowered to exercise mercy, as a prerogative, just as our juries may commend a defendant they have tried and convicted to the mercy of the court.

The custom of creating a special commission to try each criminal case led to the organization of several permanent tribunals (*questions perpetuae*), each of which had jurisdiction over certain classes of crimes. Every criminal trial was thus conducted before a magistrate and a body of *judices*, in one trial. It was the duty of the magistrate to conduct the trial according to the law which applied to the case. It was the duty of the jurors, who were private citizens selected for the occasion, to decide upon the guilt or innocence of the accused, according to the evidence.[11] Thus criminal proceedings under the republic were essentially the same as they are today.

The Roman institution during the republic was similar to the Greek in the selection of its members, their standing and compensation, but differed from it in the full separation of law from fact, in having a dual process for such determination (which differs from the modern process as well), and in the fact that jurors had no direct influence on the judgment (*sententia*); that is, they did not pronounce sentence or assess damages.[12]

One might wonder why the search for the jury does not end at Rome, where all roads seem to lead. The reason is that the remarkably modern *judex* procedure was formally abolished by the edict of Emperor Constantine in A.D. 352, and the absolute power of the magistrate was eventually incorporated into the final codification of Roman law, the Justinian Code (A.D. 533).

It is the Justinian Code which has descended to us as the essential feature or body of Roman jurisprudence. Under it, the use of the *judex* and the separation of law from fact disappeared in

European states. But it reappeared centuries later, in the process by which the English jury system was reaching its modern form. It is in that process, not the abortive Roman experience, that we must find the origins of the modern jury.13

ANCIENT GERMAN TRIBUNALS

The regression in the sophistication of the legal and political institutions on the European continent which accompanied the decline of the Greek and Roman systems was manifestly evident in the seventh century A.D. In Germany, the Teutonic polity was divided into districts called *marken*, several of which comprised a *gau*. At the head of each *gau* was a teritorial lord who led its armies into battle and sat as president of the courts of justice within his jurisdiction. But as the increasing number and frequency of the tribunals made it impossible for the lord (*suzerain*) to attend all of them in person, presidents were appointed to the various tribunals, first by the community at large and later by the king.14

Each *gau* had regular meetings of all the freemen of the district at which judicial business was considered, in addition to meetings that were summoned when there was special business to be transacted. The president of these assemblies had no voice in their decisions; his duties were ministerial. The court itself, then, originally consisted of all the freemen of the community, and later of a hundred companions of the commons assigned to the president, and still later of fixed numbers of freemen.15 But the central principle of this primitive civil polity was that all private controversies were committed to the collective freemen. This, clearly a system of self-government, was later adopted and developed by the Saxons in England. The system strongly resembled the Greek *dikasts*.

The members of the court had the right to determine all questions of law and fact, and in the early ages they did so. But as the laws became more technical and the transactions more complex, the *sachibarone* were appointed to the court as legal advisers. And with the appointment of the *scabini*, which shall be explained below in greater detail, the practice died out.

As the necessity for an increasing number of meetings became apparent, the use of a large number of freemen on the court became cumbersome and impractical. A new practice was therefore adopted in which the president appointed a specific number to the court, usually seven.16 These, the early Germanic courts (*Rachinburgen*),17 consisting of seven freemen, met in private away from the presiding officer and made their verdict upon consideration of law and fact.

Later, around the time of Charlemagne, judges or *scabini* were appointed to the courts and sat with the freemen as joint members of the court.18 (*Scibinus* is derived by Grimm from *scapan*, "to order or decree.") The *scabini* were chosen by the president with the consent of the people generally, and the number required to form a court was seven, but on solemn and important occasions the number was increased to twelve.19 The appearance of the freemen was voluntary after the introduction of the *scabini*, who gradually defined the court system, especially when they sat as twelve. They greatly resembled the modern jury, but with important distinctions.

The *scabini* were both court and jury. They determined the question of guilt or innocence, or whatever fact might be in dispute, but they also applied the legal doctrine and (something the Roman *judex* did not do) awarded and pronounced the judgment.20 In fact, the early German tribunals were often legislative as well as judicial bodies since the annual meetings were convened for legislative purposes and the state of the law in ancient Germany was extremely primitive. Thus each case was in a sense an occasion for the writing as well as the application of law; hence the Teutonic tribunals were much more like courts than juries.21

The method of proving facts in the German tribunals also was significantly different from that used in modern jury trials. In the early Anglo-Saxon system witnesses were called to speak on matters within their special knowledge, but among the ancient Germans the credibility of all competent (free) witnesses was equal. Because their testimony was deemed of equal weight, conflicting testimony might mean almost nothing.

To some extent, however, the German courts arrived at the truth by *compurgation*, which was the only method used in the early Anglo-Saxon courts. *Compurgation* will be described at more length when that system is considered, but, briefly, it was merely the assertion by a freeman, under oath, of his belief in the credibility of one of the parties. Hence the party that assembled the greater number of *compurgators* won the controversy. Thus, in failing to examine the credibility of witnesses who testified to facts, as well as in the use of *compurgators*, the German courts differed radically from modern jury practices of establishing facts.22

Finally, like the Anglo-Saxon courts, the German tribunals allowed the party against whom a judgment had been delivered to undergo the ordeal, which allowed a chance of escape. The ordeal will be described in detail when the Anglo-Saxon courts are considered.23

In three ways, then, the Teutonic tribunals differed substantially from modern juries: they considered questions of both law and fact; they employed primitive methods of proof; and they allowed the ordeal after judgment. Not only are these methods radically different from those of modern juries, they evidence a significant regression from the practices outlined under the Roman *judex* procedure. It seems clear that the Roman system had no influence on the early European tribunals, and yet it was from the Teutonic system, or its near equivalent in England, that the modern jury evolved.

The Teutonic tribunals, employed by the common ancestors of both the English and the Germans and initially characterized by *triers* selected from the community at large, flourished on English soil and eventually developed into the modern jury. Yet in Germany, and on the Continent in general, the elements of the jury fell into disuse so that the jury system never developed. The reason for this is found in two factors. The first is the gradual exclusion on the Continent of the freemen in favor of the official *scabini*, who were the sole judges of law and fact. They absorbed all the judicial functions of the court, and hence

> There was no room for another body distinct from them, whose office should be conclusively to determine questions of fact for them. And when the principle was once established of thus making the court consist entirely of a limited number of duly qualified judges, the transition . . . to single judges . . . who decided without the intervention of a jury, was a natural and almost necessary consequence.24

This process did not take place in England, perhaps because of the second factor, the Norman invasion, which brought a new and foreign influence. Before we consider the Norman influence, however, we must examine the institutions which existed in England before the invasion—those of the early Britons, those of the Anglo-Saxons, and those of the last migrants to England before the Norman invasion, the Danes.

INSTITUTIONS OF THE BRITONS AND ANGLO-SAXONS

Some of the first inhabitants of Britain were members of a Gallic or Celtic race which settled the island from the Continent. The southeast sections had already begun the creation of a civil polity at the time of Julius Caesar. The Druids, the priests of this civilization, also performed the duties of secular judges, and their influence was so deeply rooted that the Romans found it impossible to substitute their own laws for the druidical system until they resorted to stringent penal enactments.25

Caesar first invaded the island in 55 B.C., after which there were periodic military expeditions, and there is some question how much of the Roman legal institutions was imposed on the conquered Britons. It was the Roman practice to introduce the forms and provisions of its own law into every conquered province so that they might be more effectively bound to the empire. It seems at least possible, however, that while the Romans may have imposed some features of their system, the intransigence of the Britons and their priests may have precluded the self-government of the *judex* system, which was more appropriate to the native republicanism of Rome than to the administration of a rebellious province.

In any event, the centuries of Roman control of Britain witnessed the decay and near dissolution of the Roman Empire, and thus the time came when Rome could no longer spare army contingents for distant Britain. The last Roman legion was withdrawn in 448, despite the entreaties of the inhabitants, who had been safe under Roman rule but now faced eminent onslaughts from the barbarian Picts and Scots in the west and north.26

The Britons, "a people so long disused to arms [that they] had not acquired any union among themselves,"27 had little chance against the Picts and Scots, and thus turned to the Continent and the aid of Germanic tribes, the Angles and the Saxons. But the Germanic allies sought the island for themselves, and with their superior strength and experience, along with reinforcements from the Continent, routed the Britons and killed all but a few, who escaped to Wales. "[Thus] was established, after a violent conquest of near a hundred and fifty years, the Heptarchy, or seven Saxon Kingdoms in Britain; and the whole southern part of the island, except Wales and Cornwall, had totally changed its inhabitants, language, customs, and political institutions. . . . The fierce conquerors . . . threw everything back into ancient barbary."28

To the extent, then, that the Romans had established the *judex* procedure on the island, this legacy was obliterated by the Saxons (as the invaders came to be called). It is hardly surprising that this was also the fate of the trial by jury process; something so new and civilized could not have become established under the barbaric, uncivilized Saxons.29

For almost four hundred years the seven Anglo-Saxon kingdoms waged uninterrupted warfare and slaughter. Wessex finally gained supremacy over the others, and in 827 King Egbert became the acknowledged head of the heptarchy, at which point the history of England properly begins.30 In the four centuries of war, civilization in Britain did not advance, nor was its unity under Egbert sufficient to induce advancement, for the Anglo-Saxon unity was constantly threatened by the Danes, who "committed the most barbarous ravages upon them, and at last reduced them to grievous servitude."[31] As is evident from their bellicose history, the Anglo-Saxons were unable to advance the status of legal institutions, and their legal system was an outgrowth of their "national" character.

> They were in general a rude, uncultivated people, ignorant of letters, unskilled in mechanical arts, untamed to submission under law and government, addicted to intemperance, riot, and disorder. Their best quality was military courage, which yet was not supported by discipline or conduct. Their want of fidelity to the prince, or to any trust reposed on them, appears strongly in the history of their later period, and their want of humanity in all their history. Even the Norman historians, notwithstanding the low state of the arts in their own country, speak of them as barbarians.[32]

King Alfred, who headed the Saxon kingdom in 871, restored peace, settled with or expelled the Danes, and turned to the administration of justice and education. He divided all of England into counties, the counties into hundreds, and the hundreds into tithings—political subdivision on which a court system could be imposed. Alfred, and King Ethelbert before him (568-616), institutionalized two rather anomalous legal values which seem to have been borrowed from the Continent.[33]

Ethelbert introduced the *wergild*, which was simply a sum of money paid for personal injury done to another. The object of the system was to prevent the "justice of revenge" and check the right of feud, which were cherished among the Teutonic nations as inalienable rights. When a member of a family was slain, his relatives were obliged to avenge his death, creating a state of feud between two families. Ethelbert declared that the grieved family should be content with the payment of money, and later Alfred imposed severe punishments on those who took revenge.[34] It was a peculiarly humane enactment in a barbarous time.

Alfred introduced the *fridborh*, which became the judicial unit immediately below the tithing. The *fridborh* was a unit of ten neighboring householders who were responsible for one another and over whom the *headbourg*, or tithingman, presided. *Fridborh* itself came to mean a pledge or guarantee of peace, and every man was punished as an outlaw who did not register himself in a tithing to be organized into a *fridborh*. By this institution every man was obliged, for his own interest, to keep a watchful eye on the conduct of his neighbors. If a crime was committed by any member of the body, the others were to arrest him and bring him to justice. If they thought him innocent, they were to clear him by their oaths. If he was convicted and sentenced, they were to pay the *wergild*. And if he fled, they were to pay a penalty proportionate to the offense. On the other hand, if any member of the group was wronged, all received a share in the compensation.35

The judicial units of the country were the *fridborh*, the tithing, the *werborhe* (community court), the hundred, the *scir-gemot* (the shire or county), and the king. The most courtlike judicial institution was the hundred, which consisted of ten tithings, or a hundred families. The court of the hundred met at least every month and had both criminal and civil jurisdiction. It was presided over by a magistrate, and in form resembled the jury of today. Twelve freeholders were chosen who, having sworn to administer impartially, examined the cases submitted. But the practices and procedures this body was compelled to follow were distinctly unmodern, and suggest more about the Saxon character than the humanistic *wergild* and *fridborh*.

The twelve freemen who attended the hundred, county, and manorial courts (whose number was originally unlimited) varied with availability and custom. Called *sectores*, and later *pares*, they performed the judicial duties of the courts according to the following practices and procedures.

The primary method of proof originally utilized in civil trials was the *secta*, a set of witnesses who had seen the transaction in question or had personal knowledge of the dispute and testified to the truth of the plaintiff's case. The defendant's response was to rebut the presumption thus created by vouching a larger number of witnesses for his own position. At a later period, this procedure was replaced by the appointment of sworn officials in each district whose duty was to witness bargains and sales, which comprised the subject matter of the bulk of civil controversies. The equivalent of the modern notary public, they were not subject to cross examination, and their oath was decisive in case of dispute.36 The use of sworn witnesses was appropriate to their simple society, in which all events of joy and sorrow—births, deaths, marriages, and various transactions—were conducted publicly.

The problem with the *secta*, and later the sworn witnesses, was that they precipitated a "numbers game" which divested the system of judicial discretion in weighing evidence or credibility and simply granted the verdict to the party which marshaled the greater number of qualified witnesses. A hallmark of Saxon society was its great faith in the word of a freeman, which precluded distinguishing between the quality of the testimony of qualified witnesses (i.e., freemen). The use of witnesses made the functions of the *sectores* (judges) useless; it was the witnesses who alone decided a controversy—a significant difference from the weighing of evidence that characterized the Roman *judex* procedure and defines the jury system today.

The most important element of the Saxon legal system, and the one that played the largest part in the development of the jury system, was *compurgation*, which was originally limited to criminal proceedings but later came to dominate the entire legal structure. In the criminal system under Anglo-Saxon law, the charge of the accuser against the accused was sufficient to put the latter on the defensive, forcing him to disprove the charge or be punished.37 The accused's defense was called *compurgation*, which, as we have noted, was also employed by the Teutonic tribes. *Compurgators* were persons who supported, by their oaths, the credibility of the accused party, pledging their belief in his denial of the charge brought against him.38 They were in no sense witnesses for they needed have no knowledge of the facts in dispute, nor were they a jury for they considered no evidence.39 They were simply friends of the accused who attested to his character and truthfulness.

Both in criminal procedures and later in civil trials, the oaths of a party to a conflict were held to be conclusive as long as they were supported by the oaths of a certain number of *compurgators*. In important cases the number was twelve; but even if the required number of *compurgators* was produced by a party, his opponent could nullify their testimony by calling a greater number of his own. Thus in important cases the number of *compurgators* could be excessive (one trial involved a thousand witnesses to prove title to an estate).40 Hence when the numbers were evenly balanced, a method was devised to determine the legal value of the testimony. A "graduated scale" of oaths was devised and legal credit was given them in accord with the rank of the witnesses. Witnesses were ranked according to the amount of *wergild* their lives were worth; that is, how much would have to be paid to a family if they they were killed. This amount varied with the economic worth of the individuals.41

The final significant element of the Anglo-Saxon system was *ordeal*, which was also employed by the Teutonic tribes. In civil matters the witnesses and *compurgators* decided the controversy, and in criminal proceedings, if the *compurgators* decided for the accused, there was complete acquittal. But if the accused had been unable to muster a sufficient number of *compurgators*, or if he had been notoriously guilty of perjury on a previous occasion, or if he was not a freeman and hence was thought unworthy of credit, he was forced to demonstrate his innocence by an appeal to heaven, through the ordeal. The ordeal was practiced either with boiling water or a red-hot iron. The former, reserved to the common people, forced the accused to put his head or his whole arm under boiling water, depending on the degree of the offence. If he escaped unhurt, he was declared innocent. Nobles had to carry a red-hot iron nine feet, after which their hand was bound for three days. If at the end of that time there was no trace of injury, they were freed. There were other ordeals as well, all equally primitive and mystical,[42] which also indicate the status of the legal system in Anglo-Saxon England.

It seems evident that the modern jury cannot be traced to the primitive and often barbaric methods of the Anglo-Saxons. Their procedure seems to have been a hodgepodge of formulas, fictions, and tortures, and devoid of bodies that analyzed and weighed the factors surrounding a particular controversy. Rather, official witnesses, *compurgators*, and ordeals were the court and the outcome of the three processes was the decision. Hence, though we can call the Saxon system a court system, we find little evidence of a jury.[43]

With the death of King Alfred, his legal system gradually dissolved. During the reign of the next eight kings there was constant war with Denmark, which became so oppressive that in 991 King Ethelrod II agreed to pay the Danes £10,000 to buy immunity. But Ethelrod was overzealous, and eleven years later engineered a general massacre of foreigners, after which the Danes invaded and conquered all of England.[44]

The Scandinavian countries, since at least 950, had employed *compurgation* and ordeal. (It was in 950 that Bishop Poppo thrust his hand into a red-hot glove and drew it out unscathed to prove to the Jutlanders that Christianity was of divine origin.) Since that time, all the Scandinavian countries had adopted similar systems. The Norwegian *laugretto-men*, the Swedish *nambd*, the Danish *tingmaend, naevinger,* and *sunde-maend,* and the Icelandic *tolftar-quidr* generally employed a twelve-man panel which considered questions of both law and fact, more like a court than a jury.[45]

The Danes did not impose their system on the conquered English. Sweyn had conquered the island and his son Canute, who married Ethelrod's widow, mounted the throne in 1014. Canute was a lineal descendant of Alfred and, desirous of emulating him, adopted a policy of conciliation toward the English. He refrained from making essential alterations in the political or judicial systems.[46] When the Normans invaded England in 1066, they found and dealt with the Anglo-Saxon legal system as it had been introduced by Alfred and modified only by time.

The Norman Period
Though the Norman age introduced scholastic refinements and acute

and cunning argumentation,47 it was not characterized by significant legal innovations. The administration of justice became more regular under William and the study and propagation of law more general and the march of progress more distinct,48 but "it would be much nearer the truth to say that that [legal] system was unaffected by the Conquest— and continued in all its vigor for many years after that event."49 Conscious of his weak title, William strove to ingratiate himself with his new subjects by allowing them to maintain their ancient customs and laws. This seems manifest in the preamble of the laws promulgated in the reign of William (as translated by Reeves):

> These are the laws and customs which William the King granted to the people of England after the acquisition of that land: being the same [as those laws] which King Edward, his cousin, observed before him." Thus was the system of Saxon jurisprudence confirmed as the law of the country and from thenceforth it continues as the basis of the common law.50

Thus all distinguishing features of Anglo-Saxon jurisprudence were retained by the Norman king: the *wergild*, the *fridborh*, the use of legal witnesses, *compurgation*, and ordeal.51 There were, however, four changes in legal proceedings, the fourth of which can be viewed as a forerunner of the jury system, which was institutionalized by Henry II.

The first change was the separation of the spiritual and temporal courts—that is, of church business from the business of the state— which to a considerable extent curtailed the interference of the clergy with the judicial system. The second was the appointment of itinerant justiars who visited the different counties to administer justice in the king's name, thus creating an avenue for the introduction of a new system, the king's system, to replace the hundred and the county courts on a local level. The third was the introduction of the Norman practice of determining guilt or innocence and, later, the facts in civil cases. While less progressive than the other two changes, it was an improvement over the barbaric ordeal procedure.52

But the most important Norman innovation, though used only on an ad hoc basis in Normandy, was the institution of quasi-judicial inquiry on the part of the crown, from which "the later jury was immediately derived."53 These were called inquisitions, and later inquests, and were employed for specific purposes: to consider the lands of which a tenant was seised, or in lawful possession of, when he died; to test the sanity of a person; and to try matters which directly affected the crown.54 These inquiries were conducted by individuals selected from the body of the community in which the matter of the controversy existed. The inquests could be convened by a justice, sheriff, or coroner as representatives of the crown, and they selected the members according to their knowledge of the controversy, which they might supplement by the inquiry or the taking of evidence.55 The inquisition became a Norman institution after 912, when Rollo established himself in the territory that subsequently became Normandy. It crossed the Channel with the Normans in the next century.

As the general inquisition (the *inquisitoria jurata*) developed in England there arose, contemporaneously, certain accusatory tribunals (*jurata delatoria*) that handled criminal offenses committed within their district, charged offenders, and put them to trial.56

The parallel between this body and our grand juries is striking, and the general inquest also seems to be very similar to the modern jury. The members of both the *jurata* and the *delatoria* inquests were taken from the community. The *delatoria* was "an inquest of good and lawful men (*probi et legales homines*) summoned from the neighborhood were the offense was surmised to have been committed,"57 and in the *jurata* "the power and duty to decide in a particular case was entrusted to a limited number of freemen selected from the district, and this number was generally twelve or some multiple of twelve."58

The inquest was unlike the jury in that its members, called *recognitors*, decided cases almost entirely upon their personal knowledge and information, and indeed were selected for their knowledge. For the mere numerical preponderance of oaths, a decision by twelve *recognitors* was substituted, who "acted upon some cognizance of the dispute, but they derived that information from themselves; they were, indeed, a jury of witnesses testifying to each other."59 Although decision by evidence, as opposed to personal knowledge, is critical to the definition of the modern jury, and thus it would be premature to call the Norman inquest a jury, it is safe to say that if the jury was not born in the Norman inquest, it was certainly gestating.

While William and his successors took pains to avoid any official imposition of Norman institutions on the conquered Saxons, the use of the inquest seems to have appeared and developed by custom and usage because it was more familiar to Norman officials, or perhaps because it was a more rational and useful mechanism for adjudicating disputes. In either event it remained only for the inquest to be institutionalized, which came about under Henry II.

The Assise of Henry and the Judgment of Evidence

By the reign of the second Henry, England was a united nation, nationalistic and prepared for growth.60 There was, however, a major internal conflict. In the period following William's death "the assumptions of the clergy had—coincident with the growth of the Roman hierarchy—become greater than ever before; the ecclesiastics claiming exemption from the judicial process and the laws of the realm, and asserting the supreme authority of the civil law in their own tribunals."61 It may be that Henry's decision to institutionalize the form of the inquest was a simple codification of practices that already existed, or that the court system was overloaded and needed an alternative, but it seems evident that the assise was also motivated by Henry's concern with the clergy.

As we have seen, the *jurata* operated in disputes concerning land. There were times, however, when an inquest had to settle questions other than those strictly concerned with rightful seisin, such as the mental competence of an individual to own land. On these occasions the inquest was said to be decided *per assisam in modum juratae*, or through the assise in the form of the *jurata*.62

In response to the problem of the clergy and in light of the practices of the inquests, Henry II in 1164 enacted the constitutions of Clarendon, "calculated to give a rational limitation to the secular and ecclesiastical jurisprudence; and furnish a basis on which these separate jurisdictions might have been founded."63 The ninth section of the laws provided that "if there shall arise any dispute between an ecclesiastic and a layman . . . it shall be determined by the judgment of the king's chief justice, upon a recognition of twelve lawful men."64 The statute of Northampton (1176) added: "And if the lords of a fief deny to the heirs of a decendant the seisin which they demand, the justices of our lord the king shall thereupon by twelve lawful men cause to be made an inquiry."65

Thus in questions concerning seisin and clergy disputes the assise, formerly used only in aberrations of the *jurata* procedure, became institutionalized. *Assise*, which means merely a statute or enactment, was applied to the *jurata* proceeding because the *jurata* variation had been declared by statute. With the two statutes of Henry, the term *assise* was given greater legitimacy, but in reality the assise was nothing new.

In its original composition [the assie was] nothing more than a body of twelve knights, impanelled to determine by their testimony a disputed question of seisin of land, right to an *advowson*, or villenage [terms of status]. . . . In it we first find the jury in its distinct form, but the elements of which it was composed were all familiar to the jurisprudence of the time.66

The institution of the assise, now given official recognition, spread quickly by both usage and statute. Statute 13 Edward I c. 30 (1285) applied it to trespass and other pleas, which almost covered the range of civil controversies, especially when actions for false imprisonment were included in 1306.67

But as the assise was no different from the *jurata* inquests, it was no more like the jury than the *jurata*. Each lacked the judgment of evidence and relied, rather, on the personal knowledge of the twelve *recognitors*. This practice was gradually changed by a number of factors, which form the last link in the chain of events that lead to the modern jury.

First, there was a general exception to the *jurata* procedure with respect to proof of facts. In land disputes in which the issuance of deeds entered the controversy, individuals who had witnessed the deed were called upon to testify. Indeed, the statute 52 Henry III c. 14 (1267) expressly legitimized the giving of testimony in deed controversies, thereby foreshadowing the change in which juries would cease to be witnesses and would become triers of the facts.68

In all cases involving land, moreover, if the dispute were over a trifling extent and amount an ancient statute permitted the convening of a jury of twelve freemen (as opposed to the knights originally required) who were not restricted to facts within their own knowledge but could deliver their verdict upon such information as they might believe to be true.69 This was a step toward the jury's reception of evidence from witnesses in court.

A third exception to the personal knowledge requirement was found by Bracton in a rebirth of the system of *compurgation* called *et inde producit sectam*, in which witnesses were matched against witnesses by numbers. Gradually, however, the witnesses who formed the *secta* for the plaintiff began to give evidence to the court, as did the witnesses attesting to deeds.The rules for receiving such testimony were very strict, but nevertheless the precedent was established.70

Finally, it became evident that, in the strictest application of the personal knowledge requirement, not all individuals with personal knowledge of the facts would be sworn as *recognitors* and not all sworn *recognitors* would have equal knowledge of the facts. And it was certainly probable that some jurors would disagree. Thus even the general *jurata* must have involved the evaluation and consideration of the evidence. Some weighing of evidence seems inherent to the process.71

For four hundred years the *recognitors* of the assise decided cases both upon the evidence presented to them and upon their personal knowledge of the facts of the controversy. It was not until 1670 that it was held[72] that, where a juror had knowledge of facts material to an issue, he must so inform the court and be sworn as a witness. In 1816 Lord Edenborough ruled, in *Rex* v. *Sutton*,[73] that a judge who tolerated a verdict based on facts not brought out in the evidence but founded on the jury's peculiar knowledge was clearly in the wrong.[74]

The requirement that jurors consider only the evidence presented in court had wide-ranging impact on the legal profession. For one thing, the function was changed radically, from the mere mechanical receipt of knowledge to the intellectual faculty of analyzing and drawing conclusions from testimony, "a duty not only of high importance with a view to truth and justice, but also collaterally, in encouraging habits of reflection and reasoning, which must have had a great and most beneficial effect in promoting civilization."[75] This change must have infused the entire legal system with an entirely new perspective: objectivity. From decisions which first relied on the strength of battle, then on the intervention of God, then on the counting of oaths and their balance by economic worth, and finally on the intervention of the parties and the witnesses to the dispute, came a distinct, disinterested, impartial body whose job was to analyze the facts surrounding a controversy. The advancement in legal thinking was of major import.

But other, more specific procedures were also induced by the change; the entire law of evidence was born with that one change. When juries can decide only according to the evidence presented in court, very strict rules must govern exactly what evidence can influence that decision. Evidence must be excluded which will mislead or prejudice the judgment, and the manner of presentation must be governed, as well as the weight which should be given to certain kinds of evidence.[76]

The practice of hearing evidence in court must have created, or at least remarkably extended, the duty, practice, and art of advocacy. From the presentation of oaths or the drawing of technically difficult documents must have come the opening of "the flood-gates of forensic eloquence" and the ability to examine and cross examine witnesses, to present one's case to the jury, to persuade, to reason, to exhort, to shame, to emote.[77]

Thus the modern jury was born: twelve individuals, selected from the body of the community, were sworn and decided matters of fact and judged the evidence submitted to them. Distinct from the court, the development of the jury process was not arrested, and many more offshoots and institutional refinements were to be made. Methods for assembling juries, for appealing and obtaining new trials, extension of the jury to criminal cases and the development of grand and petit juries, requirements of unanimity, methods of instructing juries, the extension of jury rights to new causes of action, and of course all the development of the substantive law itself, which so vitally affects the decision in a case— all these developments and more grew with and into the jury system. The basis for their development had finally been realized, the institutional springboard without which there could be no incentive for their development: the jury system itself. It remained only for the jury to develop elsewhere in new ways.

THE AMERICAN EXPERIENCE

Trial by jury had reached maturity as an institution by the time England established its colonies which were to become the United States. The English common law (court-made law) was the explicit law of the land, "and with it . . . an inseparable adjunct, the trial by jury."[78] English laws and practices were administered by the colonial courts as part of the English legal system, and when the colonies declared their independence were permanently codified in the Constitution.

The jury existed for criminal cases in the American colonies from their first establishment as an organized government. Indeed, the Declaration of Independence chastised George III because "he has combined with others, to subject us to a jurisdiction foreign to our constitutions and unacknowledged by our laws; giving assent to their acts of pretended legislation . . . for depriving us, in many cases, of the benefit of trial by jury." Those who framed the Constitution also "must have looked upon it as an institution which must be preserved while society exists—and not as one which [as they said of the civil jury] changes in society may cause to be superseded by different modes of trial."[79] Thus Article III of the Constitution, which governs the federal judiciary, provides that

> the trial of all crimes, except in cases of impeachment, shall be by jury; and such trial shall be held in the state where the said crimes shall have been committed.

The Sixth Amendment provides:

In all criminal prosecutions, the accused shall enjoy the right to a speedy and public trial, by an impartial jury of the state and district wherein the crime shall have been committed, which district shall have been previously ascertained by law, and to be informed of the nature and cause of the accusation; to be confronted with the witnesses against him; to have compulsory process for obtaining witnesses in his favor, and to have the assistance of counsel for his defense.

And the Fifth Amendment declared that

no person shall be held to answer for a capital or otherwise infamous crime, unless on a presentment or indictment of a grand jury, except in cases arising in the land or naval forces, or in the militia when in actual service in time of war or public danger; nor shall any person for the same offense be twice put in jeopardy of life or limb.

It is curious, however, that the original articles, as adopted, were "wholly silent on the subject of trial by jury in civil actions—a principle of jurisprudence so familiar to the Anglo-Saxon mind, that we might have supposed it would be deemed an essential element in the fundamental laws of the new republic."80 Opponents of the Constitution isolated this omission for attack, claiming that the provision of Article III that "the supreme court shall have appellate jurisdiction both as to law and fact" evidenced the intention of the framers to abolish the civil jury, since the law-fact distinction was most strictly maintained in civil cases whereas criminal cases involved a jury's determination of guilt or innocence.

The defenders of the Constitution argued that the diversity of judicial systems among the different states required that the civil jury be left to the various state constitutions, or at least to the discretion of Congress. They also maintained that changes in society may render a different mode of determining questions of property preferable in many cases in which the mode of trial then prevailed. In essence, the framers of the Constitution, while preserving the basic rights of individuals subject to criminal prosecution, had left the procedure of the various civil actions to the state courts, since presumably the state laws on the substantive causes for civil action would and did vary tremendously.81

Those who desired establishment of the right to civil jury as an inalienable right persisted, and several states proposed amendments to the Constitution. The Seventh Amendment was adopted, providing that

in suits at common law, where the value in controversy shall exceed twenty dollars, the right to trial by jury shall be preserved. And no fact tried by a jury shall be otherwise re-examined in any court of the United States than according to the rules of the common law.

Thus the right to trial by jury was secured in all cases at common law; that is, whenever common law was customarily practiced and wherever the law of England applied it. The common law, a dynamic and growing institution, is applied by courts as exigencies require new procedures and laws. Thus civil juries were guaranteed unlimited expansion where courts and legislatures deemed it important to apply common law. The Seventh Amendment, however, only applied to the federal courts. Therefore, many state governments quickly incorporated similar provisions in their own constitutions.[82]

The adoption of the federal Constitution provided a unique and valuable opportunity to evaluate the British legal system, to isolate the values and assumptions upon which it is based, and—as much as possible—to give it coherency and consistency in a written document. The British experience was the ad hoc application and revision of the various legal tenets which evolved over a period of over six hundred years, all built on an unwritten constitution. The framers of the Constitution had the opportunity to rationalize the British system and consider its application or relevance from political, economic, and social perspectives, as well as the strictly legal.

CONCLUSION

The jury system, simply by its existence, implies a number of statements about the polity in which it operates. For one thing, the jury is a monument to self-government. It is composed of the citizens of the nation, not of professionals of the court or officials of the government, and thus it daily legitimizes the practices of self-government which pervade other institutions in this country. By giving individuals a part in the machinery of the legal system, the jury creates an identity with government that can hardly be achieved in any other way.

The jury system also serves a vital educational function, teaching individuals not only specific laws of conduct but also the procedures by which legal percepts are conceived and applied. In judging his neighbor, a man learns how to judge his own actions, and how to assess his own rights and responsibilities. Myriad injustices perpetrated by individuals and by the state against its citizens could be avoided if more individuals were aware of and steadfast in adherence to their legal rights. And only when individuals appreciate the nature and the reasons for our laws can they work effectively to change them.

But the jury system teaches people more than the strict legal precepts; it teaches them the rationale of the legal system and what values it treasures. To the extent that legal thinking is an admirable way of dealing with controversies, its daily expression provides an invaluable lesson in teaching citizens to approach problems in the same way by fostering an impartial, open-minded, rational, analytical attitude. While there is no doubt that many judicial functionaries could themselves learn fairness and rationality, the ideal may be well worth teaching.

The jury system, finally, is an invaluable political institution. In France, where the jury has only partial or semi-existence, "centralization swallows up and absorbs all freedom of local action. The government stretches out its polypus arms in every direction, and hardly anything is too minute or unimportant for its grasp."[83]

Not all governments are benign, and the jury system serves as a useful check on the perverse application of central power. "No matter how ardent may be its wish to destroy or crush an obnoxious opponent, there can be no real danger from its menaces or acts so long as the party attacked can take refuge in a jury fairly and indifferently chosen."[84] This is true for two reasons. First, because to the extent that a government seeks to wrest control from an unwilling populace, the jury, as both part of the legal apparatus and a representative of the people, can make decisions opposed to the government's will. Second, because the use of citizens in the judicial process guarantees publicity, which is, ultimately, the best check on governmental incursions.

And the jury can work to change governmental policies: "Jurors drawn from the masses of the people . . . may paralyze the arm of the government by refusing to bring in verdicts of guilty. . . . It might be carried to such an extent as to render a state prosecution a hopeless attempt. When this universal disinclination to convict exists, even when the evidence is clear, it is time to change the measures which have provoked such a humiliating result."[85]

If the jury does not work in these ways, if it does not teach self-government, legal precepts and rationality, if it does not prevent unwarranted governmental incursions, then perhaps the fault is not with the jury itself but with the people of the country. No judicial mechanism can be better than the people who apply it, but it must always be our goal to improve the machinery which we hold out to our people in the hope that, some day, the principles and values which underly our institutions will be assimilated and applied as a matter of course, not of law.

II Deficiencies of the Jury System

2 The Role of the Jury

The right to trial by jury has become firmly established in American legal traditions, the constitutional guarantees providing for jury trials have stood unaltered for nearly two centuries, and in that time a vast progression of court decisions and statutory provisions have established the precise conditions under which the right exists and procedures are followed in exercising the right. In the course of this long and detailed evolution the jury system, like all legal institutions, has been forced to adapt to changing circumstances and to respond to challenges to its usefulness and its very existence.

While the jury remains, for the most part, a highly valued legal institution, it would be foolish to assert that no problems are involved in its use. Nor, when its value is challenged, should we be satisfied with the defense that the demands of tradition and precedent, associated with its longevity, require its continuation. Supreme Court Justice Oliver Wendell Holmes wrote, in an oft-quoted essay:

> It is revolting to have no better reason for a rule of law than that it was laid down in the time of Henry IV. It is still more revolting if the grounds upon which it has been laid down have vanished long since, and the rule simply persists from blind imitation of the past.[1]

The logic of this conclusion is unchallengeable. If we seek justification for the jury system, it must be found in the real and current values which it serves. The jury has been challenged on numerous grounds: its lack of expertise, the danger of bias, the substantial administrative inconvenience it can involve. These and other problems will be examined in detail in this chapter, as will the modern bases for the jury. But if the system is worth retaining, it must be because of the benefits to be derived from its use in civil and criminal trials.

THE MERITS OF THE JURY

The jury's essential value can reside in either of two fundamental features. It can be viewed as a guarantor or accuracy in fact finding or as an essential political body for protecting the public from arbitrary prosecution by government. However, absolute determination of the validity of either role is impossible; cogent arguments can be made in support of and in opposition to both roles.

The jury's value as an accurate finder of fact will be of little consequence if non-jury trials can provide equally accurate and fair determinations of the guilt or innocence of an accused, and in the aggregate, studies have not indicated a significant difference between judge and jury decisions. Juries return verdicts "different from those of a judge" in less than 20 percent of all criminal cases.[2] On the other hand, the difference may well be important for those involved in the trial. Juries are more lenient than judges in 19 percent of the cases and more severe in only 3 percent.[3] Whether such leniency is desirable depends, of course upon one's view of criminal justice.

But it must be emphasized that these figures do not indicate which of the two is correct. There is no objective standard by which one can determine whether a jury makes a correct decision—no a priori method of determining guilt or innocence.[4] The jury's function is to make a determination on the basis of the evidence before it, and since most clear-cut cases are resolved by a guilty plea, without a jury trial, only the cases involving close, difficult judgments go before the jury. The jury's task therefore, is the resolution of a thoroughly arguable dispute. The court observer might disagree with the jury's conclusion, but he cannot say with any assurance that he is right and the jury wrong. The fact that twelve men can agree upon a conclusion is strong evidence that their conclusion is at least plausible. Nothing more can definitely be said.

The traditional belief that a group of twelve unbiased men will be more likely to make an accurate finding of fact than a single justice is perfectly reasonable. But in the absence of a reliable standard for determining the truth, it cannot be proved. If the non-jury trial reaches comparable decisions most of the time, the importance of the jury can hardly be declared absolute.

A second justification for the jury system is that it may serve as a democratic institution, protecting the people from arbitrary governmental prosecution. The power of jury nullification, its right to refuse to convict even where a statute is clearly violated, is an immense power. It permits the jury to deny the government ability to enforce any law which offends the sensibilities of the jurors. The government can of course outlaw any activity, but the jury can assure that the law is not enforced. The actual power of a jury to disregard the law and to refuse to convict where it feels a law or a prosecution to be unjust is not recognized in law. Juries are instructed that they must follow the law as it is given to them by the court and that they have no right to ignore a law they do not like or believe to be unconstitutional. Although the jury's duty to follow the law is largely unenforceable because a juror may not be punished simply for his vote on the verdict, jurors are required to take an oath to follow the law and are usually impressed with their duty to do so. Therefore, the power of a jury to negate the law or to obstruct a legally sound prosecution is not one that is commonly exercised.

How important this power is to the preservation of justice is open to question. As the *Columbia Law Review* indicated recently:

> The fact that the fear of unchecked government aggression led to the jury trial provision in the Sixth Amendment does not establish the present need for such protection. Mr. Justice Harlan, for one, is convinced that the need for this original virtue of the jury trial has "largely disappeared."[5]

The reasoning behind this conclusion is simple. In the United States the people elect the lawmakers directly, and if a law seems oppressive the majority can alter it through the electoral process. Though there appears to be little need for jury nullification, a strong defense for it is nevertheless possible.

In theory, the people can change the law. In practice, however, legislative bodies are often unresponsive or responsive only after lengthly delay. Hence some unpopular laws remain on the books for substantial periods. In many instances and especially if the laws are selectively enforced, little public pressure develops for their removal. Yet the selective enforcement of such laws—for example, those against political or ethnic minorities—is a major source of injustice. Although not every jury can be relied upon to object to such practices, the right to do so is nevertheless valuable.

Moreover, the potential danger of such governmental action, even if not serious now, is sufficient reason to retain the jury nullification principle. The ever increasing power and ability of the central government and police agencies to suppress certain kinds of activity (especially those involving free speech and assembly) pose genuine threats. Whether such threats have now been actualized is a matter for dispute, but the potential for abuse is undeniable.

Finally, and most importantly, the jury's power of nullification is a standing check against the domination of a minority by a callous majority. It permits a small group of men to refuse to convict if they feel that the law in question violates community standards. As the *Columbia Law Review* noted:

> The Sixth Amendment requires a jury to be composed of persons "of the state and district in which the crime shall have been committed." This requirement has little to do with accuracy. It is, rather, an affirmation of the community's prerogative not to apply criminal sanctions ordained by a superior political entity in which the voice of the community was not controlling. Thus, although this community may not determine what is criminal, the jury system gives it some ability to say what is not criminal. The jury functions as a sort of mini-legislature, to check against the tyranny of the the majority will.6

Admittedly, serious biases in juries sometimes limit this power, and this chapter will discuss such discrimination in detail. There is no question that the exclusion of blacks and other minorities should be ended if the jury is to become fully effective in protecting defendants from the tyranny of the majority. But such reforms are necessary only to improve the working of the jury system; they do not touch upon the need for the system. The potential value of juries as protection against government oppression is a real and current justification for the system.

As indicated, this justification is subject to question in light of the far from flawless nature of the contemporary American jury; and this chapter will consider some of the flaws in detail, but a brief outline of the operation of the system in criminal cases is an important prologue. The focus on criminal cases should not suggest a relative unimportance of the civil sector (which will be considered in due course), but many of the most crucial problems arise in criminal trials. And in any event, there are not enough important distinctions between criminal and civil juries to warrant a real differentiation, at least on the operational level.

THE RIGHT TO TRIAL BY JURY IN A CRIMINAL CASE

The Sixth Amendment to the Constitution requires that "in all criminal prosecutions, the accused shall enjoy the right to a speedy and public trial by an impartial jury of the state and district in which the crime shall have been committed." However, the right to a jury trial was not always universally guaranteed. Until 1968 this guarantee applied only to federal criminal trials. Jury trials were commonly used in most states, but as a function of a state statute or constitution rather than in response to the U.S. Constitution. States' application of the right to a jury trial varied: some did not require unanimous verdicts, and others limited the jury right to serious cases.

The reason for this diversity was that the rights secured by the Constitution and Bill of Rights apply only against abuse by the federal government. The rights of defendants tried in state courts were left to the determination of the states. It was not until 1868, with the ratification of the Fourteenth Amendment, that the rights provided by the Constitution could be enforced against the states. The due-process clause of the Fourteenth Amendment—no one should be deprived of life, liberty, or property without due process of law—has been interpreted by the Supreme Court to mean that those rights "essential to fundamental fairness" may not be infringed by the states.

Early interpretations of these fundamental rights were narrow, but by the middle of the twentieth century the concept had been broadened considerably. The 1960s brought enormous expansion in a variety of areas, one of which was the right to a jury trial. Prior to 1968 that right had been excluded, for reasons explained by the *Columbia Law Review:*

> The traditional and inexact standard of due process was in essence fundamental fairness. In the past, the main criterion of the test was whether a fair and equitable legal system without the particular right in question could be imagined. Applying that standard, it was easy to imagine a fair legal system without the right to trial by jury.[7]

The 1968 landmark decision in *Duncan* v. *Louisiana* reversed this position, holding that the test of fundamental fairness should be made in light of the American tradition of justice. The Supreme Court concluded:

> Because we believe that trial by jury in criminal cases is fundamental to the American scheme of justice, we hold that the Fourteenth Amendment guarantees a right of jury trial in all criminal cases . . . which, were they to be tried in a federal criminal court . . . would come within the Sixth Amendment guarantee.[8]

This application to the states of the right to a jury trial means that in all criminal cases a person has an absolute right to a jury trial, regardless of the jurisdiction that conducts the trial. The definition of criminal cases at the federal level has traditionally excluded so-called petty offenses, defined as those which impose a penalty of six months' or less imprisonment. The *Duncan* decision indicated that the jury trial is required in every case in which the potential penalty exceeds six months. The test is not the sentence actually imposed but the maximum sentence permitted by law.

SELECTION OF A JURY

The initial step in the selection of the jury is the compilation of prospective jurors from voting lists, tax rolls, assessment rolls, and the like. Efforts are supposedly made to ensure that, whatever the source of the jurors' names, the list represents a fair cross section of the community. There are few requirements other than literacy and generally good health. Minors and the elderly are generally excluded, and persons with a criminal record. The regular exclusion of any group by race, religion, or political views is forbidden. A common practice, however, which tends to lower the quality of prospective jurors, is the exemption of professional people, such as doctors, lawyers, and teachers. Public employees, such as policemen and firemen, are also generally excluded.

These lists are usually used for a year at a time. When jurors are required at the beginning of a court session, a large group of names is drawn at random from the list; this is known as the venire. A person who is notified of his selection to the venire may seek exemption for one of the reasons listed above, for personal health or hardship. Those who can serve are usually held for potential jury duty for two weeks or until they serve on a jury.

The final step is the selection of the jury from the venire: the venire is assembled and twelve names are picked at random for each trial. These twelve persons are seated as prospective jurors and the voir dire begins— a preliminary examination to determine the impartiality of the jurors. Generally, the voir dire is conducted by the lawyers, who use the privilege not only to determine the competence of the jurors but also to discover as much as possible about their personalities, with a view to what will appeal to them. In some instances, however, this questioning is done by the judge. When seated, the jury is a petit jury, which means nothing more than a trial jury, as distinct from a grand jury.

The purpose of the voir dire is to ensure a fair jury, which generally results from the process. Although lawyers cannot request a specific individual to serve on the jury, they can, and do, object to the seating of specific jurors.

There are three ways in which a juror can be removed. First, a lawyer may challenge the array, arguing that a disqualifying failure in the method by which the venire was chosen calls for a new group of jurors. For example, if a systematic exclusion of blacks from the venire is shown, the defendant would be entitled to a completely new venire—one with proper racial representation.

The second form of challenge is challenge for cause. The voir dire is the basis for this challenge, which asserts that a prospective juror should not be seated because of some bias or incompetence. Standard grounds for such bias are a personal interest in the case, a special relationship with one of the parties, or the expression of an opinion or bias which would make a fair and impartial decision impossible. A juror may also be excluded if he claims to have a personal opinion about the merits of the case. There is no limit to the number of challenges for cause which a lawyer may make. He must, however, show reasonable grounds for rejection. The final determination of the validity of these challenges is made by the judge.

The third means of challenge is the peremptory challenge. The lawyer for either party may exercise this right to arbitrarily reject a juror, without cause—to eliminate jurors they believe are unsympathetic to their cause. In most states the number of peremptory challenges is fixed by statute for both the defense and the prosecution, and usually varies according to the seriousness of the crime or the extent of punishment. This right may be exercised at any time before the jury is sworn in.

Sometimes local prejudice against a defendant may be so intense that it is impossible to obtain a truly fair and impartial jury. The horrible nature of a crime or excessive pretrial publicity may create this situation. If the defense can demonstrate that such a condition is a serious problem, it may request a change of venue. If this is granted by the judge, the trial is moved to another county, where—hopefully—an impartial jury can be impaneled.

After the jury has been selected and sworn, some jurisdictions provide for the selection of one or two alternates. These persons sit through the trial and in the event of the disqualification of one of the jurors (for illness or other reasons) replace the departed juror in determining the issues.

ROLE OF THE JURY

After the jury is sworn a foreman is elected to head the jury, to preside over its deliberations and to announce its verdict. In most jurisdictions this election is conducted by the jury, but occasionally the court will appoint the foreman.

The sole legal function of the jury is to determine the facts of a given situation, to ascertain the truth as accurately as possible. Juries are not supposed to interpret the law; this is done by the judge in his instructions to the jury, and generally in the form of hypothetical statements about the defendant's conduct. As noted previously, however, one of the primary reasons for the jury is its ability to disregard this rule of law, at least occasionally.

Jurors are supposed to base their decision on the evidence before them, and independent research outside the trial is out of the question for all juries; it constitutes reversible error. Only the evidence which the court permits to be heard is relevant to the jury's decision.

During a trial the members of a jury are generally free to return to their homes at the end of the day. They are cautioned by the court not to read news articles or expose themselves to radio or television reports about the trial as these might easily influence the jury to base its decision on evidence excluded from the courtroom. However, it is difficult to ensure that the court's instructions with respect to the news media are followed because enforcement of the juror's conduct in the privacy of his own home is impossible. Thus in "sensational" cases that are more or less exploited by the news media, the court has the option of sequestering the jury or locking it up in a hotel, with access to news reports strictly controlled, for the duration of the trial. As will be seen, the problems of pretrial publicity are a major source of strain upon the jury system.

After all the evidence has been submitted, the summations by each attorney follow, and then the court's instructions to the jury. The jury then retires to deliberate and to reach a verdict. Sequestration of the jury during its deliberations is the usual practice, and no outside sources of information are permitted. However, the jury may request that one or more of the exhibits introduced in the trial be sent to it for examination.

For all practical purposes, the jury has complete discretion in determining its verdict; it is free to consider or discard anything it chooses. It is free from every influence and cannot be told how to decide, nor even that it must decide.

To convict a defendant of a criminal violation a jury must be convinced "beyond reasonable doubt" of his guilt. This does not mean that the prosecution must present a foolproof case but merely that there must be no reasonable doubt of the defendant's guilt. The test is whether a reasonable man would conclude there is doubt of guilt, even if he believes that the preponderance of evidence favors the prosecution. There have been a few appellate decisions on the meaning of reasonable doubt, but the phrase is usually considered self-explanatory. In any event, as a practical matter, the jury is free to find as it pleases. Only where there is gross abuse of this discretion will the courts overturn its verdicts, and on that ground alone. And the court's power to overturn gross abuse of a jury is limited to verdicts of guilty; a court has no authority to upset a verdict of acquittal, no matter how obviously incorrect it may be.

In most courts verdicts in criminal cases are required to be unanimous; if the jury cannot reach unanimous agreement, a mistrial is declared and the defendant must be tried again. Although the requirement of unanimity has commonly been considered to be of constitutional magnitude, a recent decision of the Supreme Court leaves the matter in doubt. In *Williams* v. *Florida*, 399 U.S. 78 (1970), the Court held a panel of twelve jurors is not required either by the "trial by jury" provision of the Sixth Amendment or the "due process" clause of the Fourteenth Amendment. The Court did not have to decide whether unanimity is constitutionally required, but *dicta* included in the Court's opinion suggest that it is not. The Court pointed out that in adopting the Sixth Amendment, the framers purposely omitted the common-law requirements of unanimity and vicinage (399 U.S. at 96). While most states require unanimity in criminal verdicts, they vary with respect to civil verdicts. Some permit a civil verdict to stand with a two-thirds majority.

Frequently there is initial disagreement among a jury, and it may require a lengthly period of deliberation to reach a verdict. However, if a jury is unable to agree on a verdict, it is known as a hung jury, which means a mistrial and a new trial that must start from scratch. It is important to note that though the defendant is not convicted in a hung jury trial, neither is he freed: the case is retried. On occasion, however, the judge may dismiss the action. In the Black Panther trial in New Haven, Connecticut, Bobby Seale and Erika Huggins were released by the judge after the jury had deadlocked at eleven to one for acquittal.

If the jury reaches a verdict of not guilty, the defendant is discharged and the action ends; but if the verdict is guilty, there may be further work for the jury. In capital cases it is often the jury's responsibility to recommend whether or not the death penalty shall be invoked. And in several states, most notably California, the jury sets the sentence for less serious crimes at a second trial, after which the jury is dismissed with the thanks of the court.

The jury system, as described above, has been virtually unaltered since the ratification of the Constitution, during which time the criminal and civil justice systems have undergone explosive growth. A glance at the latest crime statistics reveals the rapidity of the growth in that area, and almost daily everyone sees an automobile collision that may generate a civil suit. Understandably, this vast growth in the workload of the jury system has created serious strains. Some have been met successfully but numerous others remain, and part II will focus on four primary areas of strain.

First, the huge workload which confronts the jury has led to complaints that the system is far too inefficient to handle the staggering load of cases thrust upon it. Some experts have argued that the jury is too expensive in terms of time and that administrative efficiency is now essential to justice. There is much to be said for such views, and it may be necessary to alter the system by eliminating the jury, or reducing its size, or reducing its functions.

Second, the difficulties associated with news media exploitation of a sensational trial have been alluded to already, but we will engage in a more detailed and systematic analysis of the mass communication media and the injustices they may create. Our analysis will focus on some of the more publicized recent trials, including the Calley court-martial and the trials of Charles Manson and Sam Sheppard. Other recent court decisions and their impact on pretrial publicity will also be considered.

Discrimination against the poor and minority groups in this country has long been a blot on the national reputation, and in some respects has appeared in the administration of justice. Thus we will discuss the present bail system and its alternatives in detail, the problems associated with the selection of juries, and the use of the exclusionary rule to protect minority groups in particular (although all of society in general) from the excesses of police action.

Finally, we will consider another long-neglected area of reform: the military justice system. Until 1950, military justice was conducted along approximately the same lines as during the time of Julius Caesar, and a number of experts have asserted that some of the arbitrary and unjust principles of that bygone era still persist. A thorough examination of the sources of such arbitrariness will be followed by a discussion of the possible, and civilian, alternatives.

In these four areas—overcrowded courts, pretrial publicity, poor and minority group discrimination, and military justice—part II will seek to determine the deficiencies of the jury system.

3 Court Backlogs

Although the jury is a firmly established American tradition, and solid reasons have been presented to justify its existence, a fair evaluation of the system must include consideration of the costs imposed upon the judicial system by the expensive and time-consuming procedures that jury trials involve. Studies have indicated that a jury trial, on the average, requires 40 to 50 percent longer than a trial conducted before a judge.[9] The enormous caseload that now threatens to crush our court system may mean that such an overhead, in time alone, is too high a price to pay for a jury. If equally fair proceedings can occur before a judge alone, the dangers posed to the system by the delays of a jury trial may make the right to such a trial an intolerably expensive luxury.

This chapter will attempt to balance the values of the jury against the costs that its use imposes. While many of the problems discussed are common to both civil and criminal cases, our focus will be on the delays and injustices associated with criminal jury trials. Discussion of civil cases will be deferred to chapter 11, where remedies for some of the sources of civil-case delay will be discussed.

At first glance, the suggestion that such a fundamental right as the jury trial should be abridged for mere administrative convenience and efficiency may seem rash and ill advised. Certainly, the constitutional rights of the individual have been highly regarded in this country, and the fact that their exercise may involve some cost and inconvenience has never been considered adequate reason to abridge them. As the Supreme Court held in *Bruton* v. *U.S.*, infringement of constitutional rights cannot be justified merely to "secure greater speed, economy and convenience in the administration of the law."[10]

But those who argue for restricting the right of jury trial have powerful arguments in response to this position. The essentiality of the jury for justice is not proved; many European nations operate relatively fair court systems without juries, and even in the United States the right was not considered essential until recently.[11] More importantly, what is at stake is not merely administrative convenience. Huge backlogs and lengthly delays strike at the very foundation of criminal justice, at the trial system that determines guilt or innocence, for these delays are in and of themselves a source of much injustice, to individuals and to society at large. The individual who waits for six months in jail, only to be found innocent at his trial, can hardly be said to have received fair treatment. And it is conceivable that the system could collapse under the weight of the huge backlog, with consequences for the law that we cannot imagine. Some sacrifice of individual liberty may be essential to preserve the rest of society from uncontrolled crime.

This conflict will not be settled easily. Concepts such as individual or societal rights are vague; the values we attach to them are hard to compare. Rational comprison of these conflicting values may well be impossible, and this chapter will reach no firm conclusions on which is more important. Rather, it will focus on clarifying the dangers of court congestion, the sources for that congestion, and the possible solutions within or without the context of the jury.

SOURCE AND EXTENT OF THE PROBLEM

The maxim "Justice delayed is justice denied" contains a great deal of truth although not in the context in which it is often employed. It is often used to suggest that the overburdened courts are a function of guilty criminals, who thwart the cause of justice with endless appeals by seeking every means to escape their deserved punishment. No doubt this occurs at times, but the current court crisis has much deeper roots, and its evils are far more widespread than the occasional release of a guilty felon. The injustices imposed by overburdened court calendars threaten the rights of everyone caught up in the criminal justice system, whether he is guilty or innocent.

A discussion of the problems that occur in America's courts and the source of the problems cannot be simple, primarily because the court system itself is extremely complex. Our courts have evolved in a piecemeal fashion to suit the needs of thousands of unrelated, uncoordinated, and often overlapping political jurisdictions. In addition to the large and well-organized federal court system, there is a patchwork of local, county, and state court systems whose structure and organization defy rational description. This confusion is compounded by the endless variety of courts, with each system designed to serve specific purposes. Trial courts, magistrate courts, justice of the peace courts, police courts, and traffic courts have no standard form across the nation.

For purposes of this chapter, the nation's criminal courts will be grouped in three categories according to their function. The first group is the lower courts—the local magistrates and justices who handle the mass of arrests for petty offenses, traffic offenses, and misdemeanors. These courts may also serve as an initial hearing for more serious offenses to determine whether there is sufficient evidence to hold the defendants for trial.

The second broad grouping consists of the trial courts, whose function is to try serious cases. In both state and federal systems, these courts handle felony cases and serious misdemeanors.

Finally, there are the appellate courts, to which defendants, and occasionally prosecutors, can appeal from the decisions of the trial courts. While some courts handle trials as well as appeals, the appeals process will be examined specifically because it poses a number of serious and unique problems that contribute to the general crisis of court congestion.

The lower courts handle almost all the suspects arrested by the police each year. In the early 1960s these courts were handling over 4 million misdemeanor cases a year.[12] And a large proportion of the hundreds of thousands of felony cases tried each year are initially processed in lower courts. Given the inadequate number of judges in many areas, the burden on these courts has been staggering. In 1967 the President's Commission on Law Enforcement and the Administration of Justice lamented that, until that year, one court in the District of Columbia "had four judges to process the preliminary stages of more than 1,500 felony cases, and to hear and determine 7,500 serious misdemeanor cases, 38,000 petty offenses, and an equal number of traffic offenses per year."[13] Such conditions, the commission indicated are typical of the nation's lower courts.

Since nearly every arrest creates a new case for these courts, their burdens are directly proportional to the crime rate. The FBI's crime statistics give some indication of just how rapidly the burden on the lower courts has grown in recent years. The total volume of crime increased 122 percent from 1962 through 1969, outstripping population growth by an 11 to 1 ratio.[14] in 1970 the total rose another 11 percent.[15] While not all additional crimes are solved and brought before the courts, the number of arrests has risen steadily, adding to the burdens on the already overcrowded lower courts. Judges, already handling thousands of cases, are compelled to handle more.

When the court faces such an overwhelming task, it can respond in one of two ways. It can make sure that each case is handled properly—with full attention given to the rights of the defendant, to the evidence, and to the appropriateness of the sentence. This, however, instantly creates backlogs of enormous porportions; for example, defendants might wait months or years for trial for drunkenness, disorderly conduct, and similar petty offenses. Aware of this intolerable possibility, the courts have chosen the second alternative: disposing of cases as rapidly as they are brought in. Varying degrees of consideration are given to rights and procedure, but the degree is dependent on the time available. In practice, this means rapid and often arbitrary processing of huge numbers of cases, with little regard for due process. Here administration of justice consists almost entirely of administration, with little justice. As a lower court justice explained: "The tremendous volume of cases which must pass through these arraignment courts in a given period of time necessarily limits the opportunity of the judge, city attorney, and the defendant or his attorney to give more than perfunctory attention to any individual case."[16]

The consequences of this inattention may be imagined. The vast majority of defendants are pressured into an immediate plea of guilty, often without counsel. They are often told that if they take time to consider their plea, they will be returned to jail for several weeks,[17] and attempting a defense can be dangerous. Judges, under great pressure to dispose of cases rapidly, react adversely to anything but passive acquiescence. As the commission noted: "Upsetting the routine of misdemeanor court by demanding a trial is a risky proposition. . . . It can antagonize the judge and prosecution, resulting in a stiffer sentence."[18]

Often, any attempt at defense is pointless anyway. On charges of drunkenness, disorderly conduct, or other minor offenses, it is invariably the policeman's word against the defendant's. And, with the enormous volume of such cases, the judge will invariably take the policeman's word. When cases must be handled in only a few minutes, sometimes in only seconds, a presumption of guilt is created. And, as noted above, there are penalties for challenging that presumption.

These problems are compounded by the lack of expertise that is common among lower court judges. Often they are not required to be lawyers, or even familiar with the law. In many states they are elected in partisan political campaigns by voters who pay little attention to their qualifications. The predictable result is that"the conduct of some judges reveals ineptitude and a lack of familiarity with rules of evidence or developments in case law."19 As a consequence, widespread violations of defendants' rights are common. As the federally funded Massachusetts Law Reform Institute recently reported, after a study of the lower courts: "Many poor people throughout the commonwealth are imprisoned without lawful procedures every day."20

The results can be serious for the individual. They are given jail sentences of one, two, or three months on an assembly-line basis. Post-conviction remedies for the injustices that occur at this level are almost nonexistent. No record of the proceedings is kept in most cases, and the relatively unimportant nature of the crimes and the huge number of such cases make successful appeal hopeless. The penalties imposed by lower courts are as final as they are arbitrary.

Since most of those arrested and subjected to this assembly-line justice are poor and members of racial minorities, the resulting penalties constitute more than severe personal hardship. They are viewed by the poorer communities as part of a systematic process of harassment, and therefore constitute a serious source of racial tension.

The one possible source of help for these defendants, free legal assistance, is often not available. Because of the volume of cases, cities often will not provide public defenders in misdemeanor cases. Even where they do, judges often fail to inform defendants of their right to such aid.21 And if a lawyer is provided, the volume of cases he handles makes the assistance less than effective. Patricia Wald, writing for the commission's report on the courts, notes:

> The legal aid lawyer is so hampered by the case burden he must carry in the criminal court that he will take shortcuts to the detriment of the defendant. At times, stalwart representation of a defendant requires counsel to do battle with the District Attorney or the judge. Where the penalty may be damage to the rapport between court and counsel, and defense counsel has 25 more defendants to represent, he will be reluctant to challenge . . . and eager to get the case disposed.22

Thus with no meaningful legal aid, pressure to plead guilty or face further detention, and a stiffer sentence if they defend themselves (though given little chance to do so), defendants are routinely denied their constitutional rights. The system methodically destroys any respect the defendants had for the legal system and strengthens their belief that the government is systematically repressing the poor and members of minorities. If this were a deliberate action by evil men, it might be easily remediable, but the tragedy is that it is the natural result of an over-loaded system that must run on its own momentum. We have allowed our lower courts to deteriorate for too long, even as they fall far behind in the race to dispense justice fairly but with great speed. The speed that overloaded conditions impose on the lower courts is the archenemy of justice.

Perhaps the most tragic consequence of this situation is the degree to which it contributes to our high recidivism rate. Not only does the mis-demeanant see the legal system itself as unfair, he is deprived of the assistance which might rehabilitate him. Men who appear repeatedly in the lower courts, and develop into dangerous professional criminals, are never given the assistance or opportunity for rehabilitation which they need. The lower courts simply do not have the time to attempt this. Thus, despite the fact that nearly all convicted felons have prior mis-demeanor records, and "though the chance of diverting them from a career of crime is greatest at the time of his first brush with the law, the lower courts do not deal effectively with those who come before them."[23]

To obtain the sort of information necessary to assist these individuals requires time, which the busy magistrate does not have. As one observer noted: "In the lower courts . . . when a judge wishes to see the records of individual defendants, he must send for the record and then delay the trial until it arrives. Delay and inconvenience so caused often lead to a situation where the judge merely asks the defendant what his record is and relies upon his word."[24]

Thus sentences are imposed with no real knowledge of the defendant's record. And even if potentially serious criminals could be indentified, no programs exist to counsel them. They are transferred to crowded jails for a few months to live in wretched conditions and grow bitter at the callous treatment they were given. Later, usually after several such en-counters, they find themselves in prison for a more serious offense. Only then, much too late, is an attempt made to prepare them for a return to normal life. As the President's commission concluded in 1967:

> No program of crime prevention will be effective without a massive overhaul of the lower criminal courts. The many persons who en-counter these courts each year can hardly fail to interpret that experience as an expression of indifference to their situation and to the ideals of fairness, equality and rehabilitation professed in theory

yet frequently denied in practice. The result may be a hardening of anti-social attitudes in many defendants and the creation of obstacles to the successful adjustment of others.[25]

Thus, in a tragic sort of irony, our methods for the punishment of minor crimes may be a major cause of our skyrocketing crime rates. Our failure to deal with the problems of the backlogs and crowded lower court calendars may be a primary factor in more serious crime.

A final difficulty with the lower courts is that, all too often, they add to the burden of trial courts. Of course, the serious crimes fostered by the earlier neglect will wind up in the trial court, and the lower courts do not adequately perform the screening function they are intended to. Many lower court magistrates, hampered by their own burdens and unwilling or unable to carefully examine the serious cases brought before them, routinely pass large numbers of trivial or unsupportable charges to the trial court for determination. As *Christian Science Monitor* correspondent Howard James laments:

> Thousands of minor court judges are reluctant to pass on the merits of serious cases. So many times they simply pass them on to a higher court. . . . The lack of screening results in overloading higher courts. . . . "To clog up criminal courts with 50,000 cases, 12,000 of which could be thrown out by a magistrate, is ridiculous," says Adrian Bonelly, president judge in Philadelphia's intermediate county court."[26]

Ridiculous or not, that is what often occurs.

The pressures of time that lead to arbitrary sentencing, widespread denial of rights, unjust treatment of both innocent and guilty, and a lack of effort in distinguishing between the two create disrespect among the public and resentment among the convicted. Such injustice demands that lawmakers seek diligently solutions to the crowding that threatens to crush the system of justice at its roots.

When more serious crimes are in trial, our courts have been exceptionally conscientious in protecting the rights of the accused. As a result, the trial courts deal with their larger burdens in a fair manner, but at great length. Backlogs and serious delays in processing criminal cases are the result. Because the Constitution guarantees criminal defendants the right to a speedy trial, most trial courts make every effort to keep their criminal calendars current, but generally at the expense of efficient processing of civil cases.[27] Nevertheless, the problem of criminal court delay is rising. Howard James notes that in Los Angeles, for example, "the home of one of the best court systems in the nation, criminal court volume has hit crisis proportions, and is still climbing."28 The cause has been a rapid rise in the number of arrests each year—a serious problem throughout the nation which threatens to continue.

In addition to the increased volume of cases, the broadening of the defendant's rights in the wake of recent Supreme Court decisions has been a major factor contributing to delay. In the first place, the average trial now takes longer. Broader individual rights mean more issues on which to base a defense, more motions introduced, and more time spent haggling over the admissibility of evidence.

A second and far more serious reason for the increased congestion has been that expanded individual rights breeds more trials. To understand why this occurs it must be realized that even the most efficient courts lack the time to try more than a small fraction of the cases before them. The vast majority of cases—between 70 and 85 percent of all felonies, and over 90 percent of all misdemeanors—are settled by guilty pleas.29 Such admissions of guilt constitute a waiver of the defendants' right to a jury trial; they are, instead, convicted and sentenced in a brief hearing. Thus the guilty plea saves an enormous amount of time and judicial effort by making a trial unnecessary. The recent Supreme Court decisions, however, have reduced the proportion of cases thus settled, thereby increasing the workload of the courts. The number of cases might remain stable, but the number of lengthly trials would increase.

This is precisely what has occurred as a consequence of the expanded rights. Numerous additional defendants have chosen to go to trial in order to take advantage of those rights. Perhaps the most important change allowed indigent defendants the right to legal counsel at no charge. Large numbers of the poor who were previously run quickly through the courts are now in a position to benefit from their constitutional rights. This has probably been a major factor in the rising percentage of defendants who demand jury trials instead of pleading guilty.30 A 1968 federal survey attests to the rise in the percentage of cases going to trial: "The percentage of guilty pleas has declined recently perhaps because more defendants plead not guilty in order to preserve constitutional procedural defenses."31

The decline in guilty pleas means an increase in the number of jury trials. It is possible, of course, for a judge to hear criminal trials, but the increased availability of legal aid has also increased the number of persons who demand trial by jury. As James notes in Los Angeles: "Over the past five years . . . (in which the number of criminal cases rose 30%) the number of defendants demanding jury trials has increased 300%."[32] With more criminal cases before the courts, a higher percentage requiring lengthely trials, and more of the latter demanding jury trials (which run 40 percent longer than judge-conducted trials), the trial courts are falling increasingly behind.

The courts are understandably concerned about their failure to dispense justice within a reasonable period of time. Backlogs in criminal trials create serious injustices for many individuals, and can also pose a serious threat to the society as a whole. Consider, initially, the dangers to society. Prolonged delay between arrest and trial means that many defendants, if released on bail, are free to roam the community, sometimes committing further crimes while awaiting trial. The problem is especially acute with some crimes, such as the sale of narcotics, because offenders are often addicts who must have money to support their habits. Pushers, once arrested will often redouble their sales efforts in an attempt to recover their legal fees.

The problem is not limited to narcotics, however; the President's Commission on Crime in the District of Columbia reported in 1966 that "the 1965 annual report of the D.C. Bail Project discloses that 12.3% of potential felony releases were on bond on a prior charge at the time their most recent charge originated."[33]

Yet pretrial detention of persons who have not been proved guilty in a court of law involves its own drawbacks (discussed elsewhere in this book). The best solution to the problem is to reduce the lag between arrest and trial, thereby preserving society's right to self-protection while preserving the rights of the individual defendant.

Court congestion also allows many criminals to obtain their freedom on a permanent basis, as long delays force prosecutors to drop charges even in cases in which the evidence is overwhelming. This occurs for two reasons. First, long delays can deprive prosecutors of their best evidence, such as eyewitness testimony, when witnesses fail to appear for a trial or become vague in their memory.[34] Their failure to appear is understandable inasmuch as repeated delays can seriously interfere with the defendant's private life. When backlogs and delaying motions hold up a case, the process usually involves scheduling the defendant (and witnesses) to appear in court repeatedly, each time only to be told of a continuance. The witness understandably grows resentful of this lengthly process, as his waiting is in vain, and the prospect of returning for more of the same is not appealing.[35]

Even when witnesses do appear, long delays can blur their memory and allow their testimony to be discredited by a clever defense attorney. Uncertain memory in such cases can lead a witness to unknowingly contradict his previous statements with respect to many details. The defense attorney exploits all these errors to discredit the witness. And the question "What were you doing on the night of the fifteenth?" can be embarrassingly difficult to answer many months after the date in question.

The second reason prosecutors lose cases is due to their own delays. Defendants can move that charges be dropped if they are not quickly presented. Suspects cannot, of course, invoke their right to a speedy trial as grounds for dismissal when it is the defense motions that have caused the delay. They can do so, however, if the delay is caused by the prosecution. A survey of the reasons for dismissal of charges against defendants in the District of Columbia found that excessive time lapses were responsible for seven times as many dismissals as violation of the defendant's constitutional rights.[36]

The very discovery that endless delay can create this effect provides a massive incentive for more and more defense lawyers to stall for time as long as possible. As James notes: "Criminal lawyers across the country admit they try to delay justice if they have a tough case, hoping that witnesses will forget or change their minds. They have nothing to lose and everything to gain since their clients will probably go to jail anyway."[37] Thus criminals go free as the prosecution loses witnesses, and even the right to prosecute.

The dangers to society from backlogs are not confined solely to the release of dangerous criminals who would otherwise be convicted. The moral influence and restraining force that the law should exercise on the entire citizenry is dangerously weakened. That the law seems ineffective because of court congestion can have a shattering impact upon public confidence in and respect for the law. Recent polls have indicated that the image and prestige of the nation's courts have been falling steadily.[38] Much of the responsibility can be charged to court congestion. As Illinois Governor Richard Ogilvie has noted: "Delay is itself responsible for much of the current distrust of our courts." Governor Ogilvie suggests that reform is essential "before citizens have lost confidence that justice will be done, before their faith in law is shaken."[39] This conviction that law and order are crumbling in an ineffective court system can encourage extremists to demand more and more repressive measures to maintain public safety. As Governor Ogilvie warns: "Without a generally shared confidence in the administration of justice the law could only rest on coercive power."40

Finally, there are strong indications that the deterrent effect of the law with respect to criminals is seriously endangered by the backlogs. The key to an effective legal deterrent, according to Chief Justice Warren Burger, is "the sure knowledge that a criminal act will be followed by speedy trial and punishment."41 The reason is that criminals consider the likelihood of punishment far more important than its possible severity.

To be effective as a deterrent, punishment must be swift and visibly related to the offense. Former U.S. Attorney General Ramsey Clark elaborates:

> A speedy trial is essential to protect the public and to the very meaningfulness of the system. Unless there is a clear, direct and swift connection between the commission of a crime and apprehension, trial and sentencing for the offense, the criminal will never be deterred by the fear of conviction. Swift apprehension is the greatest part of the deterrent force because anxiety is highest at the moment of the crime, and the relationship between anti-social action and deprivation of liberty is then forcefully clear. The lapse of months between arrest and conviction dissipates any significant deterrent effect.42

The damage wrought by court delays is not confined to its detrimental effects on society. Many individuals suffer immense hardship, and the pressures for efficient case disposal threaten civil liberties. The most obvious result of the long delays is that persons who are unable to post bail must be detained in prison awaiting trial, often for longer periods than the sentence that would be imposed if they are found guilty. If found innocent, the detention period is for nought. The importance of this problem was highlighted by a recent *Time* magazine article:

> Jails detain defendants awaiting trial: 52% of all people in jails have not yet been convicted of any crime. Of those, four out of five are eligible for bail but cannot raise the cash. Because courts are overloaded, unconvicted defendants linger in crowded cells for months or even years.43

For these persons, delay means only lengthened imprisonment in bad, overcrowded jails.

Persons who are released on bail are not much more fortunate. Retaining a job and the respect of one's friends is not easy when a man is under indictment for rape or robbery. For many of these people, court congestion means irrecoverable personal loss.

A more subtle but equally pervasive danger to individual liberty is posed by the strong pressures for quick disposal of cases. Prosecutors must seek to resolve as many cases as possible without trial. In order to induce more pleas of guilty, they will frequently bargain with a defendant, offering him a lower sentence or a reduction of charges in exchange for a guilty plea. This process of plea bargaining entails risks because it is so informal and invisible. Prosecutors may use their power to threaten higher charges and sentences as strong pressure upon defendants to plead guilty. These pressures are almost irresistible when the defendant has already served much of the sentence while awaiting trial.

Prosecutors have no choice. As the *Harvard Law Review* observed in 1970: "Since he is under extreme administrative pressure from an overwhelming caseload, even a conscientious prosecutor must often bargain to save time."[44]

This process poses very real dangers to the individual and to the society. Innocent individuals can be, and have been, pressured into pleading guilty.[45] Equally serious, criminals may "cop a plea" and gain quick release to continue their depredations on society. Most of these problems, due to their complexity, will be deferred for in-depth examination to chapter 11. For the moment, however, it may be noted that trial courts, although rigorously protecting an individual's rights in trial, may become so dominated by administrative considerations that justice suffers. The danger is especially serious as the seriousness of the crimes increases. The *Harvard Law Review* warned:

> The criminal justice system has become a complex bureaucracy preoccupied with its "capacity to apprehend, try, convict and dispose of a high proportion of criminal offenders whose offenses become known," and guided by the need for speed and finality. Presently, a set of informal decisions by police and prosecutors separate the apparently innocent from the presumably guilty. Because of administrative pressure, little subsequent attention can be given to these initial determinations, and they are most often confirmed quickly by a guilty plea or a dismissal of charges. The scrutiny of the criminal process is lost.[46]

Thus backlogs and court delays in the trial courts create significant dangers. They subject society to the presence of men who would otherwise be convicted and imprisoned for long periods. By destroying public confidence in the law and criminals' fear of the law, they encourage repressive measures to deal with crime. They impose severe penalties on individual defendants and threaten to replace the scrutiny of the trial process with an arbitrary and poorly regulated administrative system of justice.

In March 1971 President Nixon told the National Conference on the Judiciary:

> In case after case, the appeal process is misused—to obstruct rather than advance the cause of justice. Throughout the state systems, the average time it takes to process an appeal is estimated to be as long as eighteen months. The greater the delay in commencing a trial, or retrial resulting from appeal, the greater the likelihood that witnesses will be unavailable and other evidence difficult to preserve. This means the failure of the process of justice.[47]

While it hardly seems fair to berate convicted men for utilizing fully the appeals procedure that the law makes available, the fact that such appeals may be prolonged irritates the public immensely. Through the appeals process, a defendant can keep litigation going for a very great length of time—years in many cases.[48]

The reason for such lengthly appeals is simple: the law provides for numerous steps in the process and allows substantial time lags in each. For example, a man convicted on felony charges in a state court would commence his appeal through the state courts. This involves, initially, a notice of appeal. In some states this notice must be posted within ten days of sentencing, but others allow as much as six months.[49] The second step is the preparation of the trial record, and it is here that the first significant delay occurs. The court reporters or court clerks are responsible for the preparation os such records; yet they are among the most overworked of all judicial employees. As a recent study found:

> The major reason that the appeal is not ready for transfer on the day the appeal is noted is the fact that the stenographic report of the trial proceedings is not ready. Usually there is only one reporter for each judge, and with a series of trials or hearings to report, it may be several weeks before the reporter can suspend to prepare a transcript. . . . Depending on the length of the trial, it may be months before it can be delivered.[50]

The legally permissible time for this step varies between twenty days and two years, but continuances are liberally granted.51

The third step is the preparation of briefs by the opposing lawyers, which must await the completion of the court transcript. The permitted time for his step ranges from three weeks to 105 days52—but, again, continuances are liberal and readily available. There is, then, an additional delay between the filing of briefs and the presentation of oral argument.

The fourth and final step is the announcement of the appellate court's decision. In complicated cases, this interval may be as long as six months. A 1964 study by the American Bar Foundation found that the time between sentencing and final disposition varied from ten to eighteen months in cases where appeals were pressed.53

Even at this stage the appeals process is far from complete. Defendants whose causes are rejected by the state appellate court may appeal to the state supreme court, with the time lags attendant upon preparation of briefs and oral arguments. If the defendant is still denied, he may turn to the federal court system for relief via a petition of habeas corpus. The purpose of this legal tool is to release a person from unlawful imprisonment, and it is usually couched in language that asks the state to show cause for holding the defendant against his will. Since the state will respond by pointing to his conviction in the trial, the defendant will have the opportunity to argue that this trial was unfair in some respect—that the defendant's constitutional rights were violated in the process. This appeal again involves the usual lags.

Either side may appeal the decision of the federal district court to the federal circuit court, and from there, if necessary, to the U.S. Supreme Court. Because of the large volume of such petitions, however, and the fact that most are of questionable value, they may be dismissed by the federal court at any stage.

The vast quantity of petitions for writs of habeas corpus has become another factor increasing the workload of federal courts. As the Denver *Law Journal* asserted: "In recent years the situation in state courts seems to have improved, while the situation in federal district courts has grown worse."54 The cause for this increased crowding has been the rapid rise in habeas corpus actions. As the President's Commission on Law and the Enforcement of Justice notes:

> A tremendous increase in the number of habeas corpus petitions
> has occurred because there has been a substantial increase in the

kinds of claims which may be raised. . . . In the last two decades the Supreme Court has given vastly broader interpretation to the constitutional rules regarding the admissibility of confessions and seized evidence, the right to counsel and a number of other areas. And the Court has held that a number of specific guarantees of the Bill of Rights apply to state criminal proceedings through the due process clause of the fourteenth amendment."[55]

Chief Justice Warren Burger notes the numerical consequences:

Twenty years ago there were virtually no petitions from prisoners in state prisons to the federal courts. . . . Petitions have grown from less than 100 annually twenty years ago to approximately 12,000 this year—quite a load on the federal courts.[56]

Thus the habeas corpus process has been cited as a cause of delay in the federal court system.

Petitions for certeriorari to the Supreme Court are also possible following the exhaustion of all state remedies. But, since thousands of such appeals are made each year, the chances of being one of the 150 cases selected are remote. As should be apparent by now, the possibilities for appeal are vast, nor do they end when an appeal is granted. Appellate court reversals of trials are not equivalent to an acquittal, they are merely directions to provide the accused with a new and a fair trial. State trial courts then hear the case again, if the prosecution chooses.

This lengthly process obviously means a long period of uncertainty before an individual is finally convicted. It is equally obvious that defendants have every incentive to exhaust all avenues of appeal. Even if held in custody, defendants have nothing to lose and a great deal to gain from appeal, and it is only reasonable to expect many of them to seize any opportunity to evade prison.

These delays, of course, create familiar problems for the prosecution if the appeal is ultimately granted. All the problems of witness unavailability and memory lapse are exacerbated during the appeal, especially as these witnesses consider the case closed. Thus a retrial may be extremely difficult to win.

Such delay also aggravates the public, especially in view of the nature of the reversal, if any. From the public standpoint, the defendant has been freed on a "legal technicality" rather than on merits of his defense. Of course, higher courts have no authority to review trial court findings of fact; they must reverse on such technicalities. But the public does not appreciate this, and the appeals process therefore damages their respect for the courts. And, of course, the appeals process aggravates the loss of the deterrent effect of punishment, as the punishment is anything but swift and sure.

This lengthy process can also have detrimental effects on those who fail to win reversal—a clear majority of those who attempt appeals. Men whose primary concern should be rehabilitation are concerned, instead, with trying to beat the system. Chief Justice Burger explains:

> No system makes sense if it encourages a long-drawn-out war with society. The rehabilitation or re-education of a man cannot be carried on while he is at war with society in a process of interminable petition writs and hearings.57

Or, as Ramsey Clark concluded:

> The lapse of months between arrest and conviction . . . reduces rehabilitation possibilities.58

Our current system of appeals, which is far too time consuming, leads to a deterioration of respect for the law and a difficult burden for the prosecution in a retrial. To some degree, it impedes the rehabilitation of those it fails to free. None of these problems is reducible to numbers with any precision, but all deserve a great deal more attention than they have received in the recent past.

The Jury as a Source of Delay

The court congestion caused by the use of the jury should be considered in examining the sources of the lags just discussed; but it should be obvious from the foregoing analysis that juries cannot be the sole or even a major cause. Trial by jury was in use for decades before crowded dockets became a serious problem; and even today some courts operate efficiently with frequent jury trials. Other factors, such as the increased attractiveness of a trial, expanded trial rights, and the availability of counsel, however, have increased the use of the jury substantially. There is, moreover, no doubt that jury trials take longer than any other method of justice. They require 50 percent more time than a trial by a judge alone, and far longer than the brief hearing needed to accept a plea of guilty. The fact that the jury is not the immediate *cause* of court congestion may not be relevant, therefore, in deciding if it is a luxury that has grown too costly for the times. Even if other factors cause the delays, removing the jury may eliminate them.

It is not immediately apparent why a jury consumes so much more time than other forms of trial, although the statistics are unimpeachable. The only obvious difference is in numbers: the jury sits in the same courtroom and hears the same trial as a judge. But even the deliberations of a jury do not seem appreciably longer than those that a judge might be expected to make.

Actually, there are four reasons for the difference in time. The first, and usually the most significant, is the selection of the jury. The voir dire, or the questioning of the jurors to determine impartiality and competence, can sometimes be accomplished quickly, but in cases in which some form of prejudice may be expected against the defendant, the questioning will be long and involved, and large numbers of prospective jurors will be rejected. The murder trial of Black Panthers Bobby Seale and Erika Huggins is probably the most spectacular example on record because every conceivable form of prejudice worked against them. Black political leaders of a radical leftwing organization that was despised by many and feared by most, they were also the subject of an enormous amount of highly prejudicial publicity. The task of obtaining twelve jurors who had not developed any prior opinion on the merits of the case, who were free of racial and political bias, and who could view the issue fairly and objectively posed a herculean challenge. Four months were required and 1,035 jurors were rejected before a jury which met these requirements could be found.[59]

While the Black Panther trial was probably unique, it illustrates the potential time lag in selecting a jury. In most important or well-publicized cases, the voir dire and selection process takes a number of days and is the primary factor behind jury-time consumption. But it should be emphasized that it is precisely these trials in which the value of the jury shows most clearly. Bias by one or more jurors is not sufficient to convict; bias by a single judge would be fatal.

A second consideration is the behavior of lawyers, who, before a jury, often put on an extravagant show, calling more witnesses, questioning them in greater detail, and introducing more evidence. They will also try harder to impugn the opponents' evidence and witnesses—frequently using methods which would not impress a judge.[60]

The third factor is that, in jury trials, lawyers consume much time arguing about the admissibility of evidence. In a judge-conducted trial, that is seldom an issue. The judge, knowing what evidence is admissible and what is not, will generally allow all relevant material to be heard, then consider only that material he knows to be admissible. In a jury trial, on the other hand, inadmissible evidence, such as illegally seized goods, cannot be presented to the jury—it would be too easily influenced by evidence which should not be considered. Thus defense attorneys in jury trials spend considerable time challenging questionable evidence, in conference with the judge and the prosecutor outside the jury's hearing, to prevent the jury from considering it.

The fourth aspect of jury trials that requires increased time is their deliberations. While deliberation is sometimes swift, it can be protracted for several days as jurors argue the case among themselves. And in some instances the deliberation produces a hung jury, which requires a complete retrial.

If the jury is to be preserved, little can be done to remedy the last three of these sources of delay. The first, the time spent in selecting the jury, might be substantially improved if the questioning is limited or the number of peremptory challenges reduced. Either of these, however, would lessen the impartiality of the jury, risking bias to save time. Under such circumstances, the jury might as well be eliminated.

The only other possible solution would be to reduce the size of the jury. In March 1971 the Judicial Conference of the United States, the administrative and policy-making arm of the federal judiciary, voted to reduce the size of juries in civil cases and indicated that, if this is successful, it would be considered for criminal cases. [61] Reducing the size of the jury of course means reducing the time needed for selection in proportion to the cut. A six-man jury, presumably, would require but half the time for selection.

None of these solutions will save a great amount of time and, if that is the primary consideration, the jury may be doomed. But before such a drastic step is taken, it would be well to consider the impact that removal of the jury would have on the national problem of court congestion. In the lower courts, where overcrowding and its attendant injustices are worst of all, it would have no impact; these courts do not use juries. The right to a jury trial does not apply to petty offenses and misdemeanors, and few who are eligible for a jury elect for one.

Likewise, in the appeal and the habeas corpus processes juries are not a factor whatever. Appeal delays are written into the statutes, and appeals proceed without a jury.

Even in the trial courts, where juries are used, they influence only a small percentage of the cases. Over 90 percent are resolved by guilty pleas; and of the remaining 10 percent about half are tried by judges. The time saved from elimination of the jury would therefore apply to about only 5 percent of all cases tried. There may be some delay in these, and important national cases, such as the Black Panther trial, may consume a great deal of time, but the total of time lost in jury trials is not especially important. To abolish the criminal trial jury would hardly make a dent in the enormous backlogs now confronting our courts. The only effect might be to reduce all criminal justice to the assembly-line procedure described previously. Solutions to the congestion must deal with more fundamental causes of the problem, and to these we now turn.

ALTERNATIVE REMEDIES FOR COURT CONGESTION

Recently, when Chief Justice Walter H. McLaughlin of the Massachusetts Superior Court was asked to pinpoint the causes of the nation's judicial crisis, he responded: "It all comes down to not enough judges and not enough money to do the job."[62] The vast increase in both population and the incidence of crime in recent years makes this response the obvious one; yet oddly, in a crisis of court congestion this simple solution is commonly evaded. If the caseload exceeds the capacity of the system, the clear solution is an increase in the number of courts and judges. Yet most municipal courts continue to operate with the same number of judges as they did two or three decades ago.[63] The fact is that the executive and legislative branches of government have steadfastly refused to appropriate the funds necessary to create new judgeships, courthouses, and court staffs as they have been needed.[64]

For some reason, there seems to be a presumption that increasing the size of the judiciary is an evil to be avoided if at all possible. The most frequently cited reasons are the danger of lowering the quality of the judiciary and increasing the costs. With respect to judicial quality, it may fairly be said that, in many places, no decline is possible. Many incompetent judges have been appointed or elected to the lower courts and the trial courts, often without ability or knowledge in the legal field, and it would not lower their quality to increase their numbers. No one is advocating mass-produced judgeships, but it seems clear that new men, of whatever quality, would eventually raise the level of competence in general. Unqualified judges, with the time to learn their jobs and dispose of cases fairly, are a clear improvement over unqualified judges in a hurry to convict.

The costs of judicial expansion pose a second barrier, at least in the minds of legislators. These increases are generally expressed in percentage terms, which are misleading to say the least. The total expenditure by all state, local and federal governments on the judiciary system in 1967 totaled $260 million—less than one-thousandth of the total governmental expenditure. Effective justice would be worth many times that figure. Especially in view of the significant monetary cost imposed by crime on society, a few hundred million dollars to overhaul the system so that it effectively rehabilitates offenders would be well spent.

Additional funds are also vitally needed to provide the courts with more trained staffs and more efficient information filing and retrieval systems. Ramsey Clark urges that judges be given greater support " in the form of magistrates, referees, masters, commissioners, bailiffs, clerks, legal assistants and secretaries. . . . To deny such assistance is to impair justice and deny speedy trials." He also notes that "automatic legal data retrieval—the storage and electronic recall of pertinent briefs, decisions, and legal documents—can save every judge many hours of labor and assure higher uniformity in decision."65

In large measure, then, the congestion of our courts is simply a reflection of the short-sighted refusal of our legislative bodies to provide them with operating funds. More money and more courts, together with the suggested structural reforms, would relieve the crowded dockets and provide fairer treatment for everyone.

Even in the absence of the unpleasant task of spending more money, there are numerous administrative reforms that could speed the processing of cases without impairing individual rights. First, better coordination of the existing court systems is essential. Too often a court is overburdened while a nearby court operates well below its capacity, especially in urban areas. More efficient planning could make use of both courts simultaneously, relieving the congestion in one by utilizing the other to its capacity." Reforms could also be instituted to ensure that judges perform an acceptable amount of work. Each judge should be given some latitude in setting his workload, but better records should be kept of the courts' output, and an attempt should be made to get greater effort from the numerous judges whom the President's commission found to be working intolerably short hours while serious backlogs developed.66 Standards should also be established to limit the delay that can arise from the request for continuances. A New York court is currently experimenting with this kind of system, establishing a schedule and specifying penalties for each side if it requires more than two continuances before trial or fails to appear as scheduled.67

Several administrative remedies also appear useful with respect to the unreasonable delays encountered in the appeal process. The basis for these delays is the lengthy delay permitted at each stage; but the statutory limits could be tightened and the continuances at each stage limited to one brief period of fixed duration. Lawyers now take advantage of legally permissible delays; but if the laws were tightened it would be possible to reduce the time from conviction to determination of appeal from the present ten to eighteen months to no more than five months.[68]

The overload in the federal courts created by habeas corpus actions could be substantially reduced if trained law clerks were available to sort out the mass of frivolous requests.[69] The number of cases reviewed by the courts could be further reduced by a more careful definition of the conditions under which these appeals will be reviewed, a policy advocated by Chief Justice Burger. Some limited steps in this direction have already been taken by Congress.[70]

With respect to the lower courts, though, expansion in the size of the judiciary is absolutely essential, the most valuable reform might be in the definition of crime. Utilizing a non-criminal proceeding to deal with such "crimes" as drunkenness, or legalizing other victimless acts, might be extremely valuable in relieving the crowding of the lower courts. Drunkenness, for instance, accounts for fully one-third of the volume of these courts, and could doubtless be better handled by some form of social counseling than by criminal prosecutions. This sort of rehabilitation effort is clearly superior to the present method of dealing with alcoholics, which essentially consists of jailing them for drunkenness, releasing them to return to the gutter, then jailing them again. Aside from the enormous social benefits that rehabilitation would have, it would be an excellent means or reducing the congestion of the lower courts.[71]

Thousands of additional cases might be removed if certain private consensual activities, such as abortion, homosexuality, or possession of marijuana, were legalized. These victimless crimes are exceedingly hard to detect and prosecute, and are probably not worth the effort.[72] Legalization would remove government investigation from an essentially fruitless field and would free the law enforcement machinery, including the courts, for more serious offenses.

SUMMARY

It is evident that a wide array of solutions is available to combat the congestion that threatens to engulf our courts. While altering the jury itself can have some time-saving impact, it would not be significant in comparison to the gains available through more straight-forward methods of relief for the courts. The large volume of cases confronting the system can be dealt with through administrative reform, or even our current court system in some instances. In others, more judges and more money are essential to provide the courts with adequate staff and information systems. The funds are available, and the potential gains, even in monetary savings from reduced crime, are so impressive that more funds for the courts would be a wise investment.

The huge caseloads now overburdening the courts cannot be blamed on the jury systems. Juries simply are not significant contributors to the delays. Thus the widely accepted value of jury trials for criminal cases need not be sacrificed to end the congestion of our courts.

4 Pretrial Publicity

While pretrial publicity has not prevailed upon civil or even criminal court cases in general, or upon the news media in particular, its impact in special situations has been widespread. Although it is impossible to empirically assess the effect of this publicity on the jury system, the dangers and threats it poses to justice should be compared in light of the advantages such publicity may create in terms of enhancing justice. Today, most newspapers in America are in a large sense representatives of —so to speak—a dynamic and changing status quo,[73] but public opinion and the news media have also played an important role in establishing new precedents and in creating new departures from traditional forms of law and justice. We will not attempt to enumerate every case, but a few will be cited as illustrations.

The most recent example of a landmark case in which publicity affected judicial proceedings by influencing their nature and outcome was the trial of Lieutenant William Calley for the My Lai massacre. Today it is no secret that the United States Army has quietly convicted scores of soldiers for killing Vietnamese captives in combat situations;[74] nor is it any longer a secret that American soldiers in Vietnam shot up villages under orders and killed countless civilians.[75]

The trial of Lieutenant Calley, however, was not the first of its kind; the first United States codified laws of war were used against Confederate Captain Henry Wirz, who was hanged in 1865 for letting nearly 14,000 Union prisoners die in Andersonville prison camp.[76] And Brigadier General Jacob Hurd Smith was tried in 1902 for ordering a My Lai-style massacre during the army's anti-guerrilla campaign in the Philippines.[77]

Gratian, the twelfth-century founder of canon law, wrote that "the soldier who kills a man in obedience to authority is not guilty of murder."[78] Yet this immunity must be regulated, for as C. P. Snow once remarked: "More hideous crimes have been committed in the name of obedience than have ever been committted in the name of rebellion."79 Indeed, "for at least 800 years, men have tried to control war's excesses by transforming the rules of knightly chivalry into modern prohibitions against needless military cruelty."80

Still, Lieutenant Calley claims he was never informed of such prohibitions. If there is any validity to Calley's claim, hundreds of thousands of American troops in Vietnam (and elsewhere) would probably have continued slaughtering innocent and defenseless civilians, in ignorance of the illegality of their actions, were it not for the fact that the My Lai incident was reported in the news media. "One of the most deplorable aspects of the alleged 1968 massacre of Vietnamese villagers by American troops is that officialdom apparently was not moved to make prompt and thorough inquiries until the incident was reported in the news media."81 Even F. Lee Bailey, the defense counsel for Lieutenant Calley's company commander, Captain Ernest Medina, "accused the Army of covering up My Lai" when he spoke to the students of Northeastern University.82

Trials such as this one, which create great tension over issues under furious debate and attempt to culminate in a resolution over conflicting values, often serve as "the device by which the conscience and the phliosophy of the society are enunciated."83 Much earlier in American history, the controversy over the trials of John Brown and Dred Scott did not emerge from a vacuum but as the result of three decades of abolitionist strife that was caused by discrimination of the worst sort; and "the resultant judgment poised the nation for its imminent plunge into tragedy."84 The philosophy of society was enunciated in the conviction of John Brown, and the concern of some Americans was evident in the special chapel services that were held at the time of Brown's execution, as well as in the subsequent eulogies. The divergent influences on the Dred Scott case were cogently delineated in the *Oberlin Evangelist* on March 18, 1857:

> The Slave Power of this nation has made another bold move in a recent decision of the U.S. Supreme Court. The case has been pending several months, the announcement of their decision being postponed till after the late election, lest the indignation it must arouse should endanger the success of the pro-slavery cause at the polls.85

While it is not yet clear whether the Calley trial will accompany the termination of American military intervention under the guise of preventing communist aggression, it is quite evident that "the Scopes trial not only marked the end of the American fundamentalist cosmography but was a notably significant cause of its death."[86]

Despite the fact that as late as 1971 the executive and the legislative branches of our federal government have attempted to intimidate CBS for its controversial production of "The Selling of the Pentagon," as early as 1735 an American jury returned a general verdict of not guilty and a prisoner, John Peter Zenger, was released to the cheering spectators of the court, while through the colonies went the word of the victory of the press over the tyranny of oppressive law. The defense attorney, Andrew Hamilton, noted that while his doctrines were not allowed in court as law, they did not go unheard by the public. While Chief Justice James DeLancey denied the right of the defendant to prove the truth,

> the interest in and the approval of the outcome of the Zenger trial was a symptom of a revolutionary spirit which, nurtured by writers such as Zenger and Paine, was to sweep the country and lead to a revolution whose success would be as much due to the pamphleteer as to the minuteman. The Revolutionary and post-Revolutionary era was marked by the attempts of the newly independent colonists, influenced by their vivid memories of the oppressions of England and their recent support and applause of the radical writers, to preserve in their constitutional declarations of freedom of the press issues that had been so vital to the Revolution. The press could not be regarded as a tool of the ruling group in a democratic state. Under the democratic theory of government it had to take its place as the spokesman of the popular opinion which was to rule.[87]

Clearly, as in this case, "the trial is often the cornerstone of the institution of the future."[88] Freedom of expression thus enjoyed its legal beginning in America, though the documented defense and expression of such freedom on a substantive level continues to be subjected to general, ambiguous, and equivocal harassment by such luminaries as Spiro Agnew, Melvin Laird, F. Edward Hebert, and Harley O. Staggers, etc. [89] Thus it seems as impossible to suppress news of crime and punishment as to suppress unorthodox political views or freedom of expression. The problem, or advantage—as the case may be—"is that public interest in crime inescapably brings public influence upon the administration of justice."[90]

Friendly and Goldfarb argue that press coverage of crime and trials is believed to produce harmful effects in at least two ways.

> One comes from bringing to the attention of the actual or prospective jurors, outside the courtroom, information and opinion that is

"nonjudicial" (or "extra-record" or "extra-judicial"), namely, material they are not allowed to consider under procedures society has designed to govern and fair adjudication of a defendant's guilt or innocence. The second comes from creating an over-all atmosphere in the community, by the sheer volume or sensationalism of publication about the case, that tends to contaminate the objectivity of the jurors and the court and to subvert the dispassionate attitude prescribed for the trial procedure.91

Both of these indictments of press coverage of the Sam Sheppard trial were true, and, they will be documented at considerable length later.

Of primary importance is the frequency of such occurrences and their effect on the decision of the jury. Kalven and Zeisel suggest that "a fundamental fact about the jury trial is that it is the mode of final disposition for only a small fraction of all criminal prosecutions."92 Judge J. Skelly Wright of the U.S. Court of Appeals for the District of Columbia agreed when in 1965 he said that the problem of prejudicial publication does not exist at all in the

> great majority of the hundreds of thousands of criminal cases. . . . Less than 1 per cent of those cases receive a line of notice in the press. Of that 1 per cent, between 75 and 90 per cent of the defendants plead guilty. . . . We are dealing, therefore, with possible prejudicial publicity in only a small fraction of the less than 1 per cent of the criminal cases brought. Moreover, even as to that 1 per cent that do receive press notice, the notices are not all prejudicial.93

If Friendly and Goldfarb are correct in their position that the administration of justice is influenced by public interest, perhaps "the argument is unacceptable that infrequency justifies complacency [for] any denial at all to fair trial is too large to be ignored."94

The widespread harm of pretrial publicity, then, does not necessarily result from the wrong jury decision but rather from the lack of fairness which might produce the wrong jury decision. This has happened in several recent cases. By coincidence, decisions on the latest two such trials were released on the same day, and both were subjected to opinions indiscreetly expressed by the same person and published widely.

THE CHARLES MANSON CASE

In March 1971 death in the gas chamber was decreed by a jury for Charles Manson and three of his young women disciples for the murder of actress Sharon Tate and six other persons.[95] The jurors apparently felt that the defendants were neither insane nor so influenced by drugs that they did not know that they were committing murder, despite the fact that the three women who admitted participating in the crimes had testified that they had been influenced by LSD at the time.[96] The jurors also seemed to reject the argument that Manson did not order the crimes. In admitting their roles, the three young women claimed that Manson had known nothing of the killings that took place in August of 1969.[97] Mrs. Marie Mesmer, one of the jurors, identified the quality of the evidence upon which the jury made its assumption of guilt when she asserted: "There's no doubt that he was the leader. He was the instigator. He's a dangerous influence on society."[98] Manson never took the witness stand in the presence of the jury. The convicted women, ranging in age from twenty-one to twenty-three, all confessed their own guilt but denied that Manson had any connection with the murders.[99]

In presenting his case prosecutor Vincent T. Bugliosi contended that Manson had ordered the crimes and that the women were "mindless robots" who carried out Manson's orders. He argued that the murders at the home of Sharon Tate and wealthy supermarket owner Leno LaBianca had been ordered by Manson because of his dislike of "the establishment," and also in order to trigger a black-white race war by making it appear that the slaying of the seven white persons had been committed by Negroes.[100]

Eight months before the Manson sentence was officially announced in court, President Richard Nixon personally found him guilty, and newspaper headlines from coast to coast read "MANSON GUILTY, NIXON DECLARES."[101] Defense attorney Paul Fitzgerald's response was "we would never get an impartial jury after this."[102] The White House later attempted to correct Nixon's "slip of the tongue" by explaining that he had omitted the word "allegedly" and did not "intend to draw a premise of guilt on Manson.[103] While this official response may very well be true, the context of the speech in which Nixon made the declaration of guilt should also be considered. The *Washington Evening Star* describes it this way:

> Elsewhere in his Denver remarks he spoke feelingly of the need for preserving fairness in the judicial system. But, indicative of a verbal habit that played a part in the Manson lapse, he spoke several times of "the guilty"—rather than just "the accused"—as deserving of fair trials.
>
> Insertion of the word "alleged" does not take the curse off the fail-

ure of sensitivity that led him to discuss the Los Angeles murder trial in the first place. A President, commanding the immense powers of the federal government, has no business talking in public about a case that is pending before a jury. Besides saying that Manson was guilty, Mr. Nixon used strong language to castigate the two defense lawyers who were jailed overnight after being held in contempt of court.104

Regardless of the context of Nixon's statement, however, retraction was impossible and every member of the Manson jury soon became aware of Nixon's opinion.105 Although Manson may be undeserving of sympathy for the communication of Nixon's statement to the jury, for someone who directed the 1968 and 1970 political campaigns on the issue of law and order, President Nixon's respect for justice may be viewed as leaving something to be desired.

The American people did not have to wait long, furthermore, to learn of presidential interference in another case, this time intentionally.

LIEUTENANT WILLIAM CALLEY

Four years before the My Lai massacre, 23-year-old William Calley found a home in the army as an enlisted man, a company clerk. "It was something he could do after a long record of failures. . . . Calley Jr. saw a chance to become an officer and he took it. Three presidents saw a chance to keep communism out of South Vietnam and they took it. These circumstances conjoined in the little Viet Cong village of My Lai on March 16, 1968."106

The Calley trial began on November 12, 1970, and the government rested its case December 8, reopening it briefly for two supplementary witnesses. Calley admitted ordering the execution of a reported seventy persons in a ditch, claiming he did so under orders of his superiors. "It wasn't any big deal," Calley said of the unresisting Vietnamese men, women, and children who fell beneath the automatic rifles of five American infantrymen at the drainage ditch in My Lai. Calley testified that the main thing on his mind was "finishing off" the Vietnamese, whom he blamed for delaying the advance of his platoon and bringing Colonel Medina's criticism on his head. When asked why he ordered their execution, Calley replied: "Because that was what I was instructed to do, and I had been delayed long enough. I was trying to get out of there. Before I got criticized again, sir."107

By the end of March 1971 Calley was convicted by an army jury of the premeditated murder of not less than twenty-two Vietnamese.108

Within a couple of days, however, there were many indications that the majority of his fellow citizens felt that Calley should not have been brought to trial for the killing of South Vietnamese civilians at My Lai; and in Massachusetts a plurality of those polled believed that high-ranking American generals should be tried for their role in the killings.109 On April 4 the results of a Harris survey suggested that the public agreed, by 69 to 16 percent, with the statement that "Lieutenant Calley and the others indicted have been singled out unfairly as scapegoats."110 Three days earlier, Senator J. William Fulbright had said that, in light of the conviction of Lieutenant Calley for murdering civilians at My Lai, there was a serious question about assessing blame for Vietnam war crimes unless the United States is prepared to "go all the way" to the President as commander-in-chief of the armed forces.111 Fulbright expressed this opinion after agreeing with Senator John Sherman Cooper and other members of the Senate Foreign Relations Committee: "Now that the 1964 Gulf of Tonkin resolution has been repealed, the President has no legal or constitutional authority except to withdraw the troops from Vietnam."112

With public sentiment motivating him and the logical implications of the Calley conviction plaguing him, President Nixon could no longer wait until the jury's decision had followed the normal appeal procedure, which includes two military boards of review and review by the Secretary of the Army, before announcing that he would personally review the case and make the military's final decision vis-à-vis Lieutenant William L. Calley Jr.113 In order to remove any ambiguity about his attitude toward the conviction, Nixon also ordered Calley released from the stockade at Fort Benning, Georgia.114 Opinion Research Corporation soon announced that the percentage of Americans who approved President Nixon's performance as chief executive rose from 51 percent (in the previous month) to 54 percent.115

One of the first and most penetrating analyses of Nixon's decision to decide the Calley case was written as a letter by Captain Aubrey M. Daniel III, the prosecutor in the trial, to President Nixon himself. It deserves to be read from beginning to end.

Sir:

It is very difficult for me to know where to begin in this letter as I am not accustomed to writing letters of protest. I only hope that I can find the words to convey to you my feelings as a United States citizen and as an attorney, who believes that respect for the law is one of the fundamental bases upon which this nation is founded.

On Nov. 26, 1969, you issued the following statement through your press secretary, Mr. Ronald Ziegler, in referring to the My Lai incident:

"An incident such as that alleged in this case is in direct violation not only of U.S. military policy but is also abhorrent to the conscience of all the American people. The Secretary of the Army is continuing his investigation. Appropriate action is and will be taken to assure that illegal and immoral conduct as alleged be dealt with in accordance with the strict rules of military justice.

"This incident should not be allowed to reflect on the some million and a quarter young Americans who have now returned to the United States after having served in Vietnam with great courage and distinction." At the time you issued this statement, a general court martial had been directed for a resolution of the charges which had been brought against Lieutenant William L. Calley, Jr., for his involvement at My Lai.

On Dec. 8, 1970, you were personally asked to comment on the My Lai incident at a press conference. At that time you made the following statement: ". . . What appears was certainly a massacre, and under no circumstances was it justified.

". . . One of the goals we are fighting for in Vietnam is to keep the people from South Vietnam from having imposed upon them a government which has atrocity against civilians as one of its policies.

". . . We cannot ever condone or use atrocities against civilians in order to accomplish that goal."

These expressions of what I believed to be your sentiments were truly reflective of my own feelings when I was given the assignment of prosecuting the charges which had been preferred against Lieutenant Calley. My feelings were generated not by emotionalism or self-righteous indignation but by my knowledge of the evidence of the case, the laws of this nation in which I so strongly believe, and my own conscience.

I knew that I had been given a great responsibility and I only hoped that I would be able to discharge my duties and represent the United States in a manner which would be a credit to the legal profession in our system of justice. I undertook the prosecution of the case without any ulterior motives for personal gain either financial or political. My only desire was to fulfill my duty as a prosecutor and see that justice was done in accordance with the laws of this nation.

I dedicated myself totally to this end from November of 1969 until the trial was concluded. Throughout the proceedings there was criticism of the prosecution but I lived with the abiding conviction that once the facts and the law had been presented there would be no doubt in the mind of any reasonable person about the necessity for the prosecution of this case and the ultimate verdict. I was mistaken.

The trial of Lieutenant Calley was conducted in the finest tradition of our legal system. It was in every respect a fair trial in which every legal right of Lieutenant Calley was fully protected. It clearly demonstrated that the military justice system which has previously been subject to much criticism was a fair system. Throughout the trial, the entire system was under the constant scrutiny of the mass media and the public, and the trial of Calley was also in a very real sense the trial of the military judicial system.

However, there was never an attack lodged by any member of the media concerning the fairness of the trial. There could be no such allegation justifiably made. I do not believe that there has ever been a trial in which the accused's rights were more fully protected, the conduct of the defense given greater latitude, and the prosecution held to stricter standards. The burden of proof which the government had to meet in this case was not beyond a reasonable doubt but beyond possibility. The very fact that Lieutenant Calley was an American officer being tried for the deaths of Vietnamese during a combat operation by fellow officers compels this conclusion.

The jury selection, in which customary procedure was altered by providing both the defense and the prosecution with three peremptory challenges instead of the usual one, was carefully conducted to insure the impartiality of those men who were selected. Six officers, all combat veterans, five having served in Vietnam, were selected.

These six men who had served their country well were called upon again to serve their nation as jurors and to sit in judgment on Lieutenant Calley as prescribed by law. From the time they took their oaths until they rendered their decision, they performed their duties in the very finest tradition of the American legal system.

If ever a jury followed the letter of the law in applying it to the evidence presented, they did. They are indeed a credit to our system of justice and to the officer corps of the United States Army.

When the verdict was rendered, I was totally shocked and dismayed at the reaction of many people across the nation. Much of the adverse public reaction I can attribute to people who have acted emotionally and without being aware of the evidence that was presented and perhaps even the laws of this nation regulating the conduct of war.

These people have undoubtedly viewed Lieutenant Calley's conviction simply as the conviction of an American officer for killing the enemy. Others, no doubt out of a sense of frustration, have seized upon the conviction as a means of protesting the war in Vietnam. I would prefer to believe that most of the public criticism has come from people who are not aware of the evidence either because they have not followed the evidence as it was presented or having followed it they have chosen not to believe it.

Certainly, no one wanted to believe what occurred at My Lai, including the officers who sat in judgment of Lieutenant Calley. To believe, however, that any large percentage of the population could believe the evidence which was presented and approved of the conduct of Lieutenant Calley would be as shocking to my conscience as the conduct itself since I believe that we are still a civilized nation.

If such be the case, then the war in Vietnam has brutalized us more than I care to believe, and it must cease.

How shocking it is if so many people across the nation have failed to see the moral issue which was involved in the trial of Lieuenant Calley—that it is unlawful for an American soldier to summarily execute unarmed and unresisting men, women, children and babies.

But how much more appalling it is to see so many of the political leaders of the nation who have failed to see the moral issue or, having seen it, compromise it for political motives in the face of apparent public displeasure with the verdict.

I would have hoped that all of the leaders of this nation, which is supposed to be the leader within the international community, for the protection of the weak and the oppressed regardless of nationality, would have either accepted and supported the laws of this country as reflected by the verdict of the court or not made any statement concerning the verdict until they had had the same opportunity to evaluate the evidence that the members of the jury had.

In view of your previous statements concerning this matter, I have been particularly shocked and dismayed at your decision to intervene in these proceedings in the midst of the public clamor. Your decision could only have been prompted by the response of a vocal segment of the population, who while no doubt acting in good faith, cannot be aware of the evidence which resulted in Lieutenant Calley's conviction.

Your intervention has, in my opinion, damaged the military judicial system and lessened any respect it may have gained as a result of these proceedings. You have subjected a judicial system of this country to the criticism that it is subject to when it is a fundamental precept of our judicial system that the legal processes of this country must be kept free from any outside influences.

What will be the impact of your decision upon future trials, particularly those within the military?

Not only has respect for the legal process been weakened and the critics of the military judicial system been given support for their claims of command influence, the image of Lieutenant Calley, a man convicted of the premeditated murder of at least twenty-one, 21, unarmed and unresisting people, as a national hero, has been inhanced, while at the same time support has been given to those persons who have so unjustly criticized the six loyal and honorable officers who have done this country a great service by fulfilling their duties as jurors so admirably.

Have you considered those men in making your decisions? The men who since rendering their verdict have found themselves and their families the subject of vicious attacks upon their honor, integrity, and loyalty to this nation.

It would seem to be more appropriate for you as the President to have said something in their behalf and to remind the nation of the purpose of our legal system and the respect it should command.

I would expect that the President of the United States, a man whom I believed should and would provide the moral leadership for this nation, would stand fully behind the law of this land on a moral issue which is so clear and about which there can be no compromise. For this nation to condone the acts of Lieutenant Calley is to make us no better than our enemies and make any pleas by this nation for the humane treatment of our own prisoners meaningless.

I truly regret having to have written this letter and wish that no innocent person had died at My Lai on 16 March 1968. But innocent people were killed under circumstances that will always remain abhorrent to my conscience.

While in some respects what took place at My Lai has to be considered to be a tragic day in the history of our nation, how much more tragic would it have been for this nation to have taken no action against those who were responsible.

That action was taken, but the greatest tragedy of all will be if political expedience dictates the compromise of such a fundamental moral principle as the inherent unlawfulness of the murder of innocent persons, making the action and the court of six honorable men who served their country so well, meaningless.

> Respectfully yours,
> AUBREY M. DANIEL III
> Captain, JAGC, Trial Counsel
> U.S. v. Calley[116]

Calley's lawyer, George Latimer, naturally found Daniel's views "entirely wrong," and added: "I believe the President was exactly right in what he did."[117] Nixon's actions also won the endorsement of the judge at Calley's trial, Colonel Reid W. Kennedy.[118]

The criticism of Nixon's decision equaled that of the jury's decision. Nixon, furthermore, was to encounter considerable difficulty in attempting to justify his action. "Public reaction to the verdict was a factor in Nixon's decision, but not the determinant," said a White House aide. From another observer came the suggestion that "President Lincoln also intervened to help soldiers."[119] Mr. Nixon's special assistant and former counsel, John Ehrlichman, said this was not an unusual procedure and pointed to the precedent of several Civil War cases in which President Lincoln had concerned himself.[120] But Ehrlichman failed to point out that although Lincoln may have been lavish in his exercise of the pardoning power, there is no record of his intervening for an officer who had been convicted and sentenced to life imprisonment for murdering twenty-two unarmed civilians, including a baby, either before, during, or after the normal course of judicial review.[121]

Ehrlichman also attempted to justify Nixon's decision by explaining that it was important for him to make clear at this stage that the Calley case would include more than the legal process the military code of justice provides. Ehrlichman further said that Mr. Nixon had consulted with members of his cabinet who were also lawyers including Welfare Secretary Elliot L. Richardson, a former attorney general in Massachusetts, Treasury Secretary Connally, and presidential counselor Finch. He had also been in close touch with Secretary of Defense Melvin Laird and Attorney General John Mitchell. Ehrlichman finally suggested that the President wanted the case to go through the entire military judicial process because he had confidence in the due process of law afforded by the procedure and felt there is a "very good system of review,"[122] though apparently not good enough to make the right decision without Nixon's help. When Nixon's first set of reasons for interfering with the Calley judicial appeal were denied, he shifted his emphasis to a new set at the White House news conference one month later.

> In my view my intervention in the Calley case was proper for two reasons: One, because I felt that Captain [Lieutenant] Calley should not be sent to Leavenworth while waiting for the months and maybe a year or so that appeal would take. I thought that he should be confined to quarters. I think that was proper to do in view of the fact that under civil cases where we have criminal cases, we grant the right to bail to people that are charged with crimes.
>
> Second, I felt that it was proper for me to indicate that I would review the case because there was great concern expressed throughout the country as to whether or not this was a case involving, as it did, so many complex factors in which Captain Calley was going to get a fair trial.
>
> I believe that the system of military justice is a fair system. But a part of that system is the right of the President to review. I am exercising that right. And I think that reassured the country and that is one of the reasons that the country has cooled down on this case. I will review it.[123]

Later in the news conference Nixon was asked whether he would recommend that someone like Manson also be freed on bail. Nixon answered:

> No. I am not going to go into the specific laws of each state, and they do vary, of course, and not being a lawyer, as you know, according to every state—and some states are much more strict than others—where capital crimes are concerned, there are many states that do not allow bail at all if they feel that the individual is one who is a danger to society.[124]

It is fairly obvious that Nixon failed to respond to the point of the question—whether the facts in the Calley trial are as conclusive about guilt as those in the Manson trial. Nevertheless, it should not be implied that the comparison with freeing Manson on bail is appropriate. Admitting a defendant to bail gives him his freedom; confinement to quarters, as with Calley, is different. Moreover, a consideration in allowing bail pending appeal is whether the convicted defendant would pose a danger to society. The risk that Calley would repeat his crime if on bail appears very slim; the same could hardly be said for Manson.

If Nixon was utterly sincere in stating his second reason, he must have refused to recognize the wave of protest in response to what he had done. To argue that he was successful in cooling down "the great concern expressed throughout the country" suggests that, since many Americans feel sorry for Calley because others (including Nixon and Johnson) are also responsible, they are "cooled down" when their leader attempts to influence the jury of appeals. To believe that Calley should not have been brought to trial is not necessarily to believe that Nixon should interfere with the normal course of judicial review. Coming from all social, economic, and political elements of society, disgust over Nixon's action was expressed by representative leaders, including the professional officer corps of the United States Army.

> The trial of First Lieutenant William L. Calley, Jr., and its aftermath have left many members of the professional officer corps of the U.S. Army in a state of anguish and alarm.
>
> In the view of dozens of officers at many posts around the country, the Calley case was an isolated incident in a complex guerrilla war understood by few at home.
>
> "The Army put a couple of million men through Vietnam," a brigadier general said, "and all the people judge us on is the Calley case—one instant in a war most people don't understand or try to understand."
>
> A colonel said: "I wish politicians from the President on down would stay out of this business and let the Army police its own."
>
> . . . Many of the officers believe that the Calley case has been a catalyst for those elements of public opinion, left and right, that abuse and disparage the Army.
>
> As they see it, the right criticizes the service for cleaning its own house of the evil done at My Lai while the left cites Lieutenant Calley as a symbol of a brutal and ruthless force fighting an immoral war.[125]

Two weeks before Nixon made his statement in the White House news conference, *Newsweek* had concluded that "the case is likely to arrive on Mr. Nixon's desk in a climate far different from the one in which he moved so precipitously. It may be changing already. Some members of Congress reported that the balance of opinion in their mail had already slipped a long way from a peak of 100 to 1 pro Calley." 126 Thus a different perspective on the Calley case began to open. "The nation has gone on an emotional jag," the conservative *Detroit News* reported a week earlier.127 Recognizing the true situation more quickly, Senator Edward Kennedy spoke up for the verdict before the Daniel letter was made public, although his mail had been running solidly pro-Calley.128

If, earlier, the army had been able to convince some GI's that the My Lai massacre was justified and legal, Nixon may well have given it the highest precedent for reinforcing this persuasion and designing its future conduct. Imagine what a president could do with a volunteer army by espousing this philosophy. At any rate, the reaction abroad was not encouraging, and *Time* summarized it this way:

> Around the world, the admiration that the U.S. had won for trying and convicting Calley was quickly qualified when Nixon intervened in the case. Pro-Americans and anti-Americans were dismayed, for a kaleidoscope of reasons. East Germany's *Neues Deutschland* ran in adjoining columns pictures of Angela Davis in chains and Lieutenant Calley leaving the stockade. *Private Eye*, London's black-humor satirical review, ran a cover photograph of Charles Manson with the caption: "I should have joined the Army." In Saigon, the respected, generally critical newspaper *Duoc Nha Nam* objected: "The Nixon decision tacitly acknowledged that the savage and mass killings of Vietnamese civilians was right. A white American who killed hundreds of yellow-skinned Vietnamese was personally freed by the U.S. President."129

Newsweek elaborated:

> The reaction abroad offered no immediate comfort to the White House—and might in fact foreshadow the ultimate American verdict on the Calley affair. Foreign observers were generally impressed by the fact that America had put Calley on trial, "proof in itself of the maturity of American democracy." But the press abroad almost unanimously panned the Nixon intervention. One West German columnist called it "a monstrous rebuke to the military courts (and) a massive pressure on the appellate courts." *France-Soir* in Paris grumbled: "The intervention of a head of state in a matter of this

kind is without precedent." And in London, the *Sunday Telegraph* termed it simply: "the triumph of mob rule."[130]

It should be noted, furthermore, that the Calley case was an "isolated incident" only insofar as military justice is concerned, but *not* insofar as destruction of innocent civilians in Southeast Asia is concerned. Indeed, five months after Nixon was elected President the village of Truong Khanh II, in Quang Ngai province, was subjected to a massacre similar to the one at My Lai a year earlier. Danny S. Notley, whose discharge papers show he served in Vietnam with the American Division's 11th Brigade, said members of his squad shot villagers to death. Notley said he withdrew in a state of shock and trembling, while those who were doing the shooting moved through the village and continued to slay the occupants, about thirty Vietnamese women and children.[131]

Notley's testimony was given to a panel chaired by Representative Ronald V. Dellums, which for three days listened to former American servicemen give what they said were eyewitness accounts of indiscriminate killings of South Vietnamese and of beatings, torture, and murder in which they themselves had sometimes participated.[132]

Approximately the same time as these testimonies were being heard, a military jury acquitted Captain Eugene M. Kotouc of maiming a Viet Cong suspect during an interrogation after the My Lai assault of 1968. The captain testified that he accidentally cut off the tip of the prisoner's little finger. He said he was threatening the suspect with a hunting knife while seeking information.[133]

Similarly, Robert F. Marasco, a former captain in the United States Special Forces in Vietnam, said he shot and killed a South Vietnamese triple agent two years ago, for which he and others were accused but never tried. He said he shot the man in the head twice and, with two other officers, put him in a weighted sack and dumped him from a boat into the South China Sea (on June 20, 1969). Marasco and seven others, including the Green Berets commander in Vietnam, Colonel Robert B. Rheault, were accused by the army of the slaying. But the army later dropped the charges, saying it did so because it was told that the CIA would not permit any of its men to testify at a trial.[134]

All of this evidence seems to lend credence to the conclusion of Representative Paul N. McCloskey, who made a special trip to Vietnam and Laos, that the United States has pursued a program of deliberately destroying villages in Laos, despite official denials. "For eighteen months in 1968, 1969, and 1970 [the United States] has pursued a program of deliberately destroying Laotian villages," McCloskey said. Of the 9,000 villages in Laos, he pointed out, "it looks to me as though we may have destroyed thousands of them." McCloskey, who based his conclusion in part on interviews with refugees from seven Laotian villages, said the air force has refused his requests to produce photographs of Laotian villages. [135]

The army's claim that the Calley case was an isolated incident was not even true in terms of military justice. Nearly a month after the army made this claim, the news media revealed that "the Army is quietly proceeding with charges of premeditated murder against eight more American GIs, including a Chelmsford man—a precedent-setting case involving two helicopter crews accused of indiscriminate killing."[136] Army investigators have further listed thirty-two allegations of battlefield crimes as under investigation. And the army is also considering bringing murder charges against a brigadier general who allegedly killed Vietnamese civilians with "pot shots" from a helicopter in 1968.[137]

Thus it is difficult to believe official reports concerning the nature of our involvement in Southeast Asia, and still more difficult to accept Nixon's reasons for attempting to influence Lieutenant Calley's jury of appeals before it had the opportunity to hear his appeal. Indeed, as the *New York Times* noted:

When President Nixon addressed the nation last week, he appeared painfully aware how tenuous had become the confidence of the American people in their leadership. . . .

Governmental courage and candor have tended in recent years to give way to poll-dominated image-building and to the sugar-coating of unpleasant realities.

In a more confident past, American ideals were trusted to gain admiration and acceptance on the strength of their own values. Today, no longer buoyed by that original faith in the contagion of a better and more just society, American politicians are infecting the nation instead with a missionary obsession to support any move that seems to stand for the American way of international law and order. Such crusading fervor always breeds an erroneous belief in the omnipotence of self-righteous goals, and intolerance of those equally patriotic Americans who may disagree with either the goals themselves or the way to achieve them. This is the antithesis of an earlier, humbler faith that a free society has its own inner strength that will gain adherents of its own accord. . . .

What has happened to the American faith in freedom when the government appears convinced that its security depends on an elaborate apparatus of internal political surveillance ominously reminiscent of secret police systems? Far less significant than the actual or potential abuse of such governmental powers is the damage done to the American self-image and to the mutual trust between government and people, between citizens and neighbors.138

If Nixon feels that his attempt to influence the normal process of judicial review in the Calley case "cooled down" the American public, either he fails to recognize our reactions and ability to be reasonable or he is unaware of his failure to communicate even a semblance of justification for his actions. The *Chicago Daily News* expressed it this way:

If one can believe those chronically cheerful men who speak for the administration, President Nixon has desensitized the Calley case, drained the poison from the war, finessed his critics and broken the fever of the American people.

If one can believe an expanding army of legislators, pundits and professional doubters, the President is a hapless figure standing in debris up to his knees, heedless of a public storm that will soon consume him.139

In the past, when Nixon made indiscreet and prejudicial statements about a defendant before the completion of his trial, he has subsequently either changed his words or admitted their lack of justification. Such was the case when the comments he had made concerning three defendants were discussed in a press conference on December 10, 1970.

Question: Mr. President, at a previous news conference you said that what happened at My Lai was a massacre. On another occasion you said that Charles Manson is guilty. On another occasion you mentioned Angela Davis by name and then said that those responsible for such acts of terror will be brought to justice. My question concerns the problem of pre-trial publicity and the fact that it could jeopardize a defendant's rights at a trial. How do you reconcile your comments with your status as a lawyer?

Answer: I think that's a legitimate criticism. I think sometimes we lawyers, even like doctors who try to prescribe for themselves, may make mistakes. And I think that kind of comment probably is unjustified.140

Success was not discernible in Nixon's attempt to substantively justify his decision to make the ultimate determination on the Calley case, however, and since then there has been only reaffirmation rather than retraction by the President. Complementing the letter from Captain Daniel and the reaction of the professional officer corps of the U.S. Army, on the other hand, were numerous criticisms that were precise and worthy of consideration. Former Attorney General Ramsey Clark said that it was "inherently disrespectful of the law" for President Nixon to announce he would make the final military judgment. Clark went on: "I don't know how, in a government of laws, you can have an executive indicating his intention to intercede while the system must proceed with the case. It seems to me that's a government of men yielding to the emotion of the moment. It's inherently disrespectful of the law."141

Commenting on the public feeling which helped Nixon make his decision, Senator Edward W. Brooke put it this way: "Political judgments and public pressure must never be allowed to influence a case which is under judicial review. This is not the time for politics or emotion. This is the time for calm, reason, and above all confidence in our system of justice. I say let justice run its course."142

Senator Adlai Stevenson charged that the American people are not being "given much leadership" by the politicians, from President Nixon on down, in the Calley case. "I think the country must retain its senses. I don't know what the President's intentions are, whether he is responding to public or political pressures. I don't know whether he knows what he is doing." Stevenson, a former U.S. Marines officer, said "an order to murder women and children is not an excuse to murder innocent men, women and children." If Calley is guilty, he must pay the penalty "in his consciousness and in the courts."143

Senator Jacob Javits said the army made a difficult and unprecedented decision in charging one of its own officers with the murder of several unarmed civilians during wartime. Victors do this to the vanquished, he said, but "to enforce such disciplines on ourselves is unusual." In doing this the United States has said to the world: "We remain essentially a humane people."144

President Thieu himself said he was pleased with the conviction and would accept any sentence given Calley as just. "Now I am confident that justice has been done. The guilty [man] has to deserve his fate [*sic*]."145

In addition to Nixon's recognition of public resentment over the Calley conviction and the fact that influential public officials were pointing to the commander in chief as guilty or even more guilty than Calley, it should be emphasized that Nixon's unexpected and unprecedented announcement that he would personally review the Calley case seems to contradict the tone of his earlier reaction, when, on November 26, 1969, the White House said that an incident such as the alleged Song My massacre

> is in direct violation not only of United States military policy, but is also abhorrent to the conscience of all Americas. . . . The Secretary of the Army is continuing his investigation. . . . Appropriate action is and will be taken to assure that illegal and immoral conduct, as alleged, be dealt with in accordance with the strict rules of military justice.146

It should also be emphasized that while the White House offered a minuscule and questionable set of elusive and evasive justifications for Nixon's decision on Calley, Nixon made no substantive justification for his decision to be the final arbiter in the case or for announcing this decision before the case had followed its normal course of judicial review. Nixon's reason was simply that public anxiety was high and needed to be assuaged. However, his attempt to assuage public anxiety may well have been counterproductive or at least unsuccessful.

Whether criticism is made against or on behalf of Nixon and Calley, there seems to be virtually unanimous agreement that the guilt is too great for Calley to bear alone. Everyone is guilty, some directly and some indirectly, but each day the Vietnam war continues, its perpetrators head the list of those who are most directly responsible. According to the Soviet news agency Tass: "The main initiators of this bloodbath escaped punishment."147

In both the Manson and the Calley cases, publicity posed a problem on the national level, and it worked its way into the grass roots of American society. Some cases that involve considerable pretrial publicity create a problem which begins locally and expands to the national level. In each case, however, the problem is much deeper, and it may be reflected in publicity as much as it is caused by publicity. An example of a case in which a miscarriage of justice was caused by local pressures that were both reflected in and caused by local and national publicity is the Dr. Sam Sheppard murder trial of 1954.

THE DR. SAM SHEPPARD CASE

It is easy to criticize the sources of news reflected by the mass media while overlooking the responsibility and discretion which should be assumed by the mass media before they disseminate such information. Louis M. Lyons emphasized the significance of such a perceptual distortion when he explained that the newspaper "is the least criticized institution in our society and so strategic in its relation to all others as to require the most attention."[148] "[While] responsibile citizens would welcome public exposure of racial injustice and outspoken opposition by media and political leaders whose business it is to concern themselves with the difficult human relations problems that terrify and destroy a community . . . the attitudes of businessmen and civic leaders are overcome by the miasma of local prejudices created by a small minority of vocal bigots."[149] Such may be very well have been the case on August 28, 1954, when two detectives, Robert E. Schottke and Patrick Gareau, spent two hours on the scene and then told John Eaton, chief of police of Bay Village, Ohio: "You don't have to look any further. Sam Sheppard is your man." Meanwhile the defense attorney, William J. Corrigan, said to the family: "You don't need me or any lawyer. Sam Sheppard didn't do it."[150] If one had been reading certain newspapers at the time or had visited Bay Village in the late summer of 1954 (as this writer did), he would not have suspected that each side had such a clear case, however. Newspapers were quick to prejudice the case against Sam.

On Saturday, July 3, 1954, in the south Cleveland lake-shore home of Dr. Samuel H. Sheppard and his wife, Marilyn, neighbors Donald and Nancy Ahern visited for dinner and stayed to watch the midnight movie (*Strange Holiday*) on television. When the Aherns left, about 12:30 a.m., the 30-year-old osteopathic surgeon, clad in T-shirt and trousers, was asleep on a living room couch. After his pretty 31-year-old wife let them out, she was never seen alive again, except by her murderer.

On July 4, at 5:45 a.m., Mayor J. Spencer Houk and his wife, Esther, received a call from Dr. Sam Sheppard: "My God, Spen, come over—I think they've killed Marilyn." The Houks found Dr. Sam without his T-shirt, clutching his neck in apparent pain and his wife brutally murdered in her bed upstairs. She was four months pregnant. Dr. Sam's older brothers, Dr. Stephen A. and Dr. Richard N., confined him in the family-staffed Bay View Hospital, and searchers found Dr. Sam's watch and jewelry discarded in the brush behind the house.[151]

The testimony of Dr. Sam Sheppard at the coroner's inquest concerning his knowledge of the slaying of his wife reveals his memory of what

79

happened during the five-hour mystery.

I lay down on the couch with my head toward the television and evidently I went to sleep.

The next thing I can remember was some thought that my wife had told me she was going to bed and she asked me to come upstairs. Evidently I was not aroused very much because I must have gone back to sleep.

The next thing I know I heard her say my name loudly, but it was actually not a scream. Her voice was just louder than usual but not actually loud.

She said my name one or two times as I was going up the stairs.

In the back of my mind in my subconscious reaction I thought she was having convulsions as in the earlier pregnancy.

I rushed into the room and several things happened almost simultaneously.

I thought I saw the white form of an individual. I was grappling with it. I heard a loud moan and almost instantly I was struck down from behind and that was all.

Sometime after that, I have no way of knowing how long, I remembered coming to in a position facing the doorway. And somehow or another I saw some sort of reflection, I do not know from where, and recognized my wallet and recognized that I was injured and I was fearful for my wife.

I pulled myself up, and went back into the room, felt her pulse, and I felt sure she was gone.

I believe I rushed into my son's room to see that he was all right, because I wanted to know if anything happened to him. I am not sure, how I determined this, but I do feel sure that I established the fact that he was all right.

Coming out of his room, I thought I heard a noise downstairs, and I went down the stairs rapidly, almost running.

I felt this noise was toward the front of the house so I turned down to the north section and entered the living portion of the living room.

There I saw a figure leave the front door of the house or the porch and go toward the yard.

I was perspiring, now that I think of it.

I pursued this form as best I could and I lost sight of it down the stairs but I saw it again pointing midway down the stairs to the landing onto the beach.

I ran down these stairs and saw the form of a, I thought, I can't quite decide, but it was a big man with a relatively large head and I grabbed and tackled this individual.

The clothes were dark.

I felt as though I was choked and that is all I remember at that time.

Next thing I remember with any sort of clarity I was coming to some vague sensibility on the water's edge at the beach, my head toward the water. I felt as though I was being beat back and forth by the water and the waves slowly, how slowly I cannot say.

I got up off the beach and came to some sort of sensibility.

During this period I believe I choked and coughed some. I realized I had been injured, my wife was or probably had been injured, and I went upstairs.

I went into the room and I saw her, felt her pulse, and I thought she was gone. I don't know, I just can't explain my reaction. I thought I would wake out of this dream. I was hoping I would.

I may have walked around upstairs. I don't know just what I did. I may have gone back in again to see her.

Sometime later I realized this was not a dream and searched in my poor mind where to turn for help, and a number came into my dazed brain.

The number was that of Spencer Houk. I called him. He answered, and what I said to him I do not and cannot remember.[152]

In his summary speech at the trial, defense attorney Arthur E. Petersilge said that "no conclusive test had been made to determine whether a criminal assault preceded death, [but] a mouth wound and tooth chips indicated that Marilyn had bitten the finger of her attacker." He added: "Dr. Sam was examined head to toe and there wasn't any sign of such a wound."[153] Percy I. Lowery, chairman of the Ohio Pardon and Parole Commission, declared that "Dr. Sam's conviction of second degree murder automatically carries a life imprisonment sentence and under no circumstances can he be eligible for parole until the ten years is served. . . . The only possibility that Dr. Sam could get out of being imprisoned for less than ten years lies in the law that permits him to apply for executive clemency from the governor of the state."[154]

Before the trial began, prosecutor John J. Mahon commented: "All I want is an intelligent and fair jury that will listen to the evidence and arguments with an open mind." Defense attorney Corrigan maintained that he did not want "this boy's fate entrusted to people with prejudices against extra-marital amours, or with a tendency to take the word of detectives and public officials over that of defense witnesses."[155]

Whether either attorney was to have his wishes fulfilled depended to a large extent on whether the jury members would be influenced by overwhelmingly biased pretrial publicity. Forrest Allen of the Cleveland *Press* attempted to justify the role of his newspaper in the Sheppard murder case by arguing that "it was up to someone, in this case the *Press*, to prod them into action."[156] James Collins of the *Cleveland Plain Dealer*, on the other hand, argued that the "prodding of the *Press* in this case could very well have delayed instead of accelerated official action and said that a defendant in a murder case was entitled to unbiased procedures."[157] Thus the question seems to be not so much whether the *Press* took a position on the Sheppard trial, or the nature of its stance but the form in which this pressure attempted to manifest itself and the effects it produced.

On October 21 a prospective juror was ousted from the panel for discussing her courtroom experience with a sister and a friend, despite her claim that she could be fair and impartial. Mrs. Parker said her fellow employees at the General Electric plant had frequently discussed the case. "They 'kidded' her about being called for jury duty."[158] Yet defense attorney Corrigan was unable to acquire a change of venue, despite the fact that the jury members had been exposed to enormous amounts of highly prejudiced publicity, as well as having had their pictures, names, and addresses published in the *Cleveland Press* before they were impaneled for the trial.[159]

The problem was probably multicausal: a certain interaction among the values of the community, the expediency of the police force, and the opportunism of public officials and the press. Each of these factors contributed significantly not only to the hasty conviction of Sam Sheppard but also to his eventual acquittal.[160] Each factor however was implanted or assisted by the news media and must be viewed from that perspective.

Pressure from the Press

It is possible that no individual who has been accused of murder has received more adverse pretrial publicity than did Dr. Sam Sheppard in the late summer and the autumn of 1954. Defense attorney Corrigan was not in error when he explained, on August 27, that "day after day newspapers were filled with accusations against him. . . . His arrest was urged. One paper advocated the use of the third degree. Lurid headlines.

Every fact of his private life was exposed."161 Dr. Sheppard responded to what seemed to be a calculated attempt to gain his conviction for murder in the following words: "I am certain that there is nothing, either in her life or in mine, which will not bear scrutiny. However, I feel that there is no justification for release or publication of confidential information which the authorities may obtain."162

At first, Dr. Sheppard indicated he would prefer to have a trio of judges hear the case, and his attorneys had said that publicity on the murder would act against their client in a jury trial. Later, however, Sheppard and his attorneys decided to risk his fate before a jury.163

Within two weeks of the time Dr. Sheppard and his lawyers decided to place their faith in the objectivity and good will of a jury, common pleas judge Edward Blythin began planning how to seat the big corps of newsmen in the courtroom. The *Cleveland Plain Dealer* elaborated on these plans: "Cleveland's three daily papers, three major wire services, radio and television men plus an expected wave of correspondents from out-of-town newspapers will need a major chunk of the available space in the legal arena at the Criminal Court Building."168 Judge Blythin's preparations for hordes of newsmen meant that few spectators would find room to observe the trial.

The bias, to Sam Sheppard's misfortune, was probably most conspicuous in the *Cleveland Press*, and in several ways, both in form and substance. Newspaper editions frequently appeared with such front-page headlines as "SOMEBODY IS GETTING AWAY WITH MURDER."165 The same day it was reported that "after two weeks of futile investigation by the suburb's small police force, the Bay Village City Council voted to turn the inquiry over to the Cleveland homicide squad."166 "BUT WHO WILL SPEAK FOR MARILYN?"167 appeared as the main headline on the front page just as the trial was beginning, followed by "QUIT STALLING AND BRING HIM IN!" 168 and an anti—Sam Sheppard editorial on the front page.

The first of these headlines also was followed by an editorial, which cannot be distinguished in tone from the remainder of the *Cleveland Press* coverage of the case. The following is the text of the lead article on the front page, directly under "SOMEBODY IS GETTING AWAY WITH MURDER":

What's the matter with the law enforcement authorities of Cuyahoga County?

Have they lost their sense of reason?—or at least inexcusably set aside the realization of what they are hired to do, and for whom they work?

If ever a murder case was studded with fumbling, halting, stupid, uncooperative bungling—politeness to people whose place in this situation completely justified vigorous searching, prompt and effective police work—the Sheppard case has them all.

Was the murder of Mrs. Sheppard a polite matter?

Did the killer make a dutiful bow to the authorities and then proceed brutally to destroy the young child-bearing wife?

Why all of this sham, hypocrisy, politeness, criss-crossing of pomp and protocol in this case?

Who is trying to deceive whom?

From the very beginning of this case—from the first hour that the murder became known to the authorities by a telephone call from the husband to the town mayor—from that moment on and including this, the case has been one of the worst in local crime history.

Of course the trail is cold. Of course the clews have been virtually erased by the killer. Of course the whole thing is botched up so badly that head or tail cannot be made of it.

In the background of this case are friendships, relationships, hired lawyers, a husband who ought to have been subjected instantly to the same third-degree to which any other person under similar circumstances is subjected, and a whole string of special and bewildering extra-privileged courtesies that should never be extended by authorities investigating a murder—the most serious and sickening crime of all.

The spectacle of a whole community watching a batch of law enforcement officials fumbling around, stumbling over one another, bowing and scraping in the presence of people they ought to be dealing with just as firmly as any other persons in any other crime—that spectacle is not only becoming a stench but a serious threat to the dignity of law enforcement itself.

Coroner Sam Gerber was never more right than when yesterday he said that the killer must be laughing secretly at the whole spectacle—the spectacle of a community of a million and a half people brought to indignant frustration by Mrs. Sheppard's killer in that white house out in Bay Village.

Why shouldn't he chuckle? Why shouldn't he cover up, shut up, conceal himself behind the circle of protecting people?

What's the matter with us in Cuyahoga County? Who are we afraid of? Why do we have to kow-tow to a set of circumstances and people where a murder has been committed?

It's time that somebody smashed into this situation and tore aside this restraining curtain of sham, politeness and hypocrisy and went at the business of solving a murder—and quit this nonsense of artificial politeness that has not been extended to any other murder case in generations.[169]

Rather than an isolated example, this front-page bias against Sam Sheppard was more the rule than the exception. The front-page story following the headline "QUIT STALLING AND BRING HIM IN!" further elucidates the attempt of the *Cleveland Press* to pursue Sheppard's arrest and eventual conviction:

Maybe sombody in this town can remember a parallel for it. The *Press* can't.

And not even the oldest police veterans can, either.

Everybody's agreed that Sam Sheppard is the most unusual murder suspect ever seen around these parts.

Except for some superficial questioning during Coroner Sam Gerber's inquest, he has been scot-free of any official grilling into the circumstances of his wife's murder.

From the morning of July 4, when he reported his wife's killing, to this moment, 26 days later, Sam Sheppard has not set foot in a police station.

He has been surrounded by an iron curtain of protection that makes Malenkov's Russian concealment amateurish.

His family, his Bay Village friends—which include its officials—his lawyers, his hospital staff, have combined to make law enforcement in this county look silly.

The longer they can string this whole affair out, the surer it is that the public's attention sooner or later will be diverted to something else, and then the heat will be off, the public interest gone, and the goose will hang high.

This man is a suspect in his wife's murder. Nobody yet has found a solitary trace of the presence of anybody else in his Lake Rd. house the night or morning his wife was brutally beaten to death in her bedroom.

And yet no murder suspect in the history of this county has been treated so tenderly, with such infinite solicitute for his emotions, with such fear of upsetting the young man.

Gentlemen of Bay Village, Cuyahoga County, and Cleveland charged jointly with law enforcement—

This is murder. This is no parlor game. This is no time to permit anybody—no matter who he is—to outwit, stall, fake, or improvise devices to keep away from the police or from the questioning anybody in his right mind knows a murder suspect should be subjected to—at a police station.

The officials throw up their hands in horror at the thought of bringing Sam Sheppard to a police station for grilling. Why? Why is he any different than anybody else in any other murder case?

Why should the police officials be afraid of Bill Corrigan? Or anybody else for that matter, when they are at their sworn business of solving a murder?

Certainly Corrigan will act to protect Sam Sheppard's rights. He should.

But the people of Cuyahoga County expect you, the law enforcement officials, to protect the people's rights.

A murder has been committed. You know who the chief suspect is.

You have the obligation to question him—question him thoroughly and searchingly—from beginning to end, and not at his hospital, not at his home, not in some secluded spot out in the country.

But at Police Headquarters—just as you do every other person suspected in a murder case.

What the people of Cuyahoga County cannot understand, and The *Press* cannot understand, is why you are showing Sam Sheppard so much more consideration as a murder suspect than any other person who has ever before been suspected in a murder case. Why?[170]

Sheppard's attorney, William Corrigan, also became a prominent subject of bias in the *Cleveland Press*. Such headlines as "CORRIGAN DEFTLY BAITS CORONER IN QUIZZING,"[171] "CORRIGAN ALWAYS ON THE PROWL IN COURTROOM,"[172] "ACTOR CORRIGAN RAPS PHOTOGRAPHING OF JURY,"[173] and "SHEPPARD DEFENSE STAGES PARADE OF MEDICAL EXPERTS,"[174] which were followed by slanted articles about the trial, were not uncommon.

Volumes could be written on editorialized distortions of the facts, to the detriment of Sam Sheppard, which appeared in "noneditorial" columns of the *Cleveland Press*. Only one example will be given, but it could be easily generalized. Under the guise of reporting part of the text of the trial on the previous day, the *Cleveland Press* inserted its own opinion: "This version of how the 'tidykiller' covered up his trail hit hard at Dr. Sam's claim that he chased the intruder who killed his wife down to the beach, where he was knocked unconscious."[175] This blatant misrepresentation of reality, which appeared on the front page of the newspaper, overlooks Sheppard's claim that he had been beaten unconscious in Marilyn's room. If this is true, the killer could easily have had the time to cover his trail, and it is an eminently plausible explanation which the *Cleveland Press* obscured.

The final emphasis on the role of the *Press* in influencing the fairness of the trial through the form of its coverage is the way in which photography was presented. Photos of nearly every aspect of the murder were presented at one time or another, and they were embedded in the context of Marilyn's romantic, high school love for all-American Sam, of Marilyn's unblemished faithfulness to Sam, and of Sam's endless "cheating" on Marilyn. With the slanted articles and the editorials accompanying them, the impact seems all but overwhelming. Many of the captions for the pictures implied a subtle view, such as the following one for a picture of Marilyn: "25-DAY-OLD MURDER OF MARILYN SHEPPARD is still unsolved. The only persons held by police in that time have been two women who gave statements to police, a half dozen hitch-hikers and a couple of fishermen. The principal suspect has never been arrested."[176]

Of 146 issues of the *Cleveland Press*, only 31 failed to cover Sam Sheppard on the front page, and of 161 issues of the *Cleveland Plain Dealer* during the same period of time, only 46 failed to do the same. It would be an understatement to say that this case was a major topic of conversation at the time, particularly in the Cleveland area. Much of this interest occurred not only because of the form of the news but also because of its substance.

Extramarital aspects

Publicity on Sheppard's marital problems ranged from a possible divorce from Marilyn to extramaritial sex relations with other women. Five days after the murder, personal letters to Marilyn were found in her house and excerpts were printed in the *Cleveland Press*. The implications were suggestive of Sam's unfaithfulness to Marilyn. For example, one letter said that "his profession, a wonderful wife, and a fine son will help, we pray, to make him see how foolish anything he could do [would be]." Another letter, written by a woman relative, told Marilyn: "Something I had to learn is that men are little boys who hate to grow up." "This isn't just something that affects you and Sam," a letter from a close relative advised, "because you both have a responsibility in Chip."177 The key letters, reproduced on the front page of the *Cleveland Press*, were written to Mrs. Sheppard while she and Sam were living in Los Angeles, where he studied osteopathy.

Later, when Sheppard was attending a medical convention in Los Angeles, the Cleveland newspapers reported that he gave 24-year-old Miss Susan Hayes an expensive wrist watch. 178 Miss Hayes was formerly a medical technician at Bay View Hospital, operated by Dr. Sheppard and his family. Sam told Deputy Sheriff Carl Rossbach that he had not told Marilyn about buying the watch for Miss Hayes but that she had learned about it. He said he was unaware of who had told her, but it caused a "minor family" argument—nothing serious."179 The next day it was reported that Miss Hayes had occasionally been driven home by Sam before she had left for Los Angeles and that he had visited her in her home.180

Publicity suggesting a more intimate relationship between Sam and Susan, however, was about to emerge. After printing Sam's claim that he had neither slept in the same bedroom with Miss Hayes nor had sexual relations with her, the *Cleveland Press* pointed out that he also denied attending a strip-tease party at Lorain with Susan.181 The next day the *Lorain Journal* announced that Susan Hayes would be asked to return from California to aid the investigators.182

The public was soon to learn that Susan and Sam had spent a week as guests in a Los Angeles home the previous March and that Sam's friendship with Susan was not as casual as had first been reported.183 The same day, Coroner Gerber suggested that Marilyn had been "upset" over her handsome husband's attentions to other women,184 and he "abruptly [asked] Dr. Sheppard if he had slept four nights in the same bedroom with Miss Hayes at Dr. Miller's home."185

Not only did the *Press* explicate the facts of Sam's personal life that had no bearing on the murder, and not only did the newspapers discuss scandals which Sam denied, but the *Cleveland Press* frequently discussed questions that would be asked of Sam and testimonies that would be given against him, before the fact. One of the first times was when the *Press* discussed a visit to Tijuana, Mexico, "the gay resort where Dr. Sheppard denied having taken Miss Hayes."186

Soon Richard Lease, administrator at Bay View Hospital, denied having knowledge that Daisy Dove, an aide in the laboratory, had complained of the conduct of Sam and Susan, or that their conduct was so embarrassing that she was forced to leave the laboratory.[187] On the same day, the public was informed that Mrs. Richard A Sheppard Sr., mother of Dr. Sam, testified that Marilyn had confided in her that she "did not have a pleasant time" during the couple's California trip the previous March because of Sam's dates with Susan Hayes.[188]

On July 27 the *Cleveland Press* announced that Cleveland Police Chief Frank Story said that Miss Hayes had contradicted Sam's testimony that they had not slept together, and suggested that she admitted having had an affair. The paper also discussed Dr. Randall Chapman's statement that Sam had sought his advice on overcoming "incompatibility" with his wife, Marilyn.[189] The next day it was reported that Susan Hayes had sworn there was more to her relationship with Dr. Sheppard, and officials announced that she told them she had been intimate with the doctor.[190] On its front page, the *Cleveland Press* responded to this knowledge:

> Now proved under oath to be a liar, still free to go about his business, shielded by his family, protected by a smart lawyer who has made monkeys of the police and authorities, carrying a gun part of the time, left free to do whatever he pleases as he pleases, Sam Sheppard still hasn't been taken to Headquarters.
>
> What's wrong in this whole mess that is making this community a national laughing stock?
>
> Who's holding back—and why?
>
> What's the basic difference between murder in an "ordinary" neighborhood and one in a Lake Rd. house in suburban Bay Village?
>
> Who is afraid of whom?
>
> It's just about time that somebody began producing the answers— And producing Sam Sheppard at Police Headquarters.[191]

Thus Susan Hayes became a key witness in the case because her testimony charged the unfaithfulness of Sam to his murdered wife, Marilyn.[192]

The next day, five other women were "definitely placed by investigators in the recent life of Dr. Samuel H. Sheppard." One of the women— a 26-year-old mother of a 4-year-old daughter—had admitted to police several "kissing parties" with Sam.[193] Mrs. Lossman insisted, however, "that she—not Dr. Sheppard—was the aggressor" when their emotions flared into embraces and kisses.[194]

On the day the grand jury charged Sheppard with first degree murder, Common Pleas Judge Arthur Day admonished the jurors to keep secret "the dramatic testimony they heard behind locked doors," the *Cleveland Press* claimed.[195] It seems incredible that most, if not all, and certainly too much, of the dramatic testimony came out from behind locked doors to appear on the front pages of the *Cleveland Press*, and often even before the grand jury heard it. Yet this is true, although the *Cleveland Press* said that more was to be brought out at the trial.

In the trial, Susan Hayes admitted that she and Sam made love in his car, at his family's suburban clinic, and in the home of California friends.[196] Feeling that Susan had now released him from his commitment to secrecy, Sam admitted his affairs with her, saying he had originally claimed otherwise because he wanted to be "a gentleman." Later in the trial Sam was accused of having had still more women in his life, and finally he admitted that Marilyn and his father had become upset when he took Miss Margaret Kauzor on a date in Los Angeles, and he had suspected a friend of "trying to lead me astray."[197]

Except for demonstrating proof of motive, the evidence presented in this two-month trial was irrelevant to the murder of Marilyn Sheppard. Yet the pretrial publicity on this subject damaged Sheppard severely in the eyes of this conservative midwestern city, and it was an important contributing factor in the public demand to "get" him.

Pressure from the Community

It was only later that the community and public officials took a stand on whom they felt was guilty and should be pressed for conviction. On the day after the murder the testimony of the neighbors seemed to indicate that they were a "perfectly normal couple," and, they asked, "How could anything like that happen in Bay Village?"[198] Only two days later, however, the *Cleveland Press* announced that Dr. Stephen Sheppard was "well aware" that many people suspected his brother, The *Press* went on to say that Sam "is not telling all he knows about the slaying of his pretty wife, Marilyn."[199] By the end of the month the presumption had been taken from Sam and given to his prosecutor.

While the premise of the American jury system is that a man is innocent until proved guilty, a new interpretation emerged: "Now he can prove his innocence, if he's innocent."[200] A citizen responded to the change in public attitude this way: "He shook the confidence of plenty of people when he refused to take the lie detector test or the truth serum. I think we were all with him until he made that decision. It's hard for even the most loyal people to understand why he would do that if he's got nothing to hide."201

Sheppard refused to take the lie detector test, he said, because of his emotional condition: "It would show some disturbance."202 But Paul Holmes has suggested additional reasons to explain his reluctance.

> The polygraph is no infallible machine which by itself can determine whether a subject is lying or telling the truth. It is simply a device that records variations in respiration, pulse, and blood pressure as a subject answers questions. The knowledge and skill of the examiner are all important. It is he who must frame the questions and he who must interpret the graph by which the machine notes the subject's reactions.
>
> In the hands of an able and experienced examiner a lie test will usually give valuable information as to whether a subject is speaking frankly or is attempting to deceive. Most persons are good re-actors, but a few are able to lie without showing the kind of reactions that ordinarily indicate deception. This does not mean that they can fool an examiner who knows his business, however.
>
> When Sam's lawyers refused to let him undergo lie tests sought by the authorities, they undoubtedly had in mind that a test in the hands of a hostile examiner could be of little value in revealing the truth and might be used to harm Sam, irrespective of Sam's reactions under it. There was no enthusiasm by the authorities, even at that early stage of the case, for a test under impartial conditions, with an imported examiner in the presence of observers for both sides.203

Dr. Sheppard also spurned a request that he submit to interrogation with "truth serum."204 While he refused the lie detector test because such a test would not be accurate because of his emotional condition, "medical and psychiatric experts point out that such an objection could not be raised to truth serum," according to the *Lorain Journal*.205 Sam's reasons for refusing to submit to truth serum, however, were made public by Coroner Samuel Gerber in the *Cleveland Press*:

> He already had been subjected to interrogation shortly after the crime and while he was under barbiturate sedation. If he had anything to communicate, he believes it would have been communicated at that time.
>
> He cannot face further interrogation. His present emotional condition and his present state of fatigue make it impossible for him to agree to a further ordeal of this kind.

He is reluctant to put himself in a position in which he might make statements that would incriminate innocent people.206

The public had admittedly been influenced, though Corrigan later pointed out that "so-called truth serum examinations were not admissible in evidence."207

Nevertheless, Sheppard and Corrigan had repeatedly said that the former could not receive a fair trial in Cuyahoga County because he had "already been convicted in the court of public opinion" by newspaper reports and the statements of public officials.208

Pressure from Public Officials

On July 8, 1954, only four days after the murder, Coroner Gerber complained that "we expected cooperation from the family, but don't seem to be getting it. We'll now have to use the strong arm of the law."209 But Dr. Stephen Sheppard denied any interference with the investigation:

> If we were trying to interfere, we wouldn't have let anyone talk to him. But he's already been interviewed four times by the authorities, and told them everything he knew.
>
> Our chief concern is for his health. He's certainly been injured, having been unconscious. He's confused and unable to remember much. He'll possibly be able to remember more after his condition improves.
>
> It's fantastic to think that we're trying to impede the investigation. We tried to protect Sam physically so he could get well as soon as possible and be of more help.210

The public wanted action, however, and so public officials selected the only obvious suspect to press for conviction: Sam Sheppard. Two days later, Deputy Sheriff Carl Rossbach said: "There's one suspect so far—and that's Dr. Sheppard. Until something turns up, we'll have to keep questioning him until he gives us something to go on."211 A week and a half later, Cleveland Police Chief Frank Story announced that he would direct the investigation, and that he was "convinced of the identity of the murderer."212 Cleveland Detective Chief James McArthur said his men had gathered further evidence to prove Dr. Sheppard the slayer.213 The public, of course, was happy to hear that progress was being made.

But in order for the people to remain happy more progress was necessary, and Gershom M. M. Barber, president of the Bay Village Council, became impatient. A week later he complained that there had been "another silly 12-hour delay. Another reason for our community to be made a laughing stock by Clevelanders."214

Thus it became clear that neither the public nor the public officials would accept less than the quest of the *Press* for an early conviction. Indeed, Assistant Prosecutor John J. Mahon declared that "to grant Defense Counsel William J. Corrigan's demand that the osteopath's trial be postponed until public interest in the case has subsided would set an impossible precedent."215

In this climate, therefore, it is not surprising that while Sheppard was able to obtain temporary liberty on $50,000 bail, 216 it was only temporary. Chief defense counsel Corrigan said that, under the Ohio constitution, a defendant is entitled to bail except in first degree murder cases where "the proof is evident and the presumption of guilt is great." At the bail hearing, the burden of proof is on the defense, and Sheppard was free for only two days.217 At this point he was encouraged to seek a change of venue, which would allow his trial to be held in another location.

The Change of Venue

On August 18, 1954, Sheppard's attorney insisted that he could not be given a fair trial in Cleveland.218 Lawyers Corrigan and Garmone argued that he "was convicted in the minds of the public before he was arrested and charged."219 The defense attorneys made this charge in a lengthy public statement in which they denounced the newspapers, police, and courts for their handling of the Sheppard case.

> Newspapers are the mediums that instruct and inform the general public and to a large extent form public opinion. . .
>
> Under the guise of news the Cleveland newspapers and the newspapers generally throughout the United States have reported and editorialized on the case of Samuel Sheppard so that he was convicted in the minds of the public before he was arrested and charged.
>
> Because of this method of reporting and editorializing a case before the trial, it appears doubtful whether he will be able to secure an unbiased jury in the district where he was born and educated, and where he has led a useful life, and where his ancestors have lived for over 100 years.
>
> Day after day newspapers were filled with accusations against him. His arrest was urged. One paper advocated the use of the third degree. Lurid headlines. Every fact of his private life was exposed.

Every item that could be gathered that would make him appear unfavorably to the public [was] repeated over and over again. [He was] challenged to make a public confession of his private sins, those sins that are revealed only in confession to a minister of God, or in the privacy of one's devotion to God Himself. . . .

Although he was severely injured in the encounter with his wife's murderer and, as determined by eminent doctors, that fact was toned down and it was inferred that he had inflicted these injuries on himself. . . .

He was photographed by newspapers and television, so that his face became as familiar to the citizens of Cuyahoga County as that of the governor of Ohio, who is a Cleveland resident. He was forced to submit to Bertillon pictures, which were immediately handed out by the police to newspapers for publication, so that he appeared in one paper with a Bertillon number on his chest. . . .

His home, and home of his child, and its contents were confiscated. Admission to his home was denied him. Personal property was removed from the home without any legal warrant and no accounting made. The personal letters of his wife were taken by the authorities and given to the newspapers for publication. . . .

Sheppard was cartooned on the editorial page of one newspaper. The cartoon represented a human head on the body of an animal and around his neck was a collar representative of the orthopedic collar that Sheppard was compelled to wear a number of days after he was assaulted, and it was to give the idea that Sheppard had closed his mouth and would not talk to the police.

When the attention of the editor was called to the fact that before that cartoon appeared Sheppard had submitted to questioning by the police for over 50 hours and that he had testified publically for five and one half hours under oath before a hostile crowd of over 500 in a school gymnasium, the reply of that editor was that he considered the cartoon "fair."

Not one newspaper in Cleveland raised its editorial voice to protest.

When newspapers can do what they have done to Dr. Sheppard and to his honorable father and mother and the other members of his family, it is time for newspapers to begin to examine their conscience and consider the conditions that they are creating. Perhaps wise newspaper publishers might begin to have a slight twinge of fear in the methods resorted to in the reporting of the Sheppard case and the stirring of the public to a condition that verged on mob reaction.

If they listen closely, they may hear the creaking of the ropes back stage which can indicate that the curtain may be beginning to fall on the constitutional guarantees of the individual and the press.

> *William J. Corrigan*
> *Fred W. Garmone*
> Attorneys for Dr. Samuel
> Sheppard[220]

Corrigan persisted, in the face of considerable resistance, to have the trial changed to another county. Later, on October 18, he argued:

> I realize there are cases where it has been held that publicity alone is not the reason for granting a change of venue. But I submit that never in the history of Ohio and I doubt if in any place in the United States has a murder case been ever given this much publicity. . . .
>
> The court ought to put its stamp of disapproval on this type of publicity until the furor dies down. I also want to call the court's attention to something else unprecedented in this case. There are in this courtroom for the first time, three loudspeakers and a microphone on the witness chair.[221]

Judge Blythin answered with the assertion that "we cannot control things that are public or broadcast. Those things are beyond the power of the court. The court will not try this case through the newspapers or radio."[222]

But the validity of Blythin's position with respect to publicity was misleading at best, viewed in the light of a similar case; he had the option to initiate certain sanctions, which he ignored. For example, on November 3, 1958, the judge presiding over the trial of five men indicted for capital offenses issued the following order:

> No photograph of any party to any trial or of any defendant, prosecutor, attorney, witness, juror, spectator, or other participant in or at any trial, shall be taken at any place in the courthouse building, on the courthouse steps, or on the adjacent sidewalks and public streets. Nothing said or done by any such person at any such place shall be recorded by any television instrument, moving-picture camera . . . or other recording device or equipment.[223]

Chief defense counsel Corrigan had little encouragement from the judge, but he opened the October 25 court session "with another impassioned plea to postpone the trial and shift it to another county. He accused the *Cleveland Press* of carrying on a planned campaign, through editorials and news stories, to prejudice the community against Sam Sheppard."224 Corrigan attempted to offer as evidence copies of all Cleveland newspapers and many out-of-town papers of the preceding week in support of his claim that the case was receiving "unprecedented and undeserved publicity."225

Corrigan argued "I want to especially cite the Saturday, October 23, issue of the *Press* that contains a page-one article that is not news and doesn't pretend to be news." He said the article, headed " 'But Who Will Speak for Marilyn?' [went] into the homes of all these jurors, because all of these jurors subscribe to the *Press*." The article, he said, "would cause an animosity toward the defendant."

"There is no question but that this case has had a lot of publicity," Mahon replied. "We have no control over that. If this case were heard six months from now, we'd have the same situation. It would have to be indefinitely postponed, and it would never come to trial."226 Mahon and the judge apparently overlooked the fact that in many counties of Ohio juries could be found that did not subscribe to the *Cleveland Press*.

Having failed in his change-of-venue attempt, Corrigan argued a formal motion to have a mistrial called, based on a protest against two press stories. One, which had appeared two days earlier, included an interview with Thomas Weigle, a cousin of Marilyn Sheppard. Corrigan also protested the previous day's *Press* story concerning an interview between reporter Richard McLaughlin and the husband of Mrs. Lois Mancini, juror number 13. Corrigan said that the reporter went to the home of Mrs. Mancini with a photographer and "pictures were taken of the interior of the home, her children, her mother and her husband. A long story told of the family life while the wife was serving on this jury."227

Judge Blythin overruled the mistrial plea and Corrigan asked the court stenographer to register his formal protest.228

While Assistant County Prosecutor John Mahon and Judge Blythin were succeeding in encouraging the news media to cover the trial in detail and in preventing a change of venue, they were, at the same time, also succeeding in their respective political campaigns. On November 3 the *Cleveland Plain Dealer* reported that "the judge and the prosecutor in the murder trial of Dr. Samuel H. Sheppard appeared headed for victory early today. . . . Running for separate seats on the common pleas bench, Judge Edward Blythin was ahead by a margin of better than 3-1 and Assistant County Prosecutor John J. Mahon held a 5-to-4 advantage."[229]

Most people were not as surprised as Sam Sheppard when, on December 21, 1954, the verdict of guilty of second degree murder was announced. The jury members were interviewed immediately, but then were not anxious to justify their decisions. Jack N. Hansen commented: "The job is over. I don't want to talk about it." Frank Moravec said: "I'm going right to bed." The jury foreman, James C. Bird, went straight to the heart of the matter: "You don't know what a feeling it is to be foreman of a jury. You're not sure where to begin. You're not sure what to say. But, brother, you sure learn fast. . . . I believe in our American jury system more than ever."[230]

We cannot prove who taught foreman James Bird so quickly, but history is unequivocal about the long, hard decade of sweat, pain, suicide, and death which was to accompany the Sheppard family's difficult and expensive appeal to the highest court of judicial review, the United States Supreme Court.

So appalled was defense attorney Corrigan that he immediately demanded that the jury be polled, while his son put his arm across the osteopath's shoulder. Dr. Sheppard closed his eyes, clenched a crucifix in his hand, and shook his head in disbelief. He had been convicted of the murder of his high school sweetheart, the pregnant mother of his only son, and the pretty wife he called "the only woman I ever loved or will love." The verdict of guilty came four days before Christmas and eight days before his thirty-first birthday.

Corrigan's voice was booming: "I would like now to file a motion for a new trial and fix a time for the motion to be heard." Blythin set the hearing for December 30, the day after Sheppard's birthday. Suddenly the focus of the courtroom shifted to the young man who had just been branded a murder by a jury of his peers. The judge called Sam to come forward, and as Sheppard stood before the bench Blythin said sternly: "This jury has found you guilty of murder in the second degree. Do you have anything to say?" Speaking in a firm, clear voice, Sheppard responded: "I would like to say, sir, I am not guilty. I feel there has been evidence presented before this court that definitely proves I could not have performed this crime." Blythin answered: "This jury has found otherwise. The judgment of this court is that you be confined in the Ohio State Penitentiary for life." Corrigan objected: "I think you should hear my motion for a new trial before you pass sentence"; but the objection was denied.

Corrigan turned away angrily, blurting "This is indicative of the way the whole thing has been conducted." He paused before juror number 5, Mrs. Louise Feuchter, and accused her of having made a prejudicial remark about his client. "No, I didn't," she replied, pushing his hand off the rail. When Corrigan seemed about to engage another juror in argument, Blythin called out: "Mr. Corrigan, I wish that you would have no communication with any of the jurors while this court is in session. Please desist."

"I have a right to talk to the jurors," Corrigan shouted. "I want the record to show my exception." Blythin instructed the court stenographer to "let the record show that Mr. Corrigan tried to speak to one or more of the jurors while court was in session." Corrigan apologized.

Judge Blythin failed to shake each juror's hand while he thanked them in front of newsmen (as did the judge who presided over the Manson trial fifteen years later), but he "turned to the panel which had vindicated his judgment" and said warmly:

> I may not be an expert in finding apt words to express my feelings to you jurors. If I were the most eloquent man in the world, I would be at a loss to express the appreciation of the court for the patience, diligence and sincerity shown by you during the progress of this case. The court appreciates and the community appreciates your problem. You heard many witnesses, you heard much testimony. Your task was not a simple one.
>
> The case was complicated. It touched the heartstrings and aroused sympathy. I want to refer to your long incarceration. You are a splendid group of people. We are grateful to you for your service. You have been a credit to the community and to the jury system of our country.

Then Blythin, glancing at the eighty reporters present, gave the jurors this observation:

> Newspapermen sometimes become annoying. . . . If you do not want to be pestered by them when you leave this courtroom, decide that for yourselves right now. You may say that you do not want to be interviewed.
>
> If, after you leave here, you want to be interviewed, you may be.
>
> But I have always thought these things had a sacred element—I always thought there was a sacred element—about the things you discussed in the secrecy of your jury room.
>
> Thank you very much. You are now dismissed.

Corrigan, coming down from the jail, was asked by a reporter: "What does Sam have to say?" "Nothing printable," he replied tartly.[231]

The Appeal

It was quite clear to a few who observed the trial that Sheppard had been committed to spend the remainder of his life in jail not because he had been proved guilty but because he did not espouse the same values as his contemporaries, and because they felt he should be punished for violating their mores. This writer overheard members of Sheppard's community express their feeling that he "ought to be convicted on the murder charge for having other women in his life." Another observer described the community attitude toward the trial this way:

> There was prejudice against him because of his profession—osteo-pathy—but beyond this he was suburbia on trial, a member of a privileged gilded class dragged abruptly from his envied niche in the social scheme to suffer like a common man for his supposed misdeeds.
>
> The issue to the people of Cuyahoga County, by this writer's personal observations at the time of the trial, was not who had done it, but whether a professional man who lived in a big lake-front house in a wealthy suburb, and who had money and an influential family, could escape punishment for something he was assumed by uninformed gossip to have done.[232]

This feeling changed, however, over more than a decade of judicial review of the Sheppard case, as did the generations and their way of life. Attitudes changed while "publicity, discipline, and tragedy continued to stalk the world-famous Sheppard murder case," according to the *Elyria Chronicle Telegram* of February 14, 1963.

> While "Dr. Sam" sits behind prison walls, the impact of the July 4, 1954, murder continues . . .
>
> Jan 7, 1955—Mrs. Ethel Sheppard, Dr. Sam Sheppard's mother, shoots herself to death.
>
> Jan. 18, 1955—Dr. Richard A. Sheppard, Dr. Sam's father, dies.
>
> Feb. 13, 1963—Thomas S. Reese, father of the original victim, shoots himself to death . . .
>
> Suicide of Marilyn Sheppard's father came in the wake of some more widespread publicity.[233]

The publicity seemed to accompany each move Sam made to exonerate himself; "but I will keep fighting for my family's sake," he said two days after the verdict. "I am sorry for and worried about my father and mother and my little boy."234

Corrigan's motion for a new trial was postponed after it was decided that Judge Blythin would hear it at 9:30 a.m., December 30, 1954. In his motion, Corrigan charged Judge Blythin with forty errors in his conduct of the ten-week trial. Assistant prosecutor Sam Danaceau's response was: "We aren't even going to file any answer to this motion. This is all the same old stuff we heard throughout the trial and Judge Blythin has ruled on nearly all these points. If the defense presents anything new, we will argue it, of course."235

Corrigan's motion argued that the verdict of guilty "was not sustained by sufficient evidence, was contrary to law and was influenced by passion and prejudice." The extensive list of errors was replete with references to newspaper, radio, and TV coverage of the Sheppard case. "During the entire trial the courtroom and corridors were filled with reporters, newspaper photographers, radio commentators and television reporters. Reporters worked in full view of the jury, some within three feet of the jury box."236

The defense attorney also described as prejudicial Judge Blythin's conduct outside the courtroom in allowing himself to be "a willing part" of a TV program conducted by Robert Fabian. He also claimed the court had erred in refusing to allow Mrs. Elizabeth Borke, a juror, to ask Sheppard a question while the defendant was on the stand. The list of claimed errors recited nearly all the objections made by the defense which were overruled by the court. Corrigan finally contended that Sheppard was deprived of his rights under the Fifth, Sixth, and Fourteenth Amendments of the Constitution because of "mass hysteria that made a fair trial impossible."237

Sam's first attempt to appeal his conviction was quickly denied by Judge Blythin, who on January 3, 1955, overruled the motion in the following words: "The court has deemed this memorandum necessary, due to some statements made by counsel for the defense during the trial and repeated or enlarged in said motion." In the memorandum, he did not set forth the statements to which he referred, but he denounced them nevertheless, asserting: "Some are not factually true and some others create or tend to create impressions not representative of the true situation." He rejected one after another of the forty-odd reasons for a new trial which had been advanced in the defense motion. "There was no surprise here since he would have had to reverse himself to do otherwise."238

Blythin also explained his denial of Corrigan's appeal by saying "It is a matter of common knowledge that the case commanded the same attention throughout Ohio and the United States of America. It commanded very much attention throughout the free world. Chief counsel for the defense conceded and asserted this to be fact, and stated fervently that the defendant could not have a fair trial in the state of Ohio or even in the United States. The only conclusion from this assertion must be that the defendant cannot be tried at all on an indictment for murder in the first degree. Such a claim furnishes its own answer."[239]

Holmes, who had observed the trial and its whole milieu, responded to the judge's justification for the denial this way:

> One may wonder where Judge Blythin got the "common knowledge" that the Sheppard case got the same attention throughout Ohio and the United States that it was accorded in Cleveland. It is true that the newspapers of Ohio and the nation gave considerable space to the case, but they gave half-columns and columns at a time the Cleveland newspapers were devoting several whole pages to it daily. Moreover, the wire-service reports which went out of Cleveland were for the most part confined to authentic news developments, whereas the Cleveland newspapers overflowed with inflammatory editorials and articles based on the speculation and opinions of investigators and officials, most of them hostile to Sam.[240]

After his motion for a new trial was denied, Corrigan compiled additional evidence on the murder and used it as a basis for a second request for a new trial. In Ohio, statutory provision allows for a new trial after a verdict of conviction when new evidence is discovered which could not, with reasonable diligence, have been discovered and produced at the trial. Corrigan held that anything helpful to Sam that was found inside the house was something the defense could not have discovered with reasonable diligence, either before or during the trial, because the authorities held the house in their exclusive possession.[241]

Two days after Sam's conviction, the keys to his home were restored to him by the officials who had impounded his premises on the day of his wife's murder.[242] Corrigan now had his first opportunity to make an independent examination of the house, and to assist him he retained one of the nation's foremost criminologists, Dr. Paul Leland Kirk, professor of criminalistics of the School of Criminology of the University of California. Dr. Kirk's findings were incorporated into an affidavit nearly 10,000 words long, in addition to a substantial appendix and numerous exhibits that included charts, photographs, and sketches. Corrigan filed this affidavit in Judge Blythin's court as support for a motion to have a new trial on the grounds of newly discovered evidence.

Among other things, it pointed out many ways in which the officials failed to gather all the data available during investigations at the scene on behalf of the state.243 Furthermore, the affidavit offers persuasive evidence that a third person was in the bedroom and that at least one bloodstain in that room came from that person.244 Finally, Dr. Kirk said the theory that Sheppard's injuries were self-inflicted or were sustained in a fall was untenable.245

In the spring of 1955 three judges heard two separate appeals for a new trial for Sheppard, one an appeal from the ruling of Judge Blythin denying a new trial on forty-odd claims of error in the trial and the other an appeal from a subsequent ruling denying a new trial for newly discovered evidence, contained in the affidavit of Dr. Kirk. The judges were unanimous in rejecting both appeals.246

The prosecution asserted that the affidavit contained little or nothing of an evidentiary nature that was truly new because most of the material, with due diligence on the part of the defense, could have been obtained in time for presentation in the trial. Holmes pointedly explains the implications of the position assumed by the prosecution: "In other words, the defense should have brought Dr. Kirk to Cleveland before the trial instead of waiting until the verdict was in. The fact that the authorities seized Sam's house on the day of the murder and kept control of it until after the verdict, with access permitted to it only with police permission and supervision and then only for removal of needed belongings or inspection of its physical condition, was no excuse for defense delay, the prosecution contended."247

When the mentality demonstrated by these judges seemed to conclude that the newly discovered evidence was not new, was not discovered, and was not evidence, it must have taken unusual courage and faith for the Sheppard family to continue its expensive and trying appeal through the system of American justice. The cavalier treatment which the Kirk affidavit received in the courts may suggest that only the more fortunate or wealthy are able to pursue the resolution of the injustice that had been inflicted upon them at this point.

The Supreme Court of Ohio

When the Sheppard case reached the Ohio supreme court, Chief Justice Carl Victory Weygandt decided to disqualify himself because his son, a law director of Bay Village, had participated in the case to the extent of advising Bay Village officials to arrest Dr. Sheppard for murder. The framers of the Ohio constitution may well have felt that a chief justice who feels obliged to disqualify himself in a case should also find an uninvolved way to make the choice of a judge to replace him, but such was not the case with Chief Justice Weygandt. Consequently, Judge Montgomery, who was temporarily elevated to the bench because of Weygandt's disqualification, voted with the majority of the state supreme court to uphold the conviction of Sam Sheppard.

Representing a 5-2 majority, Justice James Finley Bell distinguished himself with the following opening paragraph, which might lead one to believe that he was going to arrive at the converse of the conclusion he supported.

> Mystery and murder, society, sex, and suspense were combined in this case in such a manner as to intrigue and captivate the public fancy to a degree perhaps unparalleled in recent annals. Throughout the pre-indictment investigation, the subsequent legal skirmishes, and the nine-week trial, circulation-conscious editors catered to the unsatiable interest of the American public in the bizarre. Special seating facilities for reporters and columnists representing local papers and all major news services were installed in the courtroom. Special rooms in the Criminal Courts Building were equipped for broadcasters and telecasters. In this atmosphere of a "Roman holiday" for the news media, Sam Sheppard stood trial for his life.
>
> The evidence in this case is largely circumstantial. In such a situation it is conceded that the law of Ohio requires that the facts upon which a verdict of guilt is based must be established beyond a reasonable doubt. The facts so established must be entirely irreconcilable with any claim or theory of innocence and admit of no other hypothesis than the guilt of the accused.[248]

Bell did not attempt to suggest a set of facts which the jury might have found to support a verdict in accordance with these limitations.[249] Holmes concludes that "with four of his colleagues, including Judge Montgomery, concurring, and two others sharply dissenting, the judgment of the Court of Appeals was affirmed and Sam's once seemingly bright chances of a new trial [were] thereby reduced to a feeble flame, flickering ineffectually but defiant still, in the darkening and deepening legal morass swirling turgidly around him."[250]

The two members of the Ohio Supreme court who refused to join the majority were Justice Kingsley A. Taft and Justice William Lincoln Hart, both of whom thought Sheppard should have been given a new trial because of the numerous prejudicial errors which they said they found in the record. The dissenting opinion, which Taft wrote and in which Hart concurred, "bristled with indignation against the majority ruling."251 Justice Taft suggested that the defense lawyers had been unjustly criticized in the majority opinion for making such a large number of assignments of error—twenty-nine—and that the supreme court should have given consideration to all of them instead of discussing only three. He claimed that the time limitation for oral argument before the court had prevented the counsel from arguing all the errors, but that all of them had been argued by brief. He indicated that it is only assigned errors, not argued by brief, which appellate courts in Ohio have a statutory right to disregard.252

The United States Supreme Court

After the Ohio supreme court rejected Sheppard's appeal there was only one resort: the U.S. Supreme Court. Final decisions of state courts may be brought for review before the highest bench in cases where questions arising under the Constitution are involved, providing the court consents to make the review. Such consent is discretionary, and when it is withheld—as it is much more often than not—there is ordinarily no explanation from the court and no disclosure of the attitude of the individual justices. Nor is there a further appeal; "It is the end of the road."253

The elaborate petition, which was almost entirely the work of Corrigan, was considered by the Supreme Court in its October 1956 term. It refused to issue a writ of certiorari, the technical name for the process by which it asserts jurisdiction in those cases which it consents to review. The denial was not entirely unexplained, however, for Justice Felix Frankfurter wrote an accompanying opinion (a rare occurrence):

> The defendant claimed that a trial so infused and enveloped by the atmosphere of a "Roman holiday" precluded a fair trial and could not but deprive him of the due process of law guaranteed by the Fourteenth Amendment of the Constitution. The Supreme Court of Ohio rejected this claim and the defendant then invoked the discretionary power of this court to review the correctness of that decision. This court now, in turn, refuses the defendant the opportunity to bring the case here for review.
>
> Such denial of his petition in no way implies that this court approves the decision of the Supreme Court of Ohio. It means and means only that for one reason and another this case did not com-

mend itself to at least four members of the court as falling within those considerations which should lead this court to exercise its discretion in reviewing a lower court's decision.

For reasons that have often been explained the court does not give the grounds for denying the petitions for certiorari in the normally more than one thousand cases each year in which petitions are denied. It has also been explained why not even the positions of the various justices in such cases are matters of public record. The rare cases in which an individual position is noted leave unillumined the functioning of the certiorari system, and do not reveal the position of all the members of the court.

At this point the Sheppard family had truly reached the "end of the road," as far as the American jury system is concerned, but there remained the so-called Court of Last Resort. Founded in 1944 by Erle Stanley Gardner and Harry Steeger for the purpose of investigating all possible miscarriages of justice in criminal cases where all avenues of relief through the courts have been exhausted, this organization agreed to consider helping the Sheppard family if it would first submit to lie tests. The Sheppards promptly agreed, and "passed the tests with flying colors."[254] Coincidentally, this happened at the same time that a Florida convict asserted that he was the murderer of Marilyn Sheppard, and a new wave of publicity erupted.

Gardner conceded that such results would not prove Sheppard's innocence, but he argued that it would show that "all of the innuendoes, all of the gossip, all of the speculation regarding the fact that these members of the family might have engaged in a cover up, have no foundation in fact." He also said that the next logical step in the Court of Last Resort's inquiry ought to be to administer a lie test to Sam in prison.[255]

Judge Blythin angrily broke the silence he had maintained since his last official connection with the case, flailing against the Court of Last Resort in a telegram to William Saxbe, the Ohio attorney general: "I believe the attorney general of Ohio should immediately take steps in the name of the state to deny any individual or group the right or privilege to designate himself or themselves as a Court of Last Resort or court under any other name in Ohio."[256]

By this time Coroner Gerber had decided he should do his part in preventing new evidence from emerging: "No unofficial outfit ought to be let in here to give anyone a lie test." John Reid of Chicago was to take charge of the polygraph, and assisting him would be C. B. Hanscom of the University of Minnesota. Sergeant William George of the state highway patrol, a polygraph operator, had been designated to attend as an observer, along with a member of the state bureau of criminal identification. All records of the test were to be state property. Such were the conditions of the test, after Governor O'Neill said he had decided to allow a lie test so he could be sure that justice would prevail.257 But the lie test was banned in Sheppard's case.

Contemplating a return to the law courts, in the late summer of 1958 Corrigan and his associates filed a petition in the state supreme court for a writ of habeas corpus. It would direct Warden Ralph Alvis to produce Sheppard for a hearing on whether his confinement was unlawful because the prosecutors had withheld or concealed evidence that would have been helpful to him in his trial. It took twenty months before it was finally decided, leaving Sam where he was when it began.258 Chief Justice Weygandt apparently saw no reason to disqualify himself in this phase of the case, as he had when the appeal was heard more than two years before.259

Corrigan had approached this appeal as another way into the federal courts, where there was a good chance for a new judicial viewpoint on some of the constitutional questions in Sheppard's trial. Federal courts are not permitted to look into a state court case on habeas corpus until all remedies in the courts of that state have been exhausted. Unfortunately for Sheppard, who remained behind bars, the counsel became so entangled in ramifications of the habeas corpus action that everyone was either too discouraged or too tired to go any further.260

After the first hearing, Chief Justice Weygandt refused to issue a writ, but he gave Sheppard's lawyers until December 31, 1958, to file an amended petition stating what evidence was claimed to have been withheld and by whom. The amended petition, filed December 30,261 contained charges that the investigating authorities had been in possession of, but had withheld, various items of evidence at the time of the trial concerning possible forcible entry into the Sheppard house, concerning a car that was parked near the house at the time of the murder, and concerning individuals who saw a bushy haired man near the house. The charge was also made that certain photographs of the interior of the house had been suppressed by the authorities. Another charge, if substantiated, would probably have induced court action:

> At the trial the state offered evidence that tests of the blood found on the wrist watch of the murdered woman, which were made by the office of the coroner of Cuyahoga County, were inconclusive, although the fact is that the original laboratory record in the cor-

oner's office states that those tests twice revealed the presence of a "B" factor in the blood taken from said wrist watch. No "B" factor is present in the blood of the relator [Sam] or in the blood of the murdered woman. The presence of the "B" factor establishes that the blood on the wrist watch was the blood of a third person who killed Marilyn Sheppard.

The state of Ohio filed a brief in February 1959 requesting dismissal of the petition, as amended, on the grounds that all the matters it brought up had been gone into thoroughly at the trial. It contended that Mary Cowan, the coroner's technician, had been cross-examined about the blood on Marilyn's watch at a time she had all the records with her and that these records had been made available to the defense.262

This position brought an answering brief from Sheppard's lawyers in March 1959, in which they charged that the state had not only withheld purported evidence of "B" blood on the watch but had concealed and suppressed it so that the defense would have no chance to cross-examine Miss Cowan about it during the trial. Proof was to be found in notations Miss Cowan made on a work card upon which she had recorded her findings of the blood from the watch, and in the fact that this card disappeared in court before Sheppard's lawyers had the opportunity to see it. The card reappeared, just as mysteriously, when the case was before the Ohio supreme court on appeal more than a year later, and was discovered among cards of similar size which had been exhibits in the trial. This card, however, had no mark on it to indicate that it had been an exhibit, whereas the other cards were clearly marked as such. Sheppard's lawyers also submitted a photostatic copy of both sides of the mystery card.263

The Supreme Court responded to these charges by making a journal entry (October 14, 1959) permitting the parties to take depositions "relating to and confined to the suppression of evidence" as alleged in regard to the blood on Marilyn's watch. When the cards were requested, the state argued that it was under no obligation to produce them, and that it might have difficulty producing all of them.264 And so the "card trick" was one more mystery in the case; the Supreme Court considered it inconsequential that the card had not been marked as a court exhibit.

This time Justice Taft concurred with the majority view because he did not believe the questions were proper in a habeas corpus action; but at the same time he wanted to make his informed analysis of the case known:

For the reasons stated in my dissenting opinion when the judgment of the Court of Appeals affirming the conviction of the petitioner was affirmed by this court, in 1956, it was definitely my opinion then, as it has been at all times since, and is now, that this court should have reversed the judgment of the Court of Appeals and at least granted the petitioner a new trial.

Holmes summarized Sheppard's predicament well when he said: "I saw it all, and for what it is worth, I think the whole business rubbed luster from American jurisprudence, and is, in its most literal and reverent sense, a God-damned shame."[265]

Retrial

More than half a decade later, the Supreme Court granted Sheppard's appeal for a new trial on grounds that prejudicial publicity and conduct in the courtroom had prevented his constitutional right to obtain a fair trial.[266] The retrial was scheduled to begin in Cleveland on October 18,[267] only four months after the Supreme Court decision.

Meanwhile, on July 5, 1966, the Southern United States District Court of Ohio, Eastern Division, "received a mandate from the Supreme Court of the United States remanding said case to the United States District Court for the Southern District of Ohio, for further proceedings in conformity with the opinion of the Supreme Court of the United States." According to the opinion of the Supreme Court: "The case is remanded to the District Court with instructions to issue the writ and order that Sheppard be released from custody unless the State puts him to its charges again within a reasonable time." In a conference on July 15, 1966, at Dayton, the petitioner, Samuel H. Sheppard, was represented by his attorney, F. Lee Bailey. The office of the prosecuting attorney of Cuyahoga County was represented by the prosecuting attorney thereof: John T. Corrigan. At the conference, the prosecuting attorney stated that he had determined to place the petitioner, Samuel H. Sheppard, on trial for second degree murder.[268]

From the beginning, conditions were vastly different from those in the Sheppard trial of 1954. Early in October, Judge Francis J. Talty barred a United Press International photographer from attending a change-of-venue hearing for the accused. Talty also took action against Ron Kuntz of the UPI Cleveland staff because he took two pictures of newsmen picking up hearing credentials in bailiff Lawrence D. Patrick's office. He further asked that the picture negatives be turned over to the court. A UPI spokesman said the negatives would be delivered to the bailiff's office "under protest." Talty said the pictures violated the rules governing newsmen who would cover the hearing.[269]

The judge also slightly changed the language concerning interviews. A ruling, on October 10, did not allow the interviewing of the witnesses at all, but a new order said: "Witnesses, jurors, and those persons summoned but excused from serving as jurors, are forbidden to participate in interviews and from taking statements for publicity from this date and until such time as a verdict in this case is returned in open court."270

The same rule applied to lawyers, court employees, and law enforcement officers, and the judge's order also prohibited the use of cameras and recording devices on the courthouse premises. Making sketches or drawings within the courthouse was not allowed, and the installation of telephone or teleprinter equipment in the courthouse was prohibited. The judge further said that no one would be allowed to enter or leave the courtroom after a session began.271

Sheppard and his attorneys had taken a large stack of newspaper clippings to the October 12 hearing in an attempt to prove that local prejudice would prevent the osteopath from receiving a fair trial in Cleveland. Nearly twenty newsmen, including fourteen reporters, had been assigned special seats for the hearing under Talty's stringent rules governing news coverage of the proceedings.272

It seemed as if virtually every aspect of the trial became more sensitive to the problem of publicity than had been the case twelve years earlier. When the jurors were examined, they were "bothering the newspaper people almost as much as the U.S. Supreme Court had when it said that there was too much publicity in the previous trial." People were saying they did not read newspapers very much: "No, they did not subscribe, or yes, they saw that article the other day about Sam but did not bother to read it." Seven of the eight persons examined said they had read about the case, but not so much that they would remember what they had read or that it would have any effect if they sat in the jury. "A reporter groaned, and a deputy came over and said that there was to be absolutely no talking." There was not the carnival atmosphere about which the Supreme Court had written in describing the earlier trial.273

Despite these precautions, six of the twelve prospective jurors who were quizzed on October 27 declared they had firm opinions on the case and could not give the former osteopathic neurosurgeon a fair trial.274 Nevertheless, twelve jurors were sworn in, though it took five days to select a jury—but only half the time it took to seat the jury of seven men and five women in Sheppard's first trial in 1954.275

On November 16, 1966, Sam Sheppard was acquitted in a second trial, the trial ordered by the Supreme Court: "We, the jury in this case, being duly impaneled and sworn, do find the defendant, Sam H. Sheppard, not guilty of murder in the second degree, as charged in the indictment." And as there was no further charge against him, he was ordered discharged.276

Sheppard's license to practice as a physician had been suspended by the Ohio Medical Board on April 2, 1957, because of his murder conviction in his first trial. J. Dennis Burns, the legal representative in the state attorney general's office in Columbus, said Sheppard must file an application requesting the board to lift the suspension. "Now that Sheppard's felony conviction has been wiped clean, it appears that lifting of the suspension by the eight-doctor board would be hardly more than a formality."277

SUMMARY

Petitioner Samuel Sheppard was tried and convicted of second degree murder in Cleveland. Prior to, and throughout the trial, he was the subject of extensive publicity which concentrated heavily on matters unfavorable to him, and often extraneous to the trial. No evidence concerning many of these matters was ever introduced in the court trial. However, this does not mean that these matters did not have something to do with his conviction.

The trial court refused to restrict the activities of the news media in gathering material, and the state was singularly unrestrained when it came to releasing information, testimony, and its opinion about Sheppard's guilt to the news media. Distorted facts, prejudiced views, and open bigotry were printed as news, and it had its impact on the public and the jury. The trial court even denied the petitioner's request to poll the jury to determine its exposure to such publicity.

On certiorari, the Supreme Court of the United States voided the petitioner's conviction and held that the failure of the trial court to insulate his trial from pervasive and prejudicial publicity, together with a disruptive courtroom environment, deprived him of the fair and impartial trial guaranteed by the due process clause of the Fourteenth Amendment.278

After spending twelve years in prison, while his only son completed grades one through twelve in school, and during which time some of his close relatives committed suicide and died of heartbreak, Sam Sheppard was retried in the same court and found innocent of the offense. Melvin Belli, the controversial criminal lawyer from San Francisco, said he had read the transcript of the federal ruling and "found it shocking to see that this man was tried and had to wait this long to get due process of law."279 It should be noted that Attorney General John Mitchell's recommendations could probably have prevented Sheppard's retrial. He suggested that there should be a "predictable time" after which a convicted man's chances for appeal would be exhausted.280

It has long been a principle of Anglo-American criminal justice that a person accused of a crime be provided a public trial. In the United States the guarantee is embodied in the Sixth Amendment: "In all criminal prosecutions, the accused shall enjoy the right to a speedy and public trial, by an impartial jury." This guarantee has also been made applicable to state courts through the due process clause of the Fourteenth Amendment, whose purpose it is to serve "as a safeguard against any attempt to employ our courts as instruments of persecution"281 by ensuring that the accused's trial will be open to members of his family and other interested parties rather than merely to officials.282 In like manner, the First Amendment guarantees that "Congress shall make no law . . . abridging the freedom of speech, or of press," which is regarded as one of the most fundamental rights guaranteed by the Constitution.283 It is held to be subject to limitation only for the purpose of preventing evils, whose potential consequences would present such a "clear and present danger" that they outweigh the maintenance of this freedom.284

The practice of balancing apparently conflicting interests was suggested by the Supreme Court when it said that "freedom of discussion should be given the widest range compatible with the essential requirement of the fair and orderly administration of justice."285 In seeking a balance, the values of the suggested remedies must be juxtaposed to the price they exact in the curtailment of public information. The more that publication undermines the right of a fair trial, the more extensive must be the nature of the remedy capable of dealing with it, and the greater the cost that society is justified in paying. When the incidence is infrequent, different remedies, which are less extensive in their impact, may be suitable and effective.286

The Supreme Court shares this judgment in its treatment of First Amendment cases. It has declared that it is incumbent on anyone who would limit First Amendment rights "to demonstrate that no alternate form of regulation would combat such abuses without infringing First Amendment rights."287

The cherished recognition of freedom of the press, and the equally important protection guaranteed the accused under the Sixth Amendment, provide the grounds for the current controversy over publicity and criminal trials. In the past, the Supreme Court has been reluctant to restrain the freedom of the news media in publicizing judicial proceedings, and even more reluctant to impose penalties for alleged excesses in the exercise of this freedom.288 In *Bridges* v. *California*, the petitioners had been convicted of contempt for the publication of newspaper stories and editorials concerning pending criminal trials: the trial court had found that such publications "tended" to interfere with the orderly administration of justice. The Supreme Court, on the other hand, rejected the application of the "tendency" test, arguing that the contempt penalty should be imposed only within the guidelines of the "clear and present danger" test. Freedom of the press is to be given the widest possible scope, and restraint is permissible only when there is an unmistakably serious probability that the substantive evil, though legitimately opposed, will occur.289

Such freedom does not exist in a vacuum, however. The Supreme Court has suggested that there are strong, countervailing interests which must be recognized, particularly in criminal trials: "With his life at stake, it is not requiring too much that petitioner be tried in an atmosphere undisturbed by . . . a wave of public passion [occasioned by extensive publicity]."290 Although the Supreme Court has recognized the conflicting values of a free press and a fair trial, it has opted to cope with the problem by remedying the ill effects of publicity on the accused through procedural safeguards rather than direct restraints on the press.291 It seems that the Supreme Court has devised such procedures as the granting of new trials292 and motions for continuances and changes of venue,293 which seem preferable to restraints upon the source of the information, which in turn gives rise to a prejudicial atmosphere.

Certain procedural restraints, which indirectly limit the latitude of the press, may also be employed. Restrictions on the news media's observation of certain investigations and the information derived therefrom are available within the status quo. For example, information in the case against Juan V. Corona during the period of time when he was suspected of having murdered 23 people was scanty. A judicial order prohibited officials from discussing the case outside court proceedings.

A year earlier, Senator Edward Kennedy was able to relate the events surrounding the death of Mary Jo Kopechne under similar conditions. In deciding to hold a secret hearing in Edgartown, the Massachusetts supreme court pointed to the great publicity about the incident. The press, and therefore the public, was barred from the probe at the behest of the attorneys for Senator Kennedy, who was driving the car in which Mary Jo died.294

Because of the reluctance of the U.S. Supreme Court to restrain the freedom of press, however, petitioners who claim they have been denied due process have generally been required to assume a heavy burden in demonstrating the prejudicial effect of publicity. In upholding such a claim the petitioner must show that his trial "was 'fatally infected' with an absence of 'that fundamental fairness essential to the very concept of justice' ";295 that such matters "aroused against him such prejudice in the community as to 'necessarily prevent a fair trial' ";296 or that the trial's environment contains a "pattern of deep and bitter prejudice."297 The Supreme Court has held that the above tests are applicable to cases involving claims of due process violation.298

Yet the Supreme Court has suggested that there are instances in which the generally applied tests should yield to a less stringent method of determining denial of due process, such as the totality of circumstances, which may be a sufficient foundation for determining prejudice, despite an inability to specify the source or impact of the prejudice.299

This happened in *Marshall* v. *United States*, when the Supreme Court reversed a conviction in a narcotics case because of the jury's exposure to newspaper articles which focused on prejudicial matters in the petitioner's past. The conviction was reversed despite the fact that the jurors, when examined, assured the trial court of their ability to discount such publicity and maintain their impartiality.300

In *Rideau* v. *Louisiana*, the petitioner's interrogation and confession were repeatedly televised. The Supreme Court reversed Rideau's conviction, stating that, even without examining the oaths taken or the competency of the jury members, the Court could decide that the publicity was inherently prejudicial. For that reason the petitioner was not required to show that a single juror had been influenced by publicity adverse to a fair trial. The mere circumstances of the publicity, aside from any demonstrable effect, were sufficient to support a claim of denial of due process.301 *Turner* v. *Louisana* is a later example in which an association of prejudice was believed to exist among individuals without actually having been proved.302

The same year in which the *Turner* decision was made, the Supreme Court reviewed the conviction of Billie Sol Estes, whose activities had been well publicized, and restated its less restrictive "probability of prejudice" or "inherently prejudicial" test.303 Despite his objection, Estes' pretrial hearing on a motion for a change of venue and his later trial were televised. The Supreme Court ruled that the widespread notoriety accompanying such media coverage was inherently unfair to Estes because of its potentially prejudicial effect on the jurors, witnesses, and judges, and without any indication that such potential effects became actualized at the trial.304

A further sanction which may be employed by the government against such activity on the part of the broadcasting industry is the power of the Federal Communications Commission to revoke licenses or fail to renew them. While newspapers usually have the protection of the constitutional freedom of the press amendment, the networks and their affiliated stations are licensed by a government which has the power to impose its notion of fair reporting by threatening to withdraw a station's license.[305]

In the case of Sam Sheppard, the Supreme Court did not require F. Lee Bailey to prove prejudice on the part of the jury in order to call for a retrial or his acquittal. Rather, the court decided that the totality of the circumstances justified application of the less restrictive probability of prejudice and inherently prejudicial tests. Comparing *Sheppard* with *Estes*, the Supreme Court declared:

> Unlike Estes, Sheppard was not granted a change of venue to a locale away from where the publicity originated; nor was his jury sequestered. The Estes jury saw none of the television broadcasts from the courtroom. On the contrary, the Sheppard jurors were subjected to newspaper, radio and television coverage of the trial while not taking part in the proceedings. . . .
>
> The press coverage of the Estes trial was not nearly as massive and pervasive as the attention given by the Cleveland newspapers and broadcasting stations to Sheppard's prosecution.[306]

It was reasoned that the totality of circumstances giving rise to a probability of prejudice had been a major factor behind the denial of due process in Sheppard's first trial. The Supreme Court also felt that the trial court had failed to exercise appropriate physical control over the courtroom. If such control had been exercised, Sheppard would have been guaranteed a fair trial, making it unnecessary (in the Supreme Court's view) to inquire into the sanctions that could have been applied to a recalcitrant press. The court's opinion suggested several steps the trial court should have taken:

> 1. Strict regulation of the presence and activities of the media representatives in the courtroom, especially their exclusion from within the bar of the court.
> 2. Insulation of witnesses from the news media.
> 3. Strict enforcement of a prohibition against court officers and prosecutors divulging non-record information to news media.
> 4. The use of procedural safeguards such as continuances and

changes of venue if it appeared that, despite the use of the foregoing methods of control, the probability of prejudice still remained.307

The problem, then, was not so much the publicity itself or the nature of the publicity but, rather, the sources of the publicity. The trial court's failure to control publicity was not in itself considered to be the basis of due process denial so much as its failure or unwillingness to regulate the sources of information to which the press consequently had access. The Supreme Court's *Sheppard* opinion, furthermore, demands that trial courts make full and effective use of their inherent power over officers of the court, witnesses, and jurors in order to insulate the accused from the effects of extraneous and prejudicial influences in the conduct of his trial.308 The "officers of the court" include the attorneys for the prosecution and for the defense in a criminal case, and the courts have broad power to regulate their contributions to the publicity surrounding a case. For example, the United States District Court for the Northern District of Illinois has adopted Local Criminal Rule 1.07, which provides in part:

[a] It is the duty of the lawyer not to release or authorize the release of information or opinion, for dissemination by any means of public communication, in connection with pending or imminent criminal litigation with which he is associated if there is a reasonable likelihood that such dissemination will interfere with a fair trial or otherwise prejudice the due administration of justice.

[b] From the time of arrest, issuance of an arrest warrant or the filing of a complaint, information, or indictment in any criminal matter until the commencement of trial or disposition without trial, a lawyer associated with the prosecution or defense shall not release or authorize the release of any extrajudicial statement, for dissemination by any means of public communication, relating to that matter and concerning [the defendant's prior criminal record, or reputation, the existence or contents of any statement or confession given by the accused, the performance of any examination or tests or the defendant's refusal to submit thereto, the identity or testimony of prospective witnesses, the possibility of a guilty plea, or any opinion as to the merits of the case and the defendant's guilt or innocence.]

[c] During the trial of any criminal matter . . . no lawyer associated with the prosecution or defense shall give or authorize any

extrajudicial statement or interview, relating to the trial or the parties or issues in the trial, for dissemination by any means of public communication, except that the lawyer may quote from or refer without comment to public records of the court in the case.

While the brunt of the Supreme Court's decision clearly falls upon the trial court, demanding that it invoke all of its inherent powers to negate any detrimental influence upon the fair determination of the accused's guilt, it is clear that it must operate within certain limitations. It was impossible for the trial court in Los Angeles to prevent the jury from learning that President Richard Nixon had, so to speak, found Charles Manson guilty of murder before it had so ruled, and without seeing the evidence and testimony. This is also the case in the military appeal procedure, with which Lieutenant Calley may soon become familiar.

In these two cases, as well as in the case of Angela Davis, it would seem unwise to disallow the press to print President Nixon's speeches; but the sanctions which could be applied to any President of the United States under these circumstances, and their causes, are not within the purview of this book.[309] Hopefully, public pressure and public reaction might serve as an effective method of deterring public officials from similar performances in the future. Nevertheless, in *Sheppard* v. *Maxwell* the Supreme Court declared that, "given the pervasiveness of modern communications and the difficulty of effacing prejudicial publicity from the minds of the jurors, the trial courts must take strong measures to insure that the balance is never weighed against the accused."[310] Thus the Supreme Court insists that the solution to the problem of pretrial publicity is preventive action at the trial level rather than curative action at the appellate level. The Supreme Court also feels that it would be unwise to attack the problem of pretrial publicity at the level of its effects (restricting the news media) and, instead, that the problem should be solved indirectly, by controlling the sources of information available to the media.

The main thrust of the *Sheppard* decision is that trial courts possess adequate powers to assure the nonintrusion of extraneous influences, and that these powers must be fully and effectively exercised for the benefit of the accused. It is in this way that the Supreme Court has attempted to equate the freedom of speech and press preserved in the First Amendment with the right to a jury trial and the due process guaranteed in the Sixth and Fourteenth Amendments. Richard Nixon came to a similar conclusion when he said:

A balance must be struck: The right of a free press must be weighed carefully against an individual's right to privacy.

All too often, the right of the accused to a fair trial is eroded by prejudicial publicity. We must never forget that a primary purpose underlying the defendant's right to a speedly and public trial is to prevent star-chamber proceedings, and not to put on an exciting show or to satisfy curiosity at the expense of the defendant.[311]

Prompted by the Warren Commission recommendations, which suggested that efforts be made to "bring about a proper balance between the right of the public to be kept well informed and the right of the individual to a fair and impartial trial,"[312] the American Bar Association's Advisory Committee on Fair Trial and Free Press prepared a tentative draft of standards in 1966, which was adopted in final form in 1968.[313] These standards were to reinforce and supplement the recent demands of the Supreme Court with regard to tempering the First, Sixth, and Fourteenth Amendments in well-publicized criminal cases.

The Reardon Committee report came to three conclusions. First, it felt that there is a substantial number of cases (greater than is generally believed) in which the dissemination of information or opinion during critical parts of the trial poses a significant threat to the fairness of the trial. This occurs in cases where it is difficult or impossible to impanel or maintain an impartial jury in the community in which the defendant has a constitutional right to be tried. One source of this information or opinion is not the media themselves but, rather, the attorneys in the case. Ill-timed public statements of personal opinion or matters that may eventually be discovered to be inaccurate, incomplete, or inadmissible as evidence in court may lead to community prejudice in a way that is totally incompatible with the right of even the "presumed guilty" to a fair and impartial trial. Hence the committee revised the canons of professional ethics.

The committee also recognized that, for the moment, it is impossible to fully understand how exposure to potentially prejudicial material affects the outlook of every attorney, judge, witness, and juror. It also conceded that the results of any study to determine these effects may well refute, rather than establish the need for drastic measures. However, it felt that its limited proposals for the conduct of attorneys in criminal cases need not be indefinitely delayed. It did not have the same attitude toward the news media, however, as was also the case (as was stated earlier) with the Supreme Court. The Supreme Court's attitude toward the news media had changed radically over several decades, to a considerably more liberal view.

While the First Amendment guarantees of freedom of the press have been allowed to continue, in some cases one of the primary sources of the problem—prosecuting attorneys—appear to have had difficulty cleaning their own houses since the Reardon Committee came to its first conclusion. Ramsey Clark expressed the problem which now exists on the federal level:

> Moral judgments are not for prosecutors to make. The district attorney, so sure he is right—and so bent on convincing the public—that he will leak stories even though he has little or no evidence on which to indict, is a menace. Of course, the press and other media render invaluable service to the public by seeking out corruption, but when they obtain and use police information, they corrupt themselves and the system of justice. We are dealing with crucial rights of privacy, reputation and liberty. Under Attorney General John Mitchell, the United States Department of Justice has regularly and often openly placed investigative information from its official sources in the press. Public announcement of pending investigations and imminent indictments may seem to be good politics, but it slowly destroys justice. It is as dangerous to liberty for the press to use police sources for news as it is for the police to use press sources for prosecution.314

Second, after making recommendations on the conduct of attorneys in criminal cases, the Reardon Committee made suggestions for the conduct of law enforcement officers, judges, and judicial employees in criminal cases. The committee felt that law enforcement officials were more responsible than attorneys in creating problems with pretrial publicity.315 Attempting to remedy the problems, the committee proposed departmental rules, court rules, or legislation for law enforcement agencies, court rules for judicial employees, and recommendations to judges that all should refrain from statements or conduct which would in any way tend to interfere with the fairness of a trial.

The third recommendation of the Reardon Committee pertains to the conduct of judicial proceedings in criminal cases. It includes a motion to exclude the public from all or part of the pretrial hearings, standards for the request, methods of proof, timing, and procedures for disposition and waiver in changes of venue or continuances, methods of examination, and standards for the acceptability and source of the panel in selecting the jury.

Finally, the committee attempted to improve the conduct of trials by recommending standards to govern a criminal trial when problems relating to the dissemination of potentially prejudicial material are raised. These include (1) the use of the courtroom; (2) sequestration of the jury; (3) cautioning parties, witnesses, jurors, and judicial employees; (4) exclusion of the public from hearings or arguments outside the presence of the jury; (5) questioning jurors about exposure to potentially prejudicial material in the course of a trial; standards for excusing a juror; and (7) setting aside the verdict.[316]

While these American Bar Association regulations have been less effective in improving the conduct of prosecuting attorneys, they have been more effective—with the assistance of several court precedents—in preventing a repetition of the injustice done to Sam Sheppard. When these standards have not been enforced sufficiently, mistrials have frequently been called. This happened, for example, in May 1971, when after "prejudicial publicity in the press, U.S. District Court Judge Frank J. Murray declared a mistrial . . . in the case of Stanley R. Bond."[317] The defense motion for a mistrial stated that the press "appears to forget that the right of the public criminal trial is that of the defendant alone."[318] (Bond was charged with breaking into the Newbury National Guard Armory, and he also faced a charge of murder in a bank-holdup slaying of a Boston policeman.) Judge Murray did not mention a possible date for the new trial, and defense counsel Robert D. Marderosian said he would press for dismissal of the indictment because Bond had not been given a speedy trial.[319]

It must be recognized that the combative proclivities of the press and bar will probably continue. Commenting on newspapers' handling of sensational cases, Clarence Darrow once said: "It is a species of mob law more insidious and dangerous than ordinary mob law."[320] More recently, the assassination of President Kennedy brought a great awakening of national interest in the performance of the press in reporting crime.[321] The Warren Commission, which pointedly rebuked the newsmen on the scene, the Dallas police, and the district attorney for irresponsible dissemination of information on the suspects in the murder, concluded that "it would have been a most difficult task to select an unprejudiced jury, either in Dallas or elsewhere."[322] Such cases as this, along with the trials of Jack Ruby, Sirhan B. Sirhan, the Chicago Seven, Angela Davis, Charles Manson, William Calley, and others, prove the irony that "while news coverage of the Court and the law has improved in some ways in recent years, such criticism has, if anything, increased."[323]

As the news media continue to improve by demonstrating more and more responsibility in their social and political attitudes, the merit of the attacks upon the news media continues to decrease. The lack of substantive criticism of the news media is probably most conspicuous in the rhetoric of their best-known critic: Vice President Agnew. After more than a year and a half of articulating colorful epithets on the news media,

Agnew shows little or no sign of mellowing.324 And while he ignores the substance of the criticism presented by the news media, newsmen such as Walter Cronkite have begun to fear a federal antipress plot.

> Evidence buttresses the suspicion that the Nixon Administration has conceived, planned, orchestrated, and is now conducting a program to reduce the effectiveness of the free press, and its prime target is television.
>
> With consummate skill it attacks on many fronts: often reiterated but unsubstantiated charges of bias and prejudice from the stump; the claim of distortion or even fakery planted with friendly columnists; the attempts to divide the networks and their affiliates; harassment by subpoena . . .
>
> As threatening as is this posture to our reputation of impartiality, the danger of silence is greater, and candor must be the order of the day.
>
> For many of us see a clear indication on the part of the Administration of a grand conspiracy to destroy the credibility of the press. No one doubts the right of anyone to seek to correct distortion, to right untruths. . . . But the present campaign, spearheaded by Vice President Spiro T. Agnew and Republican Chairman Senator Robert Dole, goes beyond that.
>
> Nor is there any way that President Nixon can escape responsibility for this campaign. He is the ultimate leader. He sets the tone and the attitude of his Administration. By internal edict and public posture, he could reverse the anti-press policy of his Administration if that were his desire.
>
> As long as the attacks, overt and subtle, continue, we must, even at the risk of appearing self-serving, rise to defend ourselves against the charges by which the enemies of freedom seek to influence a divided and confused population.325

Because of the validity of Cronkite's accusations and the recent trend toward repression of First Amendment rights, every reasonable attempt must be made, especially during such a threatening period in history, to protect rather than limit the freedom of the press. Surprisingly, perhaps, Chief Justice Burger seems to agree with the importance of news coverage in trials: "The role of the press is a crucial one. Sometimes their highest service is to reflect precisely the conduct of the brash and swaggering lawyer or intemperate, blustering judge."326

Burger also seems to agree that the primary threat to a fair trial comes from public and courtroom officials rather than the pages of the press or television screens:

I submit that we must make some basic decisions in terms of allocating the responsibility for regulating in inherently a contentious profession and then place the rigorous powers of discipline wherever we place the responsibility—whether it be in the courts or in the profession.

Lawyers, judges and law professors must see that an undisciplined and unregulated profession will destroy itself, will fail in its mission, and will not restore public confidence in the profession.

Our failure is collective and our responsibility total. The solution must be shaped and executed by lawyers, law professors, and judges.[327]

Thus it appears that it is unnecessary, unjustified, and undesirable to attempt any direct control over pretrial publicity. It would also seem unavailing to attempt to control such publicity, since—as Massachusetts senate president Kevin Harrington argues—"it is just impossible." He said newsmen believe, in effect, that "you can't tell us what to do because the Constitution guarantees the right to freedom of speech."[328]

Dr. Stephen Sheppard was reminded of this traditional value when he filed a libel suit in Lorain County common pleas court on April 26, 1963, asking $1 million from the *Elyria Chronicle Telegram*. The suit charged that an article published on February 14, 1962, wrongfully accused Stephen Sheppard of responsibility for the deaths of three people. The article, written after the suicide of Thomas Reese, the father of Marilyn Sheppard, claimed that the sensationalism drummed up by Dr. Stephen led to the deaths of Reese, Sam's father, and Mrs. Richard Sheppard (Sam's mother).[329] The Ohio supreme court, refusing to review an appeal, upheld the Lorain County court and the Ninth District Court of Appeals decisions in the case, which was dismissed four months later.[330]

It seems clear, therefore, that there are no compelling reasons for direct restrictions on press coverage of trials. Injustice to the accused can be prevented far more effectively through courtroom procedures imposed by individual judges than through general restrictions on the press. And in view of the continuing "government attacks on both the degree and the extent of freedom of the press" described by CBS president Frank Stanton,[331] further restriction might well develop into far more extensive governmental regulation. The value of a press that is free to criticize and comment on government action is certainly worth consideration. The tenuous advantages to be derived from further restriction, in the hope of improving criminal justice, do not, in the author's opinion, justify the clear dangers.

5 Justice, the Poor, and Minority Groups

"But for the excellence of the typical, single life in any society, no nation deserves to be remembered more than the sands of the sea." Thus do the sentiments of George Santayana mirror the intense concern our nation has historically exhibited for improving the quality of individual life. But while our record in protecting and improving the typical single life has been exemplary, large numbers of minority groups have been ignored. Our society has snowballed toward the promised Utopia, but those who benefit have not grown in numbers as rapidly as the snowball has grown in mass. Instead, various groups have been sidetracked on the journey to the millennium. Our society has failed the poor and the black in numerous respects, and notably—if not critically—in the judicial system.

This chapter will discuss the methods by which our judicial processes serve, or fail to serve, the minorities in our society. Special attention will be given to the poor, the black, radical political minorities, and college students. The discussion will be undertaken from three perspectives: the bail system for those awaiting trial, the jury selection system for those to be tried, and the operation of the exclusionary rule of evidence during trials. All of these areas are of fundamental importance to the poor and minorities in the administration of justice. How well the society has succeeded in protecting their rights is a question which awaits answer.

The Archaic Bail System

Recently, as one of our many overcrowded courts sat in anticipation of the defendant's 9:30 a.m. arrival, the stenographer sipped coffee and melted snow dripped from a witness's galoshes. The defendant, William

Johnson, who had allegedly attempted to rob a bank, was free on $10,000 bail and expected to return for his trial. Unfortunately, he did not appear because he was busy trying to rob another bank.332

What is society to do with its William Johnsons, who stand accused in large numbers awaiting distant trial? Forty percent of the cases pending in the U.S. district courts at the end of fiscal 1968 had been on the calendar for six months or more.333 The average wait in a typical urban county court is between six and seven months.334 This seems to be a direct denial of the constitutional guarantee of a speedy trial in all criminal prosecutions, as set forth in article VI of the Bill of Rights. The defendant who faces the prospect of an eventual trial may either be detained until the date of the trial or set free, but to make either option the exclusive method of pretrial handling of suspects would have serious drawbacks. To hold every defendant until his trial would preclude the release of dangerous criminals and those likely to commit another crime; however, it would also entail the incarceration of many who are not likely to commit another offense. As for a businessman with an otherwise impeccable record who is arrested for a financial deal, which may or may not be illegal, the experts disagree; but who would seek to detain him?

On the other hand, to set all people free pending this trial would be grossly imprudent. This method would avoid the dilemma of jailing a man who is presumed to be innocent, but it would necessarily free people who are likely to commit a crime while out on bail. For instance, narcotics cases often give rise to cyclic crimes: Pushers often return to pushing until the date of their trial since judges often give concurrent sentences for repeated offenses.

Clearly, some mix of these two policies would provide the best solution, but how should we decide whom to release and whom to detain? At present, a most irrelevant measure is often relied on—money. At first glance, it would seem that the financial status of defendants would have little bearing on whether they should be released pending trial, and this intuitive response can be borne out by a more careful analysis.

But beyond money's being a poor criterion for release, the bail system brings unnecessary suffering to those who are unable to meet bail. Indigent defendants languish in damp cells, awaiting their day in a crowded court. If they are unable to meet bail, they have little choice but to accept jailing, as if they had already been found guilty.

By the same token, an undeterminable number of organized criminals wince at the morning sun as they walk out of jails into the bright day as free men. Their Mafia friends have bailed them out. After all, they are part of the "family"; and of course the organization wouldn't want them to "talk."

Theoretically, the purpose of bail is not to deny the poor their freedom, or to service organized criminals, but to assure that once a defendant is freed he will return for trial. This theory is quite sound philosophically: it does not judge a man guilty; it assumes that he will post sufficient bail to assure his appearance on the desired date. However, on a more analytical basis there is a major flaw: the assumption that bail is low enough for a defendant to raise the money but high enough to assure his return. Clearly, only if a defendant is hard pressed to raise the money does his bail outweigh the advantage to be gained by fleeing—if he felt that conviction was likely. At this point, however, bail can be deemed excessive, and therefore in violation of article VIII of the Bill of Rights, which prohibits the setting of excessive bail.

What, in fact, happens is that a judge may set an excessive bail to prevent a person he deems dangerous from going free. While this may be a good criterion, the judge usually has little more than a general impression to go on in reaching his decision.

Once bail is set but a defendant is unable to raise the money, he may contact a bail bondsman, who might agree to post the money for him. In return, the bondsman usually receives 10 percent of the total amount of bail. This money is not returned to the defendant should he appear in court; it represents the bondsman's profit—which circumvents the purpose of the bail system. The defendant has lost this 10 percent whether he shows up for trial or not. This monetary incentive to appear, which is the whole rationale for bail, is muted.

How well has the bail system served the cause of justice? Approximately 7.5 percent of all those freed on bail do not return for trial.[335] About 3 percent commit a violent crime while on bail,[336] while various studies (of dubious value) show that 34 percent[337] committed other felonies while free on bail. On balance, it appears that the bail system does not err badly on the side of setting too many people free.

The major problem with the bail system seems to be the harm incurred by those who are not set free. Given the serious evils that result from imprisonment, there seems to be ample evidence for this conclusion. According to the President's Commission on Law Enforcement, 25 percent of all defendants are unable to make a $500 bail, which means that they can't raise even $25 or $50 (depending on the rate charged) to pay a bondsman to post bail for them.[338] In addition, 79 percent of the defendants in St. Louis cannot meet bail, 75 percent in Baltimore, 71 percent in Miami, 57 percent in San Francisco, 54 percent in Boston, and 48 percent in Detroit.[339]

The number of those subjected to the harms of incarceration is indeed significant, but before we catalogue the evils incurred by these people, it should be noted that a day in jail can cost society from $3 to $9 per prisoner.340 Hence a desirable spinoff of reforming the bail system would be to save society a very significant sum of money. More serious than this monetary consideration, though, are the personal harms that detained defendants must suffer.

First, there is economic hardship: a person who is unable to post bail is already in economic trouble, and keeping him in jail for six months automatically deprives him of half his annual earnings. Nor is this deprivation limited to the prisoner; it necessarily affects all those dependent upon him. And these economic penalties continue even after his release: since the defendant has almost surely lost his job while waiting in jail for trial, he must find a new one, but employers are not likely to receive him kindly. A recent survey disclosed that 75 percent of the employers interviewed would not hire an applicant who had an arrest record—even if he had been acquitted.341 And at present, with the unemployment rate at 6 percent, hundreds of thousands of workers, executive and blue collar alike, have been fired due to slack demand in the economy.

At least as serious as the economic losses are the psychic losses which imprisonment entails: serious crises for a marriage, a separation that makes great demands upon a family's physical and psychological resources and capacity for adaptation. Sociologists agree that separation tends to produce sharp deterioration in the relationship between husband and wife.342 Imprisonment may also alter a defendant's life style and expectations, leaving him ill equipped to cope with society when he is set free.

Finally, denial of bail affects the course of a defendant's trial, in two ways. In a charge where the sentence is likely to be short (two years or less), the defendant who is denied bail will be under more pressure to plead guilty. If he pleads guilty, his case is decided in a perfunctory hearing, and therefore, rather than wait in jail for six or seven months until trial, an innocent man may plead guilty, feeling he will be better off in the total time served. If he pleads innocent, he must still, in effect, serve the six or seven months, and still face the possibility of being wrongly convicted and serving an additional term.

Incarceration also affects the prisoner's ability to conduct his defense: he may not be able to help in the pretrial investigation and he cannot help locate witnesses or evidence which may be accessible only to him. His consultations with his lawyer are impeded by having to plan a defense in a cramped cell, within visiting hours. His pretrial experience can also affect his demeanor in the courtroom and on the witness stand, and result in jury bias against him.[343] In addition, his ability to pay the costs of his defense are limited by his loss of income during incarceration. Finally, his detention will probably cost him his job, which will in turn cost him any chance of probation if he is convicted.

A recent Philadelphia study of 946 cases revealed that 52 percent of the bailed defendants were convicted, compared to 82 percent of those jailed.[344] A Washington, D.C., study revealed that 25 percent of the bailed were placed on probation, against only 6 percent of those detained.[345] Thus it seems that denial of bail has a prejudicial effect on the jury trial and the sentencing of defendants.

But the discrimination inherent in the bail system is not limited to the poor: whenever a judge decides to set bail inordinately high, incarceration will result. In Atlanta, a 67-year-old minister who had been convicted of disturbing public worship had bail on his appeal set at $20,000. He spent seven months in jail because the court refused to accept that amount in unencumbered real estate. In another case a college student, convicted of trespass, was held on $15,000 bond; and $5,000 was required in a perjury case growing out of a civil rights boycott.[346] Minorities or demonstrators who happen to irk a judge will feel the bite of this wholly discretionary system.

The main cause for the huge backlog of court cases is not a sinister conspiracy of lazy judges but a simple lack of manpower. As Judge Hart of the U.S. District Court of Washington, D.C., complained: "We do not have the judicial manpower to even begin to reach a desirable time limit. We have to have more judge power, more clerk power, more probation power, more marshal power and more courthouses."[347]

The question, then, is how to attract funds and personnel to this neglected area. Clearly more public funds will be needed. It would seem that a society that puts law and order so high on its list of critical issues would be willing to make the financial outlays necessary to have a decent system of justice. Until now, that has not been the case, but there is cause for hope. Recent polls show that 68 percent of the people surveyed feel that the length of time that one awaits trial seriously affects the quality of justice in the United States. (This figure is eclipsed only by the 75 percent who feel that criminals get off too easily.)[348] Perhaps this outcry will be sufficient to claim some of the funds that become available in the wake of our withdrawal from Vietnam.

But there is still the question of personnel. Increased salaries could solve many personnel shortages; however—should this prove too weak an incentive—a panoply of other measures could be employed to attract qualified personnel. Loans could be offered by the federal government to help students through law school, in return for work in a choice of fields where manpower is lacking. A draft deferment could also be established if the shortages persist. While several years' work as a law clerk may not be the dream of every law student, a significant number would prefer this to duty in the army.

If this influx of people lacks the expertise and professionalism of the people currently in the field, the court system, for instance, could be divided into two parts, and crimes of lesser import could be tried by a new court system, with emphasis on administration rather than deliberation. This relief could allow the regular court system to keep current with its calendars with little increase in the number of judges.349

Finally, a thorough assessment of the potential contribution of technology to the court system should be made by the National Academy of Sciences.

All of these changes will take time; but meanwhile the bail system should be reformed, and much is being done. In 1966 Congress enacted the Bail Reform Act, which significantly liberalized the pretrial release of criminal defendants in the federal courts. The Act provides that a defendant in a noncapital case shall be released pending trial on his personal recognizance or upon an unsecured appearance bond, unless the magistrate determines that such terms of release will not reasonably assure the appearance of the defendant as required. When such a determination is made, the first of the following conditions of release shall be imposed, or a combination thereof, which reasonably assures the defendant's appearance at trial: (1) place the person in the custody of a person or organization agreeing to supervise him; (2) restrict his travel, association or place of abode; (3) require execution of an appearance bond, with up to 10 percent of such bond to be deposited as security; (4) require execution of a bail bond with sufficient surety or deposit in cash in full; (5) impose any other condition deemed reasonably necessary to assure the defendant's presence, including that he return to custody after specified hours. In determining the conditions of release, the judicial officer must take into account the nature and circumstances of the offense charged, the weight of the evidence against the accused, the defendant's family ties, employment, financial resources, character and mental condition, the length of his residence in the community, his record of convictions, and his past record of appearance at court proceedings. The landmark Bail Reform Act has safely released tens of thousands of defendants who would otherwise have remained in jail or suffered financial loss on bond premiums. Release rates in the District of Columbia district court have risen to 77 percent—and over 90 percent of these defendants stayed out of trouble until their trial.350 Department of Justice figures indicate that 35 percent of the defendants had money bail set and 42 percent were released without money bail. Only 23 percent were held over until trial.356 Bail is in its waning days in the federal court system as a result of the Bail Reform Act, which points out the irrelevance of the ability to post bail as a precondition for release.

On the state and local levels, reform has not been so sweeping; however, the pioneering work of the Manhattan Bail Project must be mentioned. Under the project (known as Vera), each defendant is granted a brief interview by a Vera worker (usually an N.Y.U. law student). The worker then converts the facts he has gleaned in the interview into a point total: +2 for a good job record, +2 for good family ties, etc. On the basis of this score, Vera recommends that the judge either release or detain the defendant, and the court follows Vera's recommendations in about 70 percent of the cases.352

During the first three years of the project, over 10,000 defendants were released on their own recognizance (with only a promise to appear for trial) due to Vera's work, and 98.5 percent of these people appeared for trial. (Nearly three times as many people who had been freed on bail during this period failed to appear.)353 In the wake of Vera's success, similar projects have been started in Chicago, Denver, Los Angeles, Des Moines, San Francisco, Syracuse, St. Louis, Orlando, and Washington, D.C., and plans for more projects are under way in many states.354

Despite Vera's success in returning the defendants for trial, many people are skeptical. Although such an interview may be relied upon to determine who will return for trial, could it disclose who would commit a felony while awaiting trial? The District of Columbia Crime Commission conducted a survey which showed that 205 persons out of 2,700, over a period of two and a half years, were alleged to have committed felonies while on bail. Because the F.B.I. records of the 205 defendants did not yield a pattern which would have allowed a judge to suspect that these men would commit crimes,355 there was a 10 percent rate of recidivism in the Vera experiment—not the most favorable ratio.

Also, by using such criteria as the type of crime committed to determine release, an implicit assumption of guilt is made. Merely using money to assure that a defendant will appear (the pure form of the bail system) does not make that assumption. Indeed, if the Vera criteria were applied universally, fewer people might be released than under the bail system. For instance, in Washington, D.C., 95 percent of the females committed and 67 percent of the males are narcotics addicts.356 Such people would probably be considered bad risks and be detained if the Vera standards were employed.

If we chose to set people free before trial, some of them will commit crimes in the interim. Clearly, however, the harm done by keeping everyone in jail, coupled with the presumption of innocence, dictate that as many people as possible be freed. The real question, then, is what criteria do we use to determine who goes free. We can use a financial criterion, which tells us nothing about the probability that the defendant will appear for trial, or commit a crime in the meantime. The alternative is to try to predict who will return for trial on the basis of constant, rational criteria. While the perfect measure has not yet been devised, the success of the Vera project should serve as a spur to research in this area. Dispatching defendants either to jail or the street can be made on a better basis than bail for the rich and jail for the poor.

Jury Selection

In 1970, with a record number of other women, Sandra Jo McMahon was raped. She identified her attacker, who also took $10 from her, as black and about 6 feet tall and 180 pounds. Raymond Holloway, a black who worked in the building where Miss McMahon was raped, was arrested for the crime and put in a lineup, where she failed to identify him as her attacker, and he was released. A sudden glimpse of Holloway in the parking lot on his way out, however, changed her mind; she identified the 5 foot 10 inch, 140-pound black as the rapist and he was rearrested. Some twelve weeks later Holloway freed himself on $20,000 bail and retained excellent legal counsel for an additional $3,800. As a prominent white attorney noted ironically, it is not unknown for blacks accused of having raped white women to be freed by a jury, but he knows of only one or two such cases.357

Although discrimination in jury selection has been a federal crime since 1875 and grounds for invalidating a criminal conviction since 1880, it remains a widespread phenomenon.358 *Swain* v. *Alabama* disclosed that although 26 percent of the persons in the fifth circuit who were eligible for jury duty were Negroes, not one had served on a petit jury in a criminal case since 1950.359 However, recent developments in jury selection have in large measure remedied the evils of jury discrimination in federal trials.

Prior to 1968, two methods of jury selection were employed: community lists and the key-man system. Community lists, which utilize a random choice of veniremen from certain public lists (such as telephone directories and lists of registered voters), are honest in method but are prejudiced against the poor and minority groups from the outset because the lists themselves are prejudiced: the poor are less likely to have telephones, and blacks have for years lagged behind whites in voter registration, especially in the South. Voting lists may also exclude a number of the young, who are disenchanted with the American political system.

Under the key-man system, court clerks or jury commissioners recommend candidates for jury service on the basis of their own knowledge or that of friends.[360] Obviously, the veniremen selected by this system are likely to be the leading citizens of the community and those who are partial to the courts, and thus the system is woefully subject to discrimination and abuse. The white, middle-class jury commissioners often allege that they know of no blacks qualified to serve on a jury—and they may well be speaking the truth: they are simply unacquainted with members of the black community. Juries, therefore, are chosen almost solely from whites. And similar abuses may be found with respect to sex: in 1957 commissioners of a California district were found to be excluding women from the jury rolls, despite state law.[361]

The 1968 Federal Jury Selection Act was an important step toward correcting these inequities and making juries proportionately representative of the communities, which of course is a fundamental goal of the jury system. The act stipulates that juries be selected at random from rolls which reflect a fair cross section of the community.[362] For the most part, this has resulted in selection from voter rolls; yet the assumption that these rolls represent a fair cross section of a community is unjustified in some areas, especially the South. While some progress in Negro voter registration has been made, many pockets of potential Negro strength have yet to take the initial steps. As late as 1961, thirteen Mississippi counties, containing 37,581 blacks of voting age, had no registered blacks.[363]

In Mississippi, Alabama, Georgia, and Louisiana, the average percentage gain in black registration was only 2.6 percent. In each state, white population per 100 outstripped black registration by a 92 to 1 ratio or more.[364] In the wake of the 1965 Voting Rights Act, black registration in these states increased to 48.5 percent of the potential in August 1967 but still trailed white registration, which stood at about 75 percent.[365] Clearly, voter registration lists—in Southern states at least—do not reflect the overall composition of the community and the goals of the Jury Selection Act. The most effective way to implement the requirements of the act would be by random selection from a community census or a statistically valid sampling.

The additional federal qualifications should also be retained: literacy examinations could be administered to the persons selected, who must also be at least twenty-one, a United States citizen, a resident of the district for at least one year, physically and mentally healthy, and free of a criminal record.366

At the state level, the key-man system is still in widespread use. Federal law holds that a person who is convicted by a jury which was selected from a panel which deliberately excluded blacks may have his conviction overturned. The key, obviously, is the deliberateness of the exclusion, and a case could be made that clerks or jury commissioners who use the key-man system must realize that blacks will be excluded, and thus discrimination is deliberate. Not only does this open the door for prosecution of a jury commissioner, but a case has been made for direct federal intervention in state courts on the ground that due process of law has not been followed. It is thus conceivable that the requirements of the Federal Jury Selection Act could be imposed upon the states.

The importance of such action does not, of course, lend itself to numerical quantification. Without a realistic standard for the determination of truth, it is not possible to declare that any one trial has been a miscarriage of justice, but one can conclude that systematic discrimination has, in the aggregate, resulted in considerable injustice. It strains credulity, for instance, to believe that nearly all blacks who are accused of raping white women are guilty, yet juries without proper community-wide origins regularly accept the doubtful eyewitness testimony of the victim and reject the testimony of the accused. To conclude that a fairly substantial number of persons are unjustly convicted is probably correct.

Such injustice is sufficient reason for action, but another social imperative requires the fairest possible juries. The young black whose first formal contact with "the system" is a jury he believes to be unfair is unlikely to accept that system as anything but unfair. As Abraham Blumberg has noted: "The existing administration of criminal adjudications in America promotes and reinforces class warfare by indicating to those at the bottom that they have no real stake in our society. Until [we] are committed to the defense of the vulnerable . . . we will have a shoddy substitute for due process."367

Reform of the jury system along the lines of the Jury Selection Act would therefore seem essential.

The Exclusionary Rule

Mrs. Mapp heard a knock at her door and, upon opening it, found a policeman waving a supposed warrant. As several other policemen began to search her apartment, she grabbed the warrant and put it down her blouse, whereupon the policeman sought to retrieve it. But Mrs. Mapp was eventually convicted on a pornography charge resulting from the illegal search and the phony warrant.

The Supreme Court recognized, as early as 1913, that the remedies available to aggrieved victims were insufficient deterrents to unconstitutional search. For reasons to be explained shortly, a citizen could not effectively sue for damages after an illegal search was made; hence this was not a deterrent to police illegality. In 1913, in *Weeks* v. *United States*,368 the court held that all evidence secured by a government official's violation of a citizen's privacy was to be excluded from federal trials. This, the court reasoned, would remove any incentive to conduct illegal searches.

That is how the matter stood until 1949, when the court decided that the exclusionary rule did not apply to the use in a state court of evidence obtained in violation of a suspect's constitutional rights, pursuant to a state crime.369 Then, in 1961, the landmark case of *Mapp* v. *Ohio*370 reversed this decision: the court said that any evidence seized in an unconstitutional search is inadmissible in any court.

The reason why exclusion is resorted to in an attempt to deter unconstitutional acts is the insufficiency of other deterrents. Two routes of recompense exist: criminal sanctions (outlined in U.S. Code Title 18, sections 241 and 242) and civil sanctions. Section 241 prohibits conspiracy to deny the civil rights of any citizen, and 242 prohibits the deprivation of rights under the color of law. Under section 242, it must be shown that the accused had "specific intent" to deprive the victim of his constitutional rights, and thus ignorance is an excuse. Section 241 applies only to conspiracies that impinge on rights deriving from an individual's relationship with the federal government. Because they do not cover Fourteenth Amendment rights,371 the application of these statutes is limited.

Even where title 18 statutes may be invoked, their application is not likely to bring conviction because prosecution is in the hands of the organization of which the offending officer is a part. No prosecutor will ordinarily seek to convict the people he relies on for evidence in all his other cases. If he angers the police, they may not cooperate with him, which will hurt his convictions record and culminate in his replacement by someone who can cooperate with the police. In light of these facts, it is not surprising that these tools have proved ineffective in curbing police misconduct.

By way of civil remedy, an aggrieved party may sue for damages incurred by having had his constitutional rights violated. This, too, is limited in at least two respects. First, it is expensive to bring suit in a court of law. As the American Civil Liberties Union points out:

> Most people who are mistreated by the police tend to be poor, friendless, out-of-the-ordinary members of society. They don't complain often, and when they do, they seldom have the money, time, confidence in the "system" or knowledge of agencies that could help them thread their way through the maze of legal steps necessary to challenge the abuse.372

For this reason, the poor and the dispossessed are not helped very much by this sanction.

Second, even when a case is brought, an officer is likely to be acquitted because juries are not likely to be sympathetic to the plaintiff. This is especially true if the plaintiff has been found guilty of a crime. When the balance is struck between the jury's distaste for the plaintiff and respect for policemen, it is easy to see why tort suits are seldom initiated or successful. Thus the court was faced with a citizenry that had no protection from unconstitutional invasion of privacy and unreasonable search, and it was in this climate that it established the exclusionary rule. If the evidence could not be used in court, policemen had no reason for gathering it—at least that is how the court saw it. However, the exclusionary rule does not seem to be effective in deterring most illegal searches. According to one observer: "The officer is not disciplined . . . for his illegal search. The federal exclusionary rule which has been in effect now for nearly fifty years has not noticeably deterred illegal searches and seizures."373 Policemen are not conviction oriented, they are arrest oriented. If the courts later free the defendants, policemen will call it a double cross and blame it on a permissive society. In addition, they may not fully comprehend the implications of the Supreme Court decisions governing search and seizure.

In all fairness, it must be said that the number of callous policemen comes nowhere close to constituting the majority. The President's Commission on Law Enforcement and the Administration of Justice recently found: "Almost all departments are headed by honest and honorable officials, and the large majority of working policemen at all levels of authority conduct themselves honestly and honorably."374 It is the minority of policemen who make this a significant problem area.

One final effect of the exclusionary rule is that, in paying the price to deter police misconduct, some genuinely guilty people may be set free because the evidence needed to convict them cannot be presented in court. Unquestionably, however, the number is small. But the fact that guilty people go free means that justice is imperfect, and this is sufficient reason to search for a better system.

Alternatives to Exclusion

One method of providing a deterrent to illegal action without freeing the guilty is the following. Each police department would be licensed, and to keep the license it would have to submit to thorough investigations by the newly created Federal Law Enforcement Commission. The departments would also be obliged to implement all recommendations of the commission. Each time an illegal search question is adversely decided in court, the victim would automatically be awarded $5,000 by the municipality as liquidated damages, but the evidence would not be excluded from the trial. After a certain number of adverse judgments, the police department would undergo a total examination by the F.L.E.C., which would examine training and promotion procedures, internal discipline and organization, etc., and make binding recommendations.

This would provide a positive incentive against illegal searches, and pressure for compliance would come from at least two levels. Municipalities will not want federal intervention and the associated reputation, which could result in forfeiture of model cities funds and various grants-in-aid, which the federal government might channel to more "deserving" communities. Also, municipalities will not pay out the considerable sum of $5,000 for each illegal search.

Second, the upper echelons in the police departments will ensure that officers do not violate the Court's standards. A chief of police does not want federal officials inspecting his organization and discovering skeletons in closets and the embarrassing idiosyncracies which accompany the discharge of power. In addition, the higher-ups know that one of the first recommendations of federal officials is likely to be "new leadership."

On the other hand, criminals would not go free because of an unconstitutional search. If their rights are violated, they should be indemnified; but if they have committed a crime they should go to jail. This plan would accomplish both aims.

INTERROGATIONS: ESCOBEDO TO HARRIS

The first area in which the reach of the exclusionary rule should be redefined is interrogation. The development of constitutional law on this subject cannot be fully treated here, but *Gideon* v. *Wainwright*[375] began an avalanche of opinions. The Gideon court claimed that all defendants have a right to a lawyer in felony cases. In the wake of *Gideon*, *Massiah*376 isolated this right as accruing immediately after indictment. *McLeod* v. *Ohio*377 extended this to the states through the Fourteenth Amendment. *Escobedo* v. *Illinois*378 further held that if the suspect has retained a lawyer and requests to see him during interrogation, that request must be honored. Danny Escobedo had asked to see his attorney but his request was denied, and Escobedo subsequently signed a confession admitting complicity in a murder. The court held that Escobedo did not realize that the penalty for complicity in a murder is as serious as that for murder, and further held that Escobedo was ignorant of his constitutional rights and had been exploited. Finally, the court held that once the adversary stage has begun, the investigatory process has been limited to one suspect, and a confession is sought, the defendant has a right to see an attorney if he requests one.379

The litigation concerning the right to counsel and interrogation culminated in *Miranda* v. *Arizona*.380 *Miranda* decided that no confession could be deemed voluntary (i.e., usable in court) unless the government could prove that the defendant had voluntarily waived his rights and decided to confess. The method the court prescribed to prove volition is demonstration that the following warnings have been given and understood:

1. You have a right to remain silent.
2. Anything you say may be held against you.
3. You have a right to an attorney.
4. If you cannot afford an attorney, the court will appoint one for you.

The penalty for defaulting on any of these provisos is exclusion, and a jury may not consider a confession that does not meet the requirements set forth in *Miranda*.

Those who predicted that *Miranda* would seriously hamper law enforcement can be proved wrong by the statistics. *Miranda*, first of all, does not impede justice because of the relative unimportance of confessions, which are part of the evidence in only 10 percent of all indictments.381 Moreover, they affect the clearance of crime by less than 1 percent.382 In 35 percent of all robberies, 45 percent of all rapes, and 80 percent of all murders, the criminals are recognized and identified as acquaintances, friends, or relatives of the victims.383 Recent studies show that, before *Miranda*, interrogation was both necessary and successful in securing confessions in only about 3 percent of the cases.384

Nor do the *Miranda* warnings thwart interrogation, which usually succeeds despite the restraints.385 In Pittsburgh, a study revealed that the warnings did not result in a statistically significant decline in confessions in the cases where they were a necessary part of the prosecution.386 In fact, an inverse trend was perceived: the cases disposed of by guilty pleas increased by 5.5 percent in the sample area during the first year following the *Miranda* decision.387 Finally, it should be noted that the F.B.I. gave warnings similar to those prescribed by *Miranda* for years before the court pronouncement made it mandatory. Yet the F.B.I. didn't find this practice pernicious; indeed, it boasts the highest conviction rate of all American law enforcement agencies.

With the passing of time, the political pendulum began its periodic and inevitable swing to the right when the Supreme Court's composition was drastically altered by Nixon's two appointments (Blackmun and Burger). The Supreme Court limited the *Miranda* decision in *Harris* v. *New York*,388 stating that if the defendant chose to take the stand, a confession obtained without the warnings would be admissible. This evidence cannot be used in the prosecution's case in chief, but it can be used to impeach the credibility of the witness. When such a confession is admitted into evidence, the jury is told to disregard it as prima facie evidence in the case and use it only to determine whether it should accept the testimony of the witness. The court stated that a record of such conversation by the witness is useful in determining the truthfulness of his testimony, and should be admitted.

This, of course, removes the deterrent effect of the exclusionary rule, and gives the police every incentive to violate the suspect's constitutional rights, on the assumption that he will seek to testify in his own behalf. If he does so, any statement that is gained, by any means, becomes useful. If the suspect does not testify, he cannot aid his own defense by introducing alibis, etc., and must face a doubly suspicious jury.

Not only does the court infringe upon the exclusionary rule by making freedom from unconstitutional activities contingent upon the forfeiture of other rights, but in admitting the evidence it expects juries to determine the truth of a statement given under oath by comparing it to a statement that was coerced. It is clear from this decision that the Court seeks to further erode the exclusionary rule via additional decisions. It would appear that the surest way to preclude this is for Congress to initiate a constitutional amendment permanently defining the rights of defendants in this area. Perhaps, when faced with public outcry and legislative action, the Supreme Court could find sufficient cause in precedent to uphold the rest of the exclusionary rule, and even redefine *Harris*.

Some libertarians have argued that even the pre-*Harris* decisions do not go far enough in protecting individual rights. They argue that a person must have the advice of counsel in order to decide intelligently whether to waive the right to counsel.[389] This assumes that many defendants don't realize the full consequences of waiving counsel; for instance, they are ignorant of the penalties involved (as was the case with Escobedo). This seems to be a reasonable objection, but the problem could be solved if a lawyer were on call at all times at the few municipal stations where most suspects are detained. He could then advise a suspect on whether to waive his rights. The exclusionary rule would then be extended to confessions obtained without a lawyer's advice on whether the defendant should waive these rights.

Miranda also makes no mention of stop-and-frisk actions and field interrogations. In San Diego alone there are reports of 200,000 police stops annually, and at least an equal number are unreported.[390] Most of the stops are made on suspicion growing out of a suspect's clothing, hair, or color.[391] The Task Force Report on the police claims that in many communities field interrogations are the major source of friction between police and minority groups.[392] A Michigan survey found that minority-group leaders and persons sympathetic to minority groups were almost unanimous in labeling field interrogation as a principal problem in police-community relations.[393]

On the other hand, police must often ask suspects questions to determine whether there are sufficient grounds for arrest, and field interrogation may be a necessary investigative device. Inasmuch as the police have the job of protecting a large and mobile population, it may be that if they fail to question a suspect there will never be another chance to solve a particular crime. In one case, for example, a person was questioned when he was seen carrying a TV and an armful of clothes down a main street at 2 a.m. From a utilitarian point of view, every community should weigh the advantages gained by field interrogation in the arrest of felons against the disadvantages of heightened social tensions, disrespect for the police, and perhaps crimes of reprisal. This is not an easy task, and the answers will differ from city to city.

The constitutionality of stop-and-frisk and field interrogation has been avoided by the Supreme Court, but sufficient precedent can be found to lead us out of this quandary. Stop-and-frisk, in short, should be discussed apart from field interrogation. In *Terry* v. *Ohio*[394] the court decided that a warrant was not needed to search for a weapon but that probable cause was necessary for any other purpose.

As for field interrogation, a distinction should be made as to the type of questioning. General questioning (e.g., What happened?) should be allowed on suspicion—there is little controversy over that. The problem pertains to questions which seek to have a suspect inculpate or exculpate himself. Investigation, at least temporarily, seems to have focused on the suspect, who according to *Escobedo* has a right to an attorney. However, *Miranda* redefined at what point the right to an attorney begins; it contends that it begins after "the suspect is taken into custody, or his freedom is limited in some significant way." The question, then, is whether field interrogation limits a suspect's freedom in a significant way.

A good case can be made that it does not: field interrogation is usually very short, the suspect is not arrested, and he does not acquire a police record. Furthermore, field interrogation does not include the components which *Miranda* says create the coercive atmosphere in custodial interrogation. The suspect is not "thrust into an unfamiliar atmosphere,"[395] and the police lack the psychological advantage of "selecting the locale for questioning."[396] In field interrogations the suspect is not "cut off from the outside world."[397] The questioning seldom (if ever) "lasts for several hours,"[398] and it is difficult to employ "physical brutality"[399] in a street setting. It does not appear that the constraints of *Miranda* should apply to field interrogation, and thus the evidence thereby gleaned by police should be admissible in court.

SEARCHING COLLEGE DORMITORIES

Having been tipped off by a telephone call, two campus security guards and the dean of men of a large state university opened all the locked doors on the second floor of a dormitory as they searched for firearms. They found none, but in one of the rooms they found a small cache of marijuana and LSD. The student occupant was expelled and now faces prosecution. This, then, was one of the many cases where the rights of minorities appear to have been violated; indeed, 4 million college students are subject to such intrusions every day of their academic life.

By way of defense, many universities point to the contract signed by incoming students wherein the university reserves the right to enter the rooms for inspection purposes. However, the *Miranda* decision applies by analogy: At what point does the student have the full implication of the waiver of his rights explained to him? Indeed, the contract is intentionally misleading. It implies that the university has the right to enter rooms and is merely retaining it, but this does not comply with the standard of voluntariness developed by the Supreme Court, and it should be struck down. Secondly, new students are not usually twenty-one and have only a limited right to sign contracts. In fact, the contracts could probably be invalidated on the grounds that they are not an agreement between two agents of even approximate equality. Duress may also enter the picture inasmuch as many universities require that all students live on campus during the first year.

The Supreme Court, which has begun to recognize the rights of college students in this area, stated in *West Virginia Board of Education* v. *Barnette* that the actions of state institutions must be tempered by respect for the students' constitutional rights. The power of schools was further limited by *Tinker* v. *Des Moines Independent School District*,[401] which stated that a school has no absolute authority and students are to be treated as persons under the Constitution. A federal circuit court decided that the Constitution requires state colleges to follow due process in expulsion proceedings and that the general disposal of authority by state colleges must be limited by the constitutional rights of the students.[402]

All of these cases provide precedents for invalidating unconstitutional housing contracts and requiring university officials to obtain a search warrant before entering a dormitory room. The penalty for illegal search would be exclusion of evidence gained for criminal prosecution and universities' punitive action (authority for this is given in the *Dixon* case), as well as recompense for violation of a student's rights. Further precedent might be the *Katz* decision, which established that it is not up to an area-granting agency to determine what constitutes an invasion of privacy in that area. The Supreme Court also held that any area a person desires to be private is protected by Fourth Amendment rights.[403] A good case can be made that since a student keeps all his papers and effects in his room, sleeps there, and locks the door when he leaves, he seeks to keep his room private.

Enforcing the Constitution in the dormitory would mean that university officials would either have to obtain a warrant or show cause why an immediate search was necessary. The rules set down by *Terry* and *Camara* v. *Municipal Court*[404] would determine the situations when a warrant is necessary. *Terry* recognized that no warrant should be required in cases where immediate danger to life or limb is perceived. In *Camara* the court held that when there is a large public interest in an immediate search (e.g., by health officials for evidence of communicable disease), no warrant is needed.

In the absence of these circumstances, a warrant should be required. A student's interest in obtaining an education should not cause him to forfeit his constitutional rights.

BORDER SEARCHES

While justice may not be blind, it has several blind spots, and one of them applies to border searches. While high standards of constitutionality are applied to ordinary searches, border searches have been almost totally excluded from the purview of these regulations. However, the U.S. Court of Appeals for the Ninth Circuit has held border searches to have been unconstitutional in three cases: *Henderson* v. *United States*, 390 F.2d 805 (1967); *U.S.* v. *Guadalupe-Garza*, 421 F.2d 876 (1970); *U.S.* v. *Johnson*, 425 F.2d 630 (1970). In the Guadalupe-Garza case, 421 F.2d at 879, the court said:

> "Real suspicion" justifying the initiation of a strip search is subjective suspicion supported by objective, articulable facts that would reasonably lead an experienced, prudent customs official to suspect that a particular person seeking to cross our border is concealing something on his body for the purpose of transporting it into the United States contrary to law.
>
> The objective, articulable facts must bear some reasonable relationship to suspicion that something is concealed on the body of the person to be searched; otherwise, the scope of the search is not related to the justification for its initiation, as it must meet the reasonableness standard of the Fourth Amendment.

The Smuggling Act of 1866[405] provided for search on suspicion that contraband was being imported "by the person, in his possessions . . . by, in or upon, any vehicle, beast or otherwise." Federal courts routinely admit evidence forcibly obtained from the human body, as well as evidence obtained far from the border and from the autos of people who have never left the country.[406] As discussed before, the avenues of remedy for these people yield little satisfaction.

The Supreme Court has held that probable cause is not needed to search people entering the country. In *Carroll* v. *United States*[407] the court held that a traveler "may be stopped in crossing an international boundary because of national self-protection reasonably requiring one entering the country to identify himself as entitled to come in."[408] In *Witt* v. *United States*[409] a circuit court held that probable cause permits searching every person at the border by reason of entry alone.

The definition of a valid border search was extended by *Alex* v. *United States*.[410] The circuit court reasoned that a border official could follow a car as much as 100 miles from the border, over a period of weeks, and search the occupants as long as the officials are convinced that the contraband was in the car when it crossed the border. While the relevant statutes apply to "any" traveler, border guards search thoroughly only on suspicion, and usually whenever a young person or person with long hair crosses the border. Once again, a minority bears the brunt of inspection.

One of the most unusual border searches gave rise to *Blefore* v. *United States*.411 The defendant was suspected of secreting heroin in his body (20 percent of all heroin crossing the Mexican-American border is secreted in body cavities),412 was forced to disrobe, and was given a rectal probe. After this failed to yield the heroin, vomiting was induced, and then a plastic tube was forced through his nose and throat and into his stomach, where the heroin was at last found. Even though the use of rectal probes, stomach pumps, and sedatives had already been held unconstitutional for regular searches, the court upheld the conviction in this instance. In fact, no border search has ever been found unreasonable.413

While there is just cause for concern about what enters the country, perhaps a balance between free entry and a police state can be reached. The necessity for some sort of search was pointed out by the President's Commission on Law Enforcement, which reported that approximately 1,500 kilograms of heroin enter the country illegally each year. And more than half of the 5,600 kilograms of marijuana seized in 1970 was taken on the Mexican-American border.414 However, the number of serious intrusions necessary to combat the problem is enormous. Approximately 180 million people and 53 million vehicles arrived in the United States in 1966.415

A possible compromise would be the following system for border searches, after standards for "intrusive" and "nonintrusive" border searches have been established. A nonintrusive search might be a cursory check of baggage; an intrusive search would be more thorough, but would exclude any methods deemed unreasonable by the Supreme Court for general searches in the United States. A nonintrusive search would be allowed on mere suspicion, but probable cause would be necessary for all intrusive searches, and the fruits of an intrusive search conducted without probable cause would be excluded from trial. Evidently, probable cause can be established, since 50 percent of all border searches are conducted on the basis of prior information.416

A country which promises freedom to individuals after they have arrived should not cause people to believe, upon arrival, that they have come under a dictatorial regime. Nor should the travel of United States citizens mean that they must forfeit their constitutional rights in order to return to their country.

ELECTRONIC SURVEILLANCE

Mrs. Anderson hung up the phone and began to prepare dinner, having heard the latest gossip from her neighbor. But her conversation was tapped. Then her son called his fiancée and they discussed their wedding plans. When Mr. Anderson arrived home, he called his broker about selling some stock. And this went on for days, as their friends called the Andersons and talked freely and confidently, unaware that their conversations were not confidential. Finally, the F.B.I. was convinced that young Anderson was not, after all, implicated in a conspiracy to incite riot. But the Andersons will never know that their line was tapped.

How did the authority to wiretap develop? The first Supreme Court announcement was handed down in 1928 in *Olmstead* v. *United States*[417] when the court ruled that electronic surveillance did not violate the Fourth Amendment's protection from arbitrary search. The court ruled that the prohibited search must be of tangible things: a person, his house, or effects. Conversation was not protected by the Fourth Amendment.

So things stood until *Irvine* v. *California*[418] reached the judicial scene in 1954 and the *Irvine* court scored the unlawful entry into the petitioner's home to plant the device as almost incredible. The conviction, however, was upheld on the grounds that evidence in violation of the Fourth Amendment was still admissible in state courts, and the *Olmstead* rationale began to cloud. At this point any tap which necessitated intrusion was unconstitutional, but otherwise taps were allowed. This became known as the "trespass standard."

In 1960 *Silverman* v. *United States* rejected the *Olmstead* rationale, claiming that the Fourth Amendment protects a person's statements as well as all his papers and property. This clearly established, as unconstitutional, unreasonable intrusions on privacy by the use of electronic devices. But this was insufficient to reverse state-court convictions, until the 1961 decision in *Mapp* v. *Ohio*[419] which declared that "all evidence obtained by searches and seizures in violation of the Constitution is inadmissible in a state court."[420]

In 1967, New York County officials installed a tap on the telephones of an attorney and an applicant for a state liquor license in the hope of securing evidence of a conspiracy to bribe the New York State Liquor Authority.[421] The Supreme Court, however, held that the New York statute permitting this action was unconstitutional on three grounds. First, it did not have satisfactory standards of particularity: the statute did not compel the agent engaging in the tap to precisely specify the statement he was seeking. The court held that the law "involved intrusion on privacy that is broad in scope."[422] Second, the statute did not require a demonstration of probable cause to obtain the order to tap, nor did it demand termination of the tap once the evidence was obtained. Third, the statute did not require that notice of the tap be served on the aggrieved party unless special facts overcame the necessity for notice. This last requirement, obviously, would render most taps useless: few persons are so foolish as to reveal anything incriminating over a telephone they know is tapped. But this case, *Berger* v. *New York*, was soon superseded by *Katz* v. *United States*.[423]

Berger established the standards that must be met to obtain a warrant, but is a warrant the sine qua non of constitutional eavesdropping? The court answered with a resounding yes in *Katz*, which recognized that technology had developed to the point that physical trespass was no longer necessary to eavesdrop. As Justice Stewart wrote for the majority: "It becomes clear that the reach of the Fourth Amendment cannot turn upon the presence or absence of physical intrusion into any given enclosure."[424] The question presented in *Katz* is the conditions under which the intrusion is justified and reasonable, which is now determined by a warrant. Only a warrant meeting the *Berger* standards could make a wiretap constitutional. *Katz*, however, modified the requirement of notice; it must still be given, but it may be given after the tap has been removed.

Until this time evidence gathered by eavesdropping was admissible in state courts, despite the fact that its collection violated federal law. *Katz* declared that all taps perpetrated without a warrant were unconstitutional. But section 605 of the Federal Code prohibited such action, and no warrants could be obtained. Hence all wiretaps were unconstitutional after *Katz*. *Mapp* had previously excluded from state courts all evidence obtained in violation of the Constitution, and thus *Katz* precluded the use of wiretap evidence.[425]

The Omnibus Crime Control and Safe Street Act of 1968 repealed section 605, but title III allowed wiretapping under specified conditions. According to its authors, this provision had two purposes. The first was to protect the privacy of the individual by regulating the conditions under which his privacy could be abridged.[426] The second was to formulate a uniform standard for the conditions under which wiretaps could occur. The act prohibits all electronic surveillance by persons other than duly authorized law enforcement officers who are investigating or preventing specific types of crimes with court orders based on probable cause. It gives the President authority to protect the nation from attack by a hostile power and to protect internal security by taking action against those who advocate overthrow of the government by unlawful means.

The Efficacy of Taps

In the face of widespread government wiretaps a panoply of methods is available to the criminal who seeks to avoid prosecution on the basis of intercepted telephone conversations. Criminals who fail to utilize one or another of these devices would in all probability be such easy arrests that the wiretap is unnecessary.

The perennial target of the wiretap is the bookie because law enforcement agencies reason that his operation is characteristically conducted over the phone and therefore vulnerable to discovery by wiretap. Professor Walter Reckless, however, has estimated that two-thirds of the illegal bookies in the United States do not use the telephone in their business. Many keep book only in their heads, have no offices, and call on their clientele personally.[427] Even when bookies don't conduct their business personally, many resort to runners on the street or in business establishments.[428]

In addition, there are numerous devices that safeguard illicit conversations, and *Popular Science* attests to the efficiency of a simple scrambler:

> Scramblers keep private phone conversations safe from wiretapping. Fitted to an ordinary handset, it needs no electrical connection and has its own power source. To hear, a person needs an unscrambler coded identically. Delcon Division, Hewlet-Packard Company, sells it for $275 and keeps your name and code locked in its vault.[429]

As wiretaps improve, so do the means of evading them: scramblers, answering services, and decoy phones. For these reasons, many observers have concluded that wiretapping is of limited use in combating organized crime. One such observer is law professor Herman Schwartz, who says: "New York has permitted its officers to tap for years, yet there is no evidence that it has coped with illegal gambling any better than has Philadelphia or Chicago where all wiretapping is forbidden."[430]

Although this tool is unreliable in combating organized crime, its potential for abuse is great, for the system of court orders does not protect Fourth Amendment rights. Wiretaps are seldom disclosed unless such evidence is brought to trial, so that law enforcement agencies make taps without warrants and use the information in other investigation techniques. Former Philadelphia District Attorney Samuel Dash has estimated that as many as 26,000 taps are made each year without court orders.[431] Indeed, the police utilize wire taps without court orders more often than with them.[432]

Even when court orders are obtained, constitutionality can be violated. A system of judge-shopping may be employed to find a judge who is amenable to authorizing taps on virtually any pretext, and district attorneys routinely employ this method. In some cases judges hand out blank orders, to be filled in after the fact by the police.[433]

Persons who engage in illegal activity can protect themselves by using the mechanical devices discussed previously. They also have protection in that convictions based on wiretap evidence may be overturned if it can be proved that the evidence was gathered illegally. It is the innocent person who is tapped but never brought to trial who has no legal recourse.

Improving the Wiretap Laws

Three provisions could be adopted to change the wiretap laws. First, since current limitations are ignored, legal authority may as well be given for all government wiretaps, and the police would not have to waste time pursuing leads derived from incriminating statements made over the telephone. The statements would be admissible as evidence and thus would shorten the time needed to construct a sound case. This, however, would require a constitutional amendment because a wiretap is search and seizure within the meaning of the Fourth Amendment, which prohibits such general warrants as this law would provide.

The second major alteration would be to curtail wiretaps, which could be accomplished by repeal of the relevant sections of the Omnibus Crime Control and Safe Streets Act. But the value of this is doubtful. The current restrictions do not deter the use of illegal taps, and it is unlikely that such a broad prohibition would have much effect on wiretaps that already are illegal.

The third and most reasonable change would involve revision of the present laws, and an obvious area for change is internal security, which presently allows wiretaps on presidential authorization. It is certainly arguable that this discretion should be revoked, at least insofar as it applies to persons who advocate the overthrow of the government by violent or unlawful means. However, the fact that the value of wiretaps against organized crime is limited may lend credence to the idea that internal security wiretaps are made primarily for harassing or checking on radical political or social minorities. It has been disclosed, for example, that Muhammed Ali, William Sloane Coffin, Benjamin Spock, and James Hoffa have been subjects of wiretaps,[434] as was the late Dr. Martin Luther King. This statute has often been used not for any real purpose of national security but for the harassment of outspoken political leaders. At a time when many persons advocate radical political change, the voices that stir our consciences should not be hushed by fear of wiretapping.

Another reform that might make significant inroads on the illegal use of wiretaps would be to exclude consideration by courts of any evidence which has been gained as a result of wiretaps. In other words, if the police develop evidence of a crime which is perfectly admissible under normal circumstances, it might be excluded if the lead which resulted in that evidence came from a wiretap. Admittedly, detection of illegal wiretaps and proof of the origin of police leads might be difficult, but such a law has at least a potential for reducing the illegal use of wiretaps.

6 Military Justice

The brilliant French prime minister Georges Clemenceau is reported to have remarked that "military justice is to justice as military music is to music." The shortcomings of Sousa may be left to musicians, but the flaws in the Uniform Code of Military Justice are of primary importance to the more than 3 million men and women in the armed services of the United States. The UCMJ is the statute which promulgates military law, and under its authority the army, navy, and air force prosecuted some 91,000 men in various courts-martial in fiscal 1970.[435] An additional 11,000 men were separated from the services by less formal legal proceedings.[436] The quality of the justice thus dispensed is therefore of fundamental concern, and not only to the individuals themselves but to the society in general.

Because a complete analysis of military law is beyond the scope of this chapter, such questions as the jurisdiction of military courts and the First Amendment rights of servicemen will not be specifically considered. Instead, the focus will be upon the problems associated with military juries and the possible gains from allowing civilian juries to decide military cases. A brief examination of the development of American military law and its present status will provide a perspective for examining operation of the military jury. The injustices associated with that process, the substantive reasons for those injustices, and possible alternatives to avoid those injustices will also be discussed.

DEVELOPMENT OF AMERICAN MILITARY LAW

Until 1950 the laws by which American servicemen were governed descended directly from the code under which the Roman Empire had made war. The Continental Congress established a cursory set of war articles in 1775, but their scope did not satisfy George Washington, who requested a more comprehensive code.[437] The task was assigned to John Adams, who borrowed the British articles of war almost verbatim for the initial legislative proposal. The British code, in turn, had been taken from the Roman articles of war, and was so harsh that Adams expected considerable liberalizing in Congress. But much to his surprise, it passed the code in toto, without regard for its illiberal nature.[438] These Articles of War governed the conduct of America's military operations during the Revolutionary War, and until their revision in 1806.

The severity of these laws, in terms of the rights denied and the punishments allowed, was clearly inconsistent with the principles enunciated in the Constitution and the Bill of Rights, a fact which did not escape observation. Secretary of War Henry Knox wrote Washington in 1789 to the effect that the code required revision to conform with the Constitution.[439] Among the rights denied service men were the First Amendment rights of free speech and assembly, and freedom to petition; the Fourth Amendment right of freedom from unreasonable searches and seizures; the Fifth Amendment right of freedom from double jeopardy; and the Sixth Amendment rights of confrontation of witnesses and assistance of counsel.[440]

It should be noted, however, that these laws, however unfair, were substantially restricted in scope and jurisdiction. The authorized total army force in 1792 was only 5,120 men, a number which was not in fact reached.[441] Moreover, the infractions with the code proscribed were limited to truly military matters, such as absence without leave or desertion; criminal matters, such as rape or robbery, were left to the civilian courts.[442]

Despite Secretary Knox's concern, no real reform of the military articles was forthcoming. Minor revisions were made in the navy's code in 1799 and 1800, upon the occasion of the undeclared war with France,[443] and a wholesale revision of the Articles of War in 1806 was little more than a rearrangement of the original code.[444] Military forces were considered to be entirely subject to the statutory authority of Congress, quite apart from the protection of the Constitution. Supreme Court Chief Justice Salmon P. Chase explicated that philosophy in his concurring opinion in *ex parte Milligin* in 1866: "The power of Congress, in the government of the land and naval forces and of the militia, is not at all affected by the fifth or any other amendment."[445] Unsurprisingly, later recodification of the Articles of War in 1874 and 1916 again was little more than a simple reshuffling of the laws.[446]

World War I, however, provided an impetus for change: the conscripts were accustomed to the safeguards of the Constitution in their civilian lives and indisposed to accept the military's abrogation of their fundamental rights. Brutal and excessive punishment, combined with charges that local commanding officers dictated the outcome of courts-martial, produced a demand for reform.447 The appearance in November 1919 of an article in the *Cornell Law Review* describing the conditions of military justice added to the outcry.448 The upshot was the enactment, in 1920, of another code. Some of the worst excesses were eliminated, and legal safeguards were provided at trials,449 but the code did not eliminate what was increasingly recognized as the major obstacle to justice: the influence of superior officers on courts-martial.450 Indeed, as an article in the *Wisconsin Law Review* noted at the end of

World War II shocked Congress into real reform when the millions to the commander to determine not only who shall be tried, for what offense, and by what court, but also what the result shall be in each case."451 The system, in short, was little improved over that of the Revolutionary War in terms of dispensing justice to the accused.

World War II shocked Congress into real reform when the millions of drafted servicemen who fought that war returned to demand change. The American Bar Association, headed by Arthur Vanderbilt, dean of New York University Law School, supported a number of explicit changes, and the result was the Uniform Code of Military Justice, which was enacted in 1950.452

The Uniform Code of Military Justice

The Uniform Code of Military Justice, as amended in 1968, is now the basis for military justice. It establishes the broad outlines of proscribed behavior, and the various services' manuals relating to courts-martial specify the particular activities which are illegal. An extensive system of legal proceedings, ranging from summary punishment by a local commander to full-scale trials by a general court-martial, is established, as well as a comprehensive appeals process.

The simplest type of punishment allowed under the UCMJ is the summary punishment (or captain's mast). Article 15 of the code establishes this option for minor infractions to enable a local commanding officer to enforce discipline quickly and without reference to higher authority. Only enlisted personnel are subject to summary punishment, in which the commanding officer is the sole official in the proceedings. There is no trial as such and no record is kept, other than the notation of punishment.

The penalties are minor: the maximum sentence an officer of less than field grade[453] may impose is seven days' loss of pay, or demotion of one rank, or fourteen days' extra duty, or restricted activity for fourteen days and seven days in correctional custody.[454] Offenders are not required to accept article 15 punishment; if they wish, they may opt for a summary court-martial.[455]

If an offense is more than a minor infraction, or if the accused requests it, one of three types of court-martial will be employed. There are no precise guidelines for determining which of these—summary, specific, or general court-martial—should be utilized in any given case. In general, however, the more serious the crime, the higher the form of court-martial.

Summary courts-martial are the lowest of the three types, the military equivalent of civilian magistrate courts, and only enlisted personnel are eligible for trial by summary court-martial. The accused is not provided with counsel, nor is he entitled to one. An officer, usually not a lawyer, serves as judge, jury, prosecutor, and defense attorney.[456] The punishment which this type of court-martial may order is limited to one month's confinement at hard labor, one month's forfeiture of two-thirds pay, extra duties, and restriction to the base.[457] A 1968 amendment to the code allows an accused to reject this court-martial in favor of a special court-martial, in which he is entitled to a lawyer.[458] This option holds even if the serviceman originally rejected article 15 punishment. Thus, with one minor exception, every serviceman who is accused of any infraction, no matter how slight, may demand and receive legal counsel.[459]

At the intermediate level is the special court-martial, whose proceedings approximate those of a civilian trial. Again, only enlisted personnel are eligible for a special court-martial.[460] However, the accused is entitled to a lawyer unless the officer convening the trial certifies that counsel is unavailable due to "physical conditions or military exigencies."[461] It might be noted, though, that such conditions or exigencies seem to exist quite often, and requests for counsel are often turned down in the Army precisely for those reasons.[462] "If the prosecutor is legally qualified, however, the defense counsel must also be a trained lawyer;[463] and the accused must be afforded a lawyer if a bad-conduct discharge is to be awarded."[464]

The special court-martial is run as a trial, with a presiding officer, a jury, and sometimes legal counsel for both parties. The presiding officer may be a general line officer, or he may be a representative of the Judge Advocate General Corps. If he is the latter, he will be a trained lawyer and an experienced judge. Special courts-martial that are authorized to award bad-conduct discharges must be presided over by this kind of experienced lawyer, unless physical conditions or military exigencies warrant otherwise.465 A verbatim trial record is also required if a bad-conduct discharge is to be awarded.466 The jury, like that in a general court-martial, is composed of local officers.

Special courts-martial are empowered to award a bad-conduct discharge (under the conditions outlined above), but alternative punishment includes a maximum six months at hard labor, six months' forfeiture of two-thirds pay, or demotion in rank.467 Special courts-martial, the most used of all courts-martial, now run at an estimated level of 75,000 per year.468

The highest level of court-martial is the general court-martial, which is reserved for the trial of officers and for the most serious crimes. General courts-martial, conducted in similar fashion to a civilian criminal trial, are presided over by a member of the Judge Advocate General Corps (which is the armed services' legal branch). As a result of the 1968 amendments to the UCMJ, officers in the JAGC are subject only to the Judge Advocate General himself, not to the local military commanders.469 The presiding officer's function is similar to that of a federal district judge: he rules on all questions of military law and on all motions before the court. Since 1968, he cannot be overruled by the jury on these points.470

The jury is comprised of no less than five members, generally all officers, selected by the local commanding officer.471 The numerical size of the jury can and does vary, but there is a fixed requirement for conviction: two-thirds of the panel must agree on conviction, or else the defendant goes free.472 Thus if a seven-member panel votes 4 to 3 for conviction, the verdict is not guilty. Enlisted personnel may request that one-third of the jury be enlisted men, but this option is rarely exercised because the senior noncommissioned officers who serve as the enlisted representatives are almost always more severe than the officers they replace.473 Defendants may also—except in capital cases, and with the approval of the judge—request trial by the military judge alone.474

The general court-martial is empowered to pass any sentence commensurate with the offense that it desires, up to and including capital punishment. It is the only court-martial which can sentence a man to death, and the only one which can award a dishonorable discharge.475 Legal counsel for defendants is mandatory.476

Prior to a general court-martial the convening authority (generally the local commander) is required by article 32 of the code to conduct a thorough investigation of the charges. This investigation includes, of course, a thorough review of the events in question and an evaluation of them by a staff officer of the Judge Advocate General Corps as to the validity of the charges. But it also requires a formal preliminary hearing in which sworn testimony of prosecution witnesses is heard, which the defendant has the right to cross-examine.477 The accused also has full access to the investigator's file, but is not required to reveal his own defense. In the opinion of a civilian defense attorney, this system offers "considerably more pretrial discovery rights than federal rules afford a civilian defendant."478 Then, on the basis of the article 32 hearing, the staff judge advocate evaluates the issues and recommends trial on the initial charges, on reduced charges, or dismissal. The final authority which passes on these recommendations, however, is the local convening authority, not the legal staff.479

Another article in the UCMJ applies to courts-martial in general and is of special interest. Article 37 contains a flat prohibition of interference in courts-martial by a superior command:

> No authority convening a general, special or summary court-martial, nor any other commanding officer, may censure, reprimand, or admonish the court, or any member law officer or counsel thereof. . . . No person subject to this chapter may attempt to coerce, or by any unauthorized means, influence the action of a court-martial, or any other military tribunal or any member thereof.480

The purpose of this article is obvious: to deny local commanding officers any and all power to influence the outcome of courts-martial. Whether, in fact, the code lives up to this intent will be discussed shortly.

The UCMJ also provides an extensive appellate procedure for convicted defendants. The initial stage is automatic review of the trial transcript and findings by the convening authority, usually the local commanding officer. Every case that has been tried before a court-martial is reviewed at least once by the convening authority, which has the authority to approve, disapprove, or suspend a sentence in whole or in part. If the accused has been found guilty, the commanding officer may even reverse the verdict.481 Of course, the convening authority is also the individual who ordered the court-martial initially and thus it is unlikely that he will overturn many convictions. Also, the staff judge advocate who heard the trial must file a lengthy posttrial interview with the accused for the information of the higher authorities who will review the trial.482

After the convening authority examines the record, further appeals may be taken to the Courts of Military Review, which are comprised of three-man panels of officers, from the Judge Advocate General Corps —any number of which may be assigned to a particular case by the Judge Advocate General.483 Review by this body is mandatory for any punitive discharge or imprisonment of one year or more which is awarded by a general court-martial, and for any bad-conduct discharge which a special court-martial imposes.484 The board may review questions both of law and fact, and may reduce any sentence; it may also set aside a verdict and order a rehearing, or dismiss the charges entirely.485 Some 7 percent of all courts-martial are reviewed by the Courts of Military Review.486

The final review tribunal of courts-martial is the Court of Military Appeals (unfortunately abbreviated COMA), which is composed of three civilians who are appointed for fifteen-year terms by the President. It reviews approximately 1 percent of all courts-martial, limiting itself (like the Supreme Court) to cases of special importance or cases which illuminate important legal issues.487 Mandatory review by this body includes all cases involving general officers and all cases in which the death penalty has been imposed. It may also hear cases which the Judge Advocate General certifies for it, or any case in which the accused presents a petition alleging good reasons for review.488 This court is the last resort for a defendant within the military hierarchy.

Another aspect of military justice deserves comment although it does not fall within the UCMJ. This is the administrative discharge, by which some 11,000 men are annually separated from the services with less than honorable discharges.489 The administrative discharge is most common in AWOL cases and convictions by a civilian court, where a court-martial might not have jurisdiction. None of the UCMJ safeguards, which at least on paper, protect the serviceman, are applicable here, nor is there the right of appeal.490 The basis for these exclusions is the administrative nature of the proceedings which are designed to promote the efficiency of the armed services rather than judicial objectives. Hence, the military argues, no restriction should be placed on the use of the administrative discharge, and none are.

On paper, therefore, the military has constructed an admirable system of justice, which is superior in many respects to the quality of justice dispensed by civilian courts. In the words of a former member of the Judge Advocate General Corps, Frederick B. Wiener:

Over the years, Congress has gradually extended the serviceman's protection by statute, and today the Court of Military Appeals is giving to the statutory provisions a content which in most instances is indistinguishable from that of the constitutional norms regularly formulated and applied in the federal courts. Today the person in uniform enjoys the effective assistance of counsel, he is accorded the full privilege against self-incrimination, he has the right of compulsory process for witnesses, his right to freedom from unreasonable searches and seizures is receiving recognition, his protection against double jeopardy is greater than that accorded civilians in many states, due process in the sense of essential fairness is a concept fully enforced in court-martial proceedings, and servicemen are granted considerable freedom of speech within the limits of a military society.491

Indeed, as Wiener notes, one of the few substantive constitutional rights not granted the serviceman is the right to trial by a petit jury.492 Unfortunately, that omission, combined with the military's stringent sense of discipline, has in many cases vitiated the safeguards of the UCMJ.

INEQUITIES OF MILITARY JUSTICE

The UCMJ, of course, operates within the military structure; judge, jury, defense counsel are all military officers first and officers of justice second. Such a system therefore, must be prejudiced against the defendant, and prejudice arises from two separate and distinct phenomena. First, the focus of the army in its judicial proceedings is on maintaining discipline within the ranks; courts-martial are merely one means by which discipline may be enforced. A jury of career officers, by virtue of their preeminent concern for discipline, will ordinarily enter the courtroom with a clear though unconscious bias in favor of conviction. As the head of the American Civil Liberties Union, himself a veteran of the court-martial system, observed: "It's impossible to have true justice in the military because courts-martial are almost totally dedicated to the preservation of discipline at the expense of justice."493 It is not that the officers who sit on courts-martial are evil or dishonest; it is merely that their training conditions them to regard discipline as the primary goal, so that the truth of the charges before them becomes a secondary question.

The other basis for inequity is the phenomenon known as command influence or command control of the trial, which operates not only upon the jury but also upon the defense counsel, and encourages conviction.

Command control is a natural phenomenon of courts-martial: The local commanding officer supervises the pretrial investigation for a court-martial, and on the basis of that information decides if the charges will be pressed. Thus the mere order for a court-martial serves notice to all that the commanding officer believes the defendant is guilty as charged. He then appoints a jury of his subordinates to try the case, who cannot help but be aware of his views.

As Robert Sherrill writes:

> General courts-martial are not convened unless the commanding officer believes the defendant is guilty; and since the officers who make up the trial panel know that the commander is of this persuasion—and because they must often look to the commandant for promotion—they will most often come through with the verdict he wants. It is, in fact, that simple.494

Moreover, the military's concern with discipline often leads commanders to attempt subtle direction of a trial. Again, they do not act for any evil purpose but merely to maintain discipline in their commands. The chief of the Court of Military Appeals, Robert Quinn, observed:

> Command control may take many forms. Most obvious is the conference before the start of the trial in which the commander's views about the accused or the offense are brought directly home to the court members. Subtle psychological pressures at all levels of the court-martial process are less direct, but just as effective. One of the most troublesome forms of indirect pressure is the policy statement. A policy can be framed as a positive order, or it may be phrased as indicating what is merely desirable. As members of a hierarchical system, with promotion and type of duty largely dependent upon the ratings of superiors, military personnel would virtually tend to regard all policy as mandatory.495

Or as defense attorney Emile Zola Berman has argued: "The commanding officer never says, 'I want to get this son of a bitch.' But he doesn't have to. The members of the court understand that they are there to convict."496

Nor is command influence limited to members of the jury, though it is most obvious there. The military counsels who defend servicemen who are unpopular with the higher command frequently find that a successful defense is rewarded with a transfer of duty. When former Senator Charles Goodell won an acquittal for a soldier who was charged with desertion, he was promptly reassigned to the prosecution.497

Captain Brendan Sullivan, defense counsel in the Presidio mutiny case, was reassigned to Vietnam following his efforts on behalf of the "mutineers."[498] Harassment such as this, although forbidden by the UCMJ, makes a mockery of the right to a fair and impartial jury and a skilled defense counsel. Thus ACLU attorney Charles Morgan observes ironically: "The Uniform Code of Military Justice is uniform, is a code, and is military, and therefore has nothing to do with justice."[499]

Examples of command control are not difficult to find, and the case of Private Bruce Peterson is typical. Peterson, who was on poor terms with his commander, was the editor of an underground newspaper which was revealing a number of disturbances at Fort Hood that the army preferred to keep secret. Arrested for possession of marijuana, Peterson was tried and given an eight-year sentence (the normal sentence was six months)—for having an amount so small that it was entirely destroyed in the chemical test that proved it was marijuana.[500] His conviction was overturned—thirteen months later—on a technicality.

Equally obvious were the machinations of the army in the Presidio mutiny trial. Despite the recommendations of the army's investigator, Captain R. H. Millard, that the charges against the Presidio demonstrators be reduced, the commanding general insisted on a court-martial for mutiny. Not surprisingly, in view of such insistence, most of the twenty-seven demonstrators were convicted of mutiny, and some received sentences of as much as sixteen years.[501]

The military, of course, defends the system as fair and equitable, and has some support from more unbiased authorities. Rear Admiral William Mott, the navy's Judge Advocate General, has argued: "No more than an extremely small percentage of commanders, either directly or indirectly, attempt to influence the actions of the courts-martial."[502] Yale law professor Joseph W. Bishop asserts: "The members . . . are usually honorable men, unlikely to perpetrate deliberate injustice merely to curry favor with the commanding officer."[503] Thus, he says, "my experience leads me to the conclusion that most [courts-martial] are as fair as most civilian criminal trials . . . and their members as fair as civilian juries."[504]

In support of this position, the defenders of the military point to the statutory prohibition of interference in article 37 of the UCMJ. Certainly, if statutes can prevent commanding officers from meddling in courts-martial, the present system is adequate. The problem, however, is that statutes cannot prevent command control because the process is not amenable to legal correction. Command control, it will be recalled, arises from the perception of the jurors that their commander, who is in large measure able to control their career, desires a certain outcome for a trial, and the mere convening of the court-martial indicates that he believes the accused to be guilty. As the Senate's leading expert in the Bill of Rights, Sam Ervin, argues:

> Over the years there have been numerous complaints of command influence in trials by court-martial. . . . The interpretation by courts of Article 37 of the UCMJ, which purports to prohibit command influence, with respect to trials by court-martial . . . is not sufficient to provide the requisite protection against the subtle influences affecting the impartiality of the members of the court-martial.505

To the mind of a commanding officer, a vote to acquit when the "facts" point so obviously to the contrary can only indicate poor judgment (a fact to be noted in the juror's next fitness report). As Fred B. Smith, general counsel for the Treasury, noted:

> The proposed prohibition [to end command influence] would be largely ineffective. If a reporting officer observes either good or bad performance by a member of a board or a court, this would inevitably contribute to his opinion of that person, and this opinion would —also inevitably—be reflected in any evaluation the reporting officer makes of that member. The impression made on a reporting officer by either good or bad performance cannot be erased from his mind by a statutory provision.506

Since fitness reports play a major role in an officer's career, he must subconsciously, if not consciously, give weight to his commander's views —article 37 to the contrary notwithstanding.

The 1968 amendments to the UCMJ have made some changes in this condition: they allow an accused serviceman (except in capital cases) to request trial by the Judge Advocate General Corps military judge alone, provided the latter agrees, and a military jury is not empaneled. Inasmuch as JAG officers are now, legally at least, independent of the local commands, they are presumably not subject to the same pressures as military juries. Senator Ervin, who suggests that this insulation from local command will make JAG presiding officers virtually immune from command influence,507 is seconded by Professor Bishop: "The accused in a non-capital case may elect to be tried by a military judge, whose fitness reports are not written by the commander who convened the court."508

There is reason, however, to believe that even JAG officers are not free of the influence of local commanding officers. For example, the case of Roger Priest, a seaman whose underground newspaper offended the late House Armed Services Committee chairman L. Mendel Rivers and Defense Secretary Melvin Laird, was dismissed by the military judge. But under pressure from the local commander, the JAG officer reinstituted the charges six days later, and Priest was ultimately convicted.509

Furthermore, the number of defendants who will elect this alternative is unknown. In civil courts, only about a third of all contested criminal cases are heard by a judge alone.510 Moreover — as is argued elsewhere in this book — the collective wisdom of a jury has been deemed (in Anglo-Saxon law at least) to be superior to the judgment of a single official, be he ever so fair-minded. The point is, of course, that the sacrifice of the right to a jury trial is a high price to pay for an unbiased decision.

The military's defenders also argue that the extensive appeals procedures ensure that if command influence has been exerted, the error can be corrected. Admiral Mott, for instance, claims that while command influence is occasionally encountered, "it is invariably corrected [by appeal] when it comes to light."511

The problems encountered in relying on the appeals mechanism to correct command control are threefold. Appeals review only a small portion of cases: 7 percent for the intermediate Court of Military Review; 1 percent for the Court of Military Appeals. The automatic review of all cases by the convening officer is, of course, useless: a man who is guilty of command influence will hardly overrule himself. It is not sufficient to argue that appeals mechanisms review all the important cases involving long prison terms—inasmuch as the undeserved six-month jail sentence is quite as unjust to the individual involved. So is the less than honorable discharge handed down by an administrative tribunal, which is never reviewed by the military appeals process.

Moreover, appeals are based on the written record of the courts-martial, which is a poor instrument for detecting command influence. Rarely does a commander exert his influence so blatantly that it appears in a written record. The process operates indirectly, it should be remembered; it commences when the convening officer orders the court-martial, and it operates more subconsciously than openly. Thus many instances of command control will remain hidden from the most rigorous and conscientious review. As Professor Bishop says: "Illegal command influence is often intangible and hard to find in the record."512

Finally, appeals are inevitably after the fact; they cannot prevent command influence; they can merely attempt to correct it. As Justice Clark of the Supreme Court wrote in the landmark pretrial publicity case, *Sheppard* v. *Maxwell*: "But we must remember that reversals are but palliatives; the cure lies in those remedial measures that will prevent the prejudice at its inception."513 Sole reliance on appeals mechanisms cannot, of course, cure prejudice at its inception, nor even later, in many cases. Military appeals procedures, therefore, are not capable of eliminating command control.

The military, however, is not limited to the judicial system to work its will, justly or otherwise, upon servicemen it regards as offenders; an alternative device, increasingly utilized, is the administrative discharge. This, it will be recalled, is a three-man board, appointed by the local commanding officer, that has power to discharge individuals under less than honorable conditions. In 1968, the last year for which statistics are available, some 11,000 men were separated from the services by this procedure.514

The administrative discharge is the ideal means for the military to shortcut the lengthy procedures of courts-martial and their attendant safeguards. Moreover, these proceedings have no safeguards whatever because they are viewed by the military as administrative in nature rather than judicial. As Senator Ervin noted: "The serviceman who is brought before an administrative board considering the issue of an undesirable discharge may not be represented by legally qualified counsel, may not have the opportunity to confront adverse witnesses or to subpoena witnesses in his own favor, and may receive an undesirable discharge on the basis of evidence which would be inadmissible before a court-martial."515

Moreover, the administrative boards do not have even the appearance of freedom from command influence. In contrast to the UCMJ, there is no prohibition of interference from superior officers; and since the commanding officer appoints the board, command control is pervasive. According to Senator Ervin: "There is no prohibition at the present time against command influence with respect to administrative proceedings, even though these procedures can have a tremendous impact on the future of a serviceman, and may result in discharges under other than honorable conditions."516

It is not surprising, therefore, that the military is making increasing use of this device to rid itself of servicemen it deems undesirable. A former Air Force Judge Advocate General has admitted: "The tremendous increase in undesirable discharges by administrative proceedings was the result of effort by military commanders to avoid the requirements of the Uniform Code."517 The attitude of the military seems to be that the administrative discharge is ideal for disposing of individuals who, in the minds of their commanding officers, are clearly guilty but cannot be convicted by a court-martial because of lack of evidence. The implications of this attitude for the presumption of innocence in the absence of proof of guilt are obvious.

Examples of this behavior are not wanting, and the case of the Fort Jackson Eight is typical. Eight soldiers were charged with mutiny at Fort Jackson, South Carolina, for conducting a loud "bull session" on Vietnam and white racism, and Secretary of the Army Stanley Resor was ultimately called upon to investigate the matter. As a result of his recommendation, the mutiny charges were dropped, but six of the eight were quietly discharged via the administrative board.518

What is the effect of command control upon courts-martial and administrative proceedings? It is, simply, injustice. Thousands of American citizens are deprived of their liberty, their veterans' benefits, and their reputations on the basis of unfair trials. They are convicted because their commander believes them to be guilty, whether in fact they are or not. These soldiers, on any reasonable grounds, are not proved guilty beyond any reasonable doubt. Nevertheless, they are given less than honorable discharges or jail sentences which will handicap them for life.

The effects of an undesirable discharge are felt long after the individual departs the service. Any discharge less than honorable eliminates the veterans' benefits for which the ex-serviceman is otherwise eligible.519 Pension rights, VA hospitalization, and GI Bill assistance are lost. And the blot on the individual's record makes it difficult or impossible for him to obtain a decent job.

Florida criminologist Leonard Hippchen discovered that 53 percent of the businessmen in his survey would not even consider employing a person with a less than honorable discharge from the military.520 Even among those companies willing to consider applicants with less than honorable discharges, their rigid screening requirements create major difficulties.521 And, in addition to tangible losses, one should not overlook the effects of six months' hard labor in a military prison. To allow all this to happen to a person who has not been proved guilty is to perpetrate a huge injustice.

Such penalties are sufficient reason for change, yet military injustice creates a further problem for society at large. In an age of conscript armies, a significant portion of the citizenry puts some time in the military, and this experience undoubtedly leaves a lasting impression. If part of that impression is indifference to justice, there may well be an infection of civilian justice by the excesses of the military. Indeed, Robert Sherrill argues that if military justice is corrupt—and it is—sooner or later it will corrupt civilian justice. Perhaps this has already begun. The Supreme Court was wrong when it said that "the military constitutes a specialized community governed by a separate discipline from that of the civilian." When one fifth of all adults have had military experience, the two ways of life cannot be separated so distinctly. There is inevitable seepage, by means of movement of civilians in and out of the military and of the indoctrination that lingers a lifetime. . . . Military justice is in fact an experience in totalitarian expediency, a persuasive experience from which the insecure America of today emphatically does not benefit.522

The conclusion must therefore be that command influence, the inevitable focus upon discipline at the expense of justice, creates injustice and the need for remedies, to which we now turn.

POTENTIAL SOLUTIONS

In view of the intrinsic inability of the military to correct its injustices, civil alternatives are required, and the two most obvious alternatives are civil court review and complete civil jurisdiction.

Even at present, a convicted serviceman can appeal to a federal court to issue a writ of habeas corpus, which directs the military to show cause for holding the serviceman in prison. If the cause is constitutionally defective, he is ordered freed. Thus, in theory, a serviceman can demonstrate that he was convicted in an unfair trial and can win civil release. Nor is the Supreme Court as averse to appeals from military courts as it was in Salmon P. Chase's era. In 1953 its decision in *Burns* v. *Wilson* held that "military courts, like state courts, have the same responsibilities as do federal courts to protect a person from the violation of his constitutional rights."523

Although habeas corpus actions are useless in cases of administrative discharge, these discharges can also be challenged in civil courts. A serviceman can sue for a writ of mandamus to the secretary of the service involved and request the court to order the secretary to issue an honorable discharge. Since the Supreme Court in the 1958 case of *Harmon* v. *Bruckner* ruled that judicial review of administrative discharges is permissible, a number of ex-servicemen have challenged their undesirable discharges in court.524

The right to a civilian hearing may thus be open but success in a federal court is another matter. The Supreme Court, even under the liberal Earl Warren, took a conservative position with respect to such matters. As the former Chief Justice told a New York University Law School class:

> The basic attitude of the court has been that our jurisdiction is most limited. Thus, the Supreme Court has adhered consistently to the 1863 holding of *ex parte Vallandigham* that it lacks the jurisdiction to review by certeriorari the decisions of the military courts. The cases in which the Court has ordered the release of persons convicted by court-martial have, to date, been limited to instances in which the defendant was found to be such that he was not constitutionally, or statutorily, amenable to military justice.[525]

The practical effect of this stance, according to Joseph Bishop, is that the unfairness must be more than "the common garden variety of error"[526]—but common garden variety unfairness, such as command influence, is apparently tolerable. In any event, no military convict has yet been freed by a federal court on the grounds of an unfair trial.[527]

Even if such a landmark decision were to be made by the Supreme Court, its practical effect might be extremely limited. The problem of detection and proof of command influence, in any given trial, is all but insoluble. The military's appellate courts have acted where command influence is obvious,[528] but the root of the problem, of course, is that command influence is exercised so subtly that it is rarely apparent. Even where it is overt, it may go unchallenged: the numerical limitation of appeals applies as much to federal as to military courts. The delay involved in deciding an appeal may also prove fatal, for a habeas corpus action automatically becomes void when the appellant is released from prison.

Finally, there is the basic problem that appeals are an ex post facto solution. As COMA's chief justice Robert Quinn admitted: "Pronouncements by the highest court of legal doctrine are sterile exercises in semantics, if there is only grudging compliance with the letter, and little respect for the spirit of the law."[529] So pervasive is the desire for discipline and so intrinsic is the influence of command that a number of critics have concluded that justice is impossible as long as it remains independent of the civilian court system.[530]

An alternative to military injustice, which avoids the problems of the civil courts for appellate purposes only, might be to transfer the entire military legal process to civil courts. Thus the court-martial of military offenders would be conducted in a civilian courtroom, before a federal judge, by a jury of civilians. Civilian jurors, of course, would be free from the military's emphasis on discipline and the command influence on career officers. It is precisely this freedom that is one of the strongest arguments in favor of the jury in general, and in military cases it would eliminate the sources of injustice. Administrative boards which award undesirable discharges would also be subject to civilian jury trials at the request of the defendants.

Do civilian courts have the capacity to handle such trials? Robert Sherrill argues that they do:

> Deserters can be tried in civilian courts just as easily as draft evaders are today. Servicemen whose disturbance of base operations is too serious to be adequately punished by Article 15 can be taken care of in civilian courts just as easily as are those civilians today who disrupt church services or create a public nuisance or disturb the peace. Civilian courts can handle servicemen who rape, murder, rob, gamble, get drunk, fornicate in public, abuse animals, expose themselves, fight, steal cars or commit any other notable mischief just as easily as they handle civilians who do these things.[531]

Certainly, if expansion of the civil courts or reform of their procedures is necessary to accommodate military cases, it could be accomplished by the procedures discussed elsewhere in this book. Such a system has been successfully used in West Germany since 1946.[532]

The military has objected to such a civilian usurpation of military law principally on the grounds that it would disastrously weaken discipline in the ranks. A typical position was that of the New York State Bar Association's Committee on Military Justice in 1949: "Experience has demonstrated that the success of an army depends on its commander. No one but he can be responsible for discipline within his command. To assure discipline, he must have the authority and responsibility for the manner in which justice is exercised in his command."[533] Such emphasis on discipline is, in fact, the primary source of the command influence, which in turn is a principal source of military injustice.

However, there is little objective basis for the conclusion that the army will disintegrate if court-martial offenses are subject to the civilian jury. Germany's experience, as noted above, has been to the contrary. Punishment is still imposed for proved offenses and the proof must merely be fair. Also, the military retains its article 15 summary punishment powers, which can be administered by the local commander, and this should certainly suffice to maintain discipline.[534] And, finally, if the military is determined to discharge an individual, it still has the option of issuing an honorable discharge through an administrative board.

In short, civilian trials for military offenses could eliminate one of the principal elements of injustice in the military because they would be invulnerable to the pressures that inevitably operate in a military trial. Such an expansion of the jury system therefore deserves careful consideration.

SUMMARY

The present jury system is far from perfect but is capable of remedy, and the courts are not functioning efficiently. Accordingly, the failure to dispense justice in more than a cursory fashion creates innumerable tensions for society and gross injustices to individuals.

In the area of pretrial publicity, juries can be influenced by the news media if judges are not diligent in protecting the defendants' rights, and the solution to this problem rests with the judges. How well they solve it may well be determined by how well society provides them with the necessary time and staff.

Closely related to the problems of court congestion are the inadequacies of the bail system, which makes the right to bail an arbitrary exercise in class discrimination. Discrimination is all too common in jury selection as well. In light of the recent encroachments on the exclusionary rule by the Supreme Court, defendants now—even more than before—require intelligent, perceptive, fair-minded juries.

Fair juries are also essential to military justice, but the military's hierarchical structure and its emphasis on discipline sometimes preclude fair courts-martial. Their transfer to the civilian courts seems a logical alternative, but only after the civil courts have disposed of their backlog of cases.

These separate and distinct problems may nevertheless be considered as different aspects of a fundamental problem: ensuring a fair trial and all the constitutional safeguards for the defendant. How well we succeed in this may be of vital importance in preventing further social and political upheaval in the nation.

The focus on the structural deficiencies of the jury system should not, of course, blind us to alternative means of reform, which might come from an investigation of the powers of the jury, including the power (in many states) to execute a defendant. There is a very real question about the jury's right to hold such an awesome power, and it is to consideration of that power that we now turn.

7 Capital Punishment

Over 650 men and women now languish on death rows throughout the United States.535 A society that is able to transplant vital organs and to telecast from the moon is nevertheless primitive enough to dispatch its more unsavory characters to places where they will be less troublesome. A nation civilized enough to outlaw child labor and to give aid to its poor still resorts to a form of legal murder.

Is the practice of capital punishment, or even the threat of punishment, any deterrent to would-be capital offenders? Is there a basis for declaring capital punishment unconstitutional? If the Supreme Court refuses to act, what role can governors and state legislatures play in wiping this immoral blot from our laws and our souls? These are only a few of the issues in the capital punishment debate, and the debate is by no means one-sided.

The number of people executed in the United States has been steadily declining for a generation, and the figures depict the evolving standards which are finding capital punishment abhorrent:536

1930	155	1955	76	1964	15
1935	199	1960	56	1965	7
1940	124	1961	42	1966	1
1945	117	1962	47	1967	2
1950	82	1963	21	1968	0

The last execution in the army was April 13, 1961; the navy hasn't executed anyone since December 1, 1842.537 In addition, one-fourth of the states have abolished capital punishment, following a trend set by eighteen nations. Of the eighty-nine countries that allow capital punishment, thirty-six have not had an execution since 1958, and the eighty-nine countries average six executions per annum.538

THE EIGHTH AMENDMENT, THE COURTS, AND CAPITAL PUNISHMENT

The Eighth Amendment of the United States Constitution prohibits cruel and unusual punishment, but this vague heading is subject to the evolving standards of society. In *Wilkerson* v. *Utah* the Supreme Court ruled that torture was cruel and unusual punishment and therefore fell within the Eighth Amendment's prohibition.[539]

In 1910 the court expanded the scope of the Amendment. In *Weems* v. *United States*[540] it said that twelve to twenty years of hard and painful labor in wrist or ankle chains is cruel and unusual punishment, and two criteria developed. First, its scope was expanded to include all circumstances of degradation. Second, the court affirmed that punishment cannot be disproportionate to the crime.[541] But neither criterion automatically applied to the death penalty. Evidently, death was not considered degradation or disproportionate punishment. The court made this specific in *in re Kemmler:* the Eighth Amendment does not preclude capital punishment.

In *Trop* v. *Dulles*[542] the court ruled that expatriation was cruel and unusual punishment. Court judgments causing undue distress were also proscribed. While some would argue that loss of citizenship is not worse than death, the court refused to strike down capital punishment.[543]

Sandwiched between the *Mapp* decision (1961), which gave Fourth Amendment protection in state trials, and the *Miranda* decision (1966), which did the same with the Sixth Amendment, was the case of *Robinson* v. *California* (1962), which affirmed that state courts could not order punishment in violation of the Eighth Amendment.

ISSUES IN THE CAPITAL PUNISHMENT DEBATE

Is the Death Penalty a Valuable Deterrent?

Those in favor of retaining the death penalty claim that the threat of execution deters criminals from committing capital crimes, particularly when the threat is occasionally carried out. They also argue that, in the absence of capital punishment, blood feuds would begin as friends and relatives of the victim sought revenge. Opponents of capital punishment argue that no deterrent effect is discernible, and that capital punishment may even increase the incidence of capital crimes. There are two reasons for this. First, once a person has committed a murder, he will not hesitate to kill as many more times as necessary (e.g., in making his escape) since he is already liable to be executed. Second, it has been argued that the death wish of criminals is at least as strong as their urge for self-preservation.[544]

Statistics give us little help; they do not distinguish the abolitionist states from those that use the death penalty:[545]

	Murder	(Rates per 100,000) Aggravated Assault	Violent Crime
Minnesota (ab.)	1.6	54.7	132
North Dakota (ab.)	0.2	18.3	29
South Dakota	3.7	6.2	86.9
New York (ab.)	5.4	165.8	403.4
Pennsylvania	3.8	63.6	138.4
New Jersey	3.9	92.4	188.5
Rhode Island (ab.)	2.2	90	128.4
Massachusetts	2.8	65.2	127.6
Connecticut	2.4	55.7	95.9

Aggravated assaults and violent crimes are included in the above figures because the perpetrators may have been willing to commit murder in the process. (Of course, this sample does not consider various sociological factors.)

A recent study compared the number of homicides in the United States in a sixty-day period before an execution to the number of homicides in a sixty-day period after the execution. If capital punishment is an effective deterrent to capital crimes, one would expect fewer homicides in the second period, but the statistician found 91 and 113 homicides, respectively.[546] A similar study, which used the day of sentencing instead of the day of execution, found 43 and 41 homicides, respectively.[547]

Iowa abolished the death penalty in 1964; the crime rates in that state are as follows:[548]

	Murder	Aggravated Assault
1963	1.3	8.7
1964	1.3	19.0
1965	1.3	20.1

Iowa's murder rate did not change as the legislature moved to abolish capital punishment, and even after abolition there was no perceptible change. Aggravated assaults more than doubled after 1963, but leveled off in 1965. This would seem to indicate that criminals took more chances as the state moved to abolish capital punishment. However, since the murder rate did not increase, one can reasonably conclude that murderers in Iowa were neither encouraged nor discouraged by the death penalty. And since there was no increase in homicides, lethal weapons and premeditation were probably not involved in the increased assaults. These assaults would probably have occurred regardless of the state's method of dealing with murderers.

New York abolished the death penalty in 1965, and its relevant statistics are the following:549

	Murder	Aggravated Assault
1964	4.6	104.4
1965	4.6	147.8
1966	4.8	155.2

Thus New York's experience almost exactly parallels Iowa's. As it became obvious that the state would abolish the death penalty, aggravated assault jumped while the murder rate remained constant. Proponents of the death penalty have trouble explaining why capital punishment does not deter criminals from committing murder but lowers the rate of aggravated assault.

West Virginia abolished the death penalty in 1965, and its statistics are:550

	Murder	Aggravated Assault
1964	3.7	50.1
1965	4.0	55.4
1966	4.2	61.5

These figures are evidence of a steadily increasing crime rate that was not exacerbated by abolition of the death penalty.

On balance, there is no strong statistical evidence that capital punishment is a valuable deterrent; however, a word about the limited usefulness of statistics is in order. The number that is sought by this study is the number of capital crimes that would have been committed in the absence of the death penalty but would not have been committed under it—the number of "uncommitted crimes." The statistics can show us only the basic trends in the crime rates of the abolitionist states; but if the penalty had a large deterrent effect its proponents would surely inform us of the fact.

Is Execution Immoral?

Proponents of the death penalty view execution by the state as society's attempt to protect itself. Some even turn to the Old Testament for justification: "He that striketh a man with a will to kill him, shall be put to death."551 They contend that the methods are quick and painless, as in electrocution, which usually takes about one minute.552 The victim lurches in the chair as the current first hits him and often struggles with surprising strength. Usually, one or two jolts will kill the victim. If a third is needed, the body will almost certainly burn, and the smell of charred flesh fills the death chamber.

Death by gas may take up to five minutes. The victim typically clenches his fists in a reflex action as the fumes begin to fill the chamber. He struggles and coughs, and often remains conscious until very near the end.553

But beyond the physical pain is the greater pain of the knowledge of impending death. However, it is the task of each reader to determine the morality of the death penalty.

Is the Death Penalty Unconstitutional?

The Supreme Court has gone to great lengths in recent years to avoid this issue, but judicial precedent states that capital punishment is not unconstitutional, as described in the Eighth Amendment. And proponents of the death penalty point to the Fifth Amendment, which states that no person shall "be deprived of life, liberty, or property, without due process of law. However, the Fifth Amendment also says "No more shall any person be subject for the same offense to be twice put in jeopardy of life or limb," which implies that a person *may* be put in jeopardy of losing an arm or leg.

All of this, then, is subject to the evolving standards of decency of society: what may have been permissible in 1789 may not be permissible in 1971.

On the other hand, capital punishment may be "cruel and unusual" in light of the current purpose of punishment. The California supreme court, in the case of *in re Estrada* (1965), held that punishment should serve one of three ends: deterrence, confinement, or correction. But since there is no clear evidence that capital punishment has a deterrent effect, it achieves confinement in a most unique way, and totally thwarts any attempt at correction. Life imprisonment, then, achieves confinement as well as the death penalty. Therefore, if a punishment is cruel and unusual if a less severe penalty would achieve the same end, and if life imprisonment can be judged less severe than the death penalty, capital punishment is cruel and unusual, and should be declared unconstitutional.

Life imprisonment, obviously, preserves the prisoner's freedom to choose whether he will live or die (he may choose suicide if he feels that death is less severe than life imprisonment). And life imprisonment may eventually lead to parole, if this punishment fulfills its role of correction. Furthermore, though life imprisonment deprives the criminal of many of the joys of life, many prisoners are able to write novels or memoirs, to paint, to ponder and study—to develop their potentialities as human beings. Clearly, life imprisonment is not as severe a punishment as death.

As for confinement, a murderer is confined by his prison term, or until he is judged rehabilitated, and the only people who are not protected by this arrangement are the prison guards and other prisoners. In 1965, for example, there were sixty-one deaths from altercations in U.S. prisons. Six abolitionist states had no such deaths and eight had one death each. Seventeen states that allow capital punishment had no such deaths, while nineteen states permitting capital punishment and the federal prisons accounted for fifty-three of sixty-one deaths.[554]

Since the lesser punishment of life imprisonment can perform the functions of deterrence, confinement, and correction as well as the death penalty, there is ample reason to declare that the latter is cruel and unusual punishment.

Are the Innocent Executed?

Proponents argue that if innocent people are convicted, this is an argument against our judicial system as a whole and not an indictment of capital punishment. Many also feel that the number is negligible and therefore these lapses are not a sound basis for changing the system. On the other hand, abolitionists contend that the charge is particularly relevant due to the irreversible nature of the punishment.

Those who seek to abolish capital punishment cite the cases of innocents who have been convicted, such as Roger Dedmond, who spent eighteen years in jail for the murder of his wife, until Lee Roy Martin confessed to the crime in May 1967.[555] James Foster was twice identified by the widow of Charles Drake as his slayer and was sentenced to death in 1956; but in 1958 a former police officer confessed to the crime.[556] Robert Watson stood convicted of a homicide until a reporter found the real criminal.[557] Paul Pfeffer was convicted of murder in 1953, but in 1954 Philip Roche confessed to the crime.[558] And several weeks after a court sentenced John Rexinger to death for torture and rape, the real criminal confessed.

Although we try to minimize the number of our judicial mistakes, we are fallible and will inevitably convict some innocent men. All punishment, however, except the death penalty, allows for reversal when error is found, and since error is inherent to the system, reversibility should be an essential feature of all forms of punishment. It is illogical and tragic to make the most severe punishment the system is capable of so permanent and irreversible.

Is the Death Penalty Exacted in a Discriminatory Fashion?

Again, proponents of the death penalty argue that discriminatory punishments are an indictment of the judicial system and not a sound argument against the death penalty. They also point out that even if the charge of discrimination is true, this does not preclude capital punishment from fulfilling its deterrent function. Presently, however, only 1 percent of those accused of capital crimes receive the death penalty.559 To proponents of capital punishment, the charge of arbitrariness means simply that the use of the death penalty should be increased.

Opponents of capital punishment, on the other hand, feel that the death penalty is used in a discriminatory fashion and conclude that no system which allows such capriciousness should be able to inflict this ultimate penalty.

The history of the death penalty reveals that of the 455 men executed for rape since 1930, 405 were black.560 Of all those executed since 1930, 53.5 percent were black.561 The major reason for this preponderance is the discrimination built into our investigatory and judicial procedures—the propensity to complain about Negro offenders. Also, the police are more inclined to arrest blacks, and there is often a prejudicial desire among juries to convict black suspects.562 When the connection between executions and poverty is made, the correlation is close to 100 percent.563

One of the more celebrated cases of discrimination is the Groveland case, in which four Negroes were charged with raping a white woman. The first man was killed by a posse. The second, a 16-year-old, received life imprisonment and refused to allow an appeal because he feared his sentence would be changed to the death penalty. The third was sentenced to death, but when the Supreme Court granted him a retrial the sheriff killed him on the way to court. The fourth man was also sentenced to death, but after the prosecutor stated that he doubted the man was involved, his sentence was commuted to life imprisonment.564

In the famous case of *Hamilton* v. *Alabama*,565 Hamilton, a Negro, evidently entered the apartment of an elderly woman, but there was no claim at the trial that he had touched her. Nevertheless, he was sentenced to death for burglary with intent to commit rape. The Supreme Court overturned his conviction because he had been denied a lawyer at arraignment, and upon retrial he was sentenced to life imprisonment.

Again, statistics and examples are not perfect proof; they cannot determine which juries invoked the death penalty because the defendants were blacks. However, the statistics seem to indicate that something is very wrong, that the system encourages prejudice. Wide discretion is given juries in deciding when to use the death penalty; they pass sentence without instruction from the judges and with no added reports from the attorneys (as in noncapital cases).566 Recently, the Supreme Court even upheld this discretion in the case of Dennis McGauther: in a 6 to 3 decision it held that such power is not offensive to the Constitution.567 But Justice Brennan, in dissenting, held this discretion to be "unguided, unbridled, unreviewable naked power" in violation of due process.568

Thus the structures permit more or less arbitrary application of the death penalty and the prejudices of juries guarantee that this power can be used in a discriminatory fashion. To remedy this, a set of standards could be established and explained to the jury by the judge. Then the defense and the prosecution would submit briefs to the jury to explain why this case did or did not meet these standards. In a questionnaire, the jurors would have to defend their decision.

This method might be of limited value, however, since it may be very difficult to devise equitable standards for deciding who shall live and who shall die. However inaccurate these criteria are, though, they are likely to be a quantum leap in the right direction and better than making the decision on the basis of skin color or income. And the use of the questionnaire would probably preclude jurors from making the life-death decision on prejudicial grounds since they would have to defend their views on a rational basis.

What Should Be Done?

In light of the foregoing analysis, it is the conclusion of the authors that capital punishment has always been cruel and unusual punishment. The fact that the number of executions has decreased makes it a less pressing problem, but only for the present. In a cyclic swing toward repression and "law and order," the number could rise dramatically. Therefore the opportunity to abolish capital punishment should be seized before the evolving standards of decency regress to those of a less enlightened time.

Who Should Do It?

The Supreme Court, characteristically, has avoided the issue of capital punishment. Although a number of petitions are before the court claiming that capital punishment is cruel and unusual punishment and thus is forbidden by the Eighth Amendment,569 the court has not indicated whether it will hear arguments on these petitions. And it appears unlikely to do so in the present session.570 However, many states have delayed executions until the court reaches some decision on this matter. The court has had many chances to declare itself on this issue, but always chose to confine itself to the narrow issues of the cases involved.

It is the court's duty to note the evolving standards of society, and there is mounting evidence that those standards have changed since the court last ruled on the constitutionality of capital punishment. First, the number of people executed has been decreasing steadily. Second, it is becoming increasingly difficult to obtain jurors for capital cases. In a recent case in Pennsylvania, 142 prospective jurors were interviewed before twelve could be selected. Over and over, the jurors stated that they could not order the death penalty under any circumstances. The latter problem should be substantially alleviated by the Supreme Court's decision in *Witherspoon* v. *Illinois*, 391 U.S. 510 (1968). The Court held that it is unconstitutional to exclude all persons who are conscientiously opposed to capital punishment from juries that fix the penalty in capital cases.

Because it is the court's duty to pass on the constitutionality of the death penalty, and because there are grounds for declaring it unconstitutional, and because such a pronouncement does not seem to be forthcoming, Congress could take the initiative and abolish capital punishment on the grounds of section 5 of the Fourteenth Amendment. Such a decision would have to be based on the rationale that capital punishment constitutes a violation of the equal protection clause. From the discriminatory manner in which the death penalty is inflicted, there appear to be adequate grounds for such a finding.

It has been argued, however, that there are two constraints on this congressional power. First, it applies only to state laws which deprive minorities of their rights. Second, the power resides with Congress only when it has special ability to gather the pertinent facts.[571] The first limitation has been questioned of late, since in *Katzenbach* v. *Morgan*[572] the court made note of this power of Congress but no mention of limiting it to enforcing the rights of minority groups. However, to the extent that the limitation is admitted, it would appear that Congress is acting well within its power in striking down a law that is as pernicious to the well-being of the poor and the black as capital punishment appears to be.

The second criterion is also met by Congress, which could utilize its committee mechanism to conduct exhaustive hearings that would help it decide whether the equal protection clause has been violated and whether capital punishment is of any value or runs counter to society's evolving standards of decency.

It appears, therefore, that Congress has the jurisdiction to make a ruling in this area.

Another avenue of abolition is the executives and legislators of the thirty-two states that allow capital punishment. Indeed, governors have the power to affect the process in four ways. First, they can initiate legislation to abolish the death penalty. Second, they can sign such a bill if passed by the state legislatures. Third, they can refuse to enforce the death penalty. Fourth, they can grant clemency in any case where capital punishment is invoked.

The lower courts appear to be unwilling to blaze any new trails with respect to cruel and unusual punishment and the death penalty, preferring to wait until the Supreme Court agrees to decide the issue. For example, the United States Court of Appeals for the Eighth Circuit said in *Maxwell* v. *Bishop*, ". . . if the death penalty for rape is to be nullified on constitutional grounds, that step in the first instance is for the Supreme Court and not for this inferior federal court."   The Supreme Court has declined many invitations to decide that question; on June 28, 1971, however, the Court granted certiorari in four state-court criminal cases on the question, "Does the imposition and carrying out of the death penalty in this case constitute cruel and unusual punishment in violation of the Eighth and Fourteenth Amendments?"[573]

While executive or legislative action may be desirable, capital punishment is too rarely imposed to trigger sustained legislative or executive opposition. In addition, "convicted murderers make a singularly ineffective constituency."[574] Action on this level, therefore, is not likely.

SUMMARY

While the incidence of execution has been declining dramatically, capital punishment is not likely to be abolished, mainly because of attitudinal and political factors. Capital punishment has never been found to be a significant deterrent to capital crimes, but the Supreme Court has avoided the issue of its constitutionality, although there are ample grounds for declaring it unconstitutional. Thus the penalty for this may be the killing of some innocent people, and such sentences are almost certainly applied in a discriminatory fashion.

While it may be that such deaths are a small price to pay, society does not hasten the arrival of the millennium by exacting this penalty by capricious standards. The price we pay should advance the pursuit of perfection, societal and biological. To obtain a better future, we should not resort to the brutal methods of the past.

III Alternatives to
   the Jury System

8 Plea Bargaining

The primary responsibility of any criminal court must be the accurate separation of the innocent from the guilty. The second responsibility, then, is to deal appropriately with those that it determines to be guilty. Under the Constitution, a defendant has a number of important rights which are intended to ensure him a fair trial, and elaborate procedural safeguards have been incorporated into the criminal trial to protect those rights. The prolonged adversary proceeding which results, whether before a judge or a jury, carefully examines the facts of a given case, in a manner consistent with the accused's rights. In those cases in which a court convicts him, he has been given a fair hearing, and his sentence is determined only after careful examination of the offense and the defendant's background. No steps are spared in assuring that criminal trials are conducted fairly.

Most persons imprisoned by the courts today, however, find these elaborate procedural safeguards to be meaningless, because a trial never takes place. The right to trial before a jury, of course, is by no means an obligation; the defendant may exercise the right or he may waive it, as he chooses. If he waives it, no trial need take place. Indeed, the vast majority of criminal convictions are obtained without a trial. Roughly 90 percent of all criminal cases are resolved without trial by a guilty plea.[1]

The mechanics of entering a plea of guilty are quite simple. Each defendant, when brought before a court, is asked to enter a plea, and a plea of not guilty, in effect, constitutes a demand for a trial. But if the plea is guilty, the trial—so to speak—is over before it starts. Unlike a confession given to the police before trial, which is merely evidence, the guilty plea is the entire trial. The defendant waives all right to a trial, to the privileges against self-incrimination, to challenging the evidence against him, and to the offering of a defense of his conduct. The plea admits to all the charges against him. "The plea, once entered, becomes a conviction, and no further evidence is needed to prove the defendant's guilt."2 All that is necessary is the defendant's consent and his assurance that he understands the charges against him and the extent of the legal penalties which could be imposed on him.

The judge, however, is not obligated to accept the plea. If he feels that it is not made voluntarily or that the defendant is not competent to make such a plea, he may refuse to accept it and order a plea of not guilty. This action, however, is rare, for reasons that will shortly be explained. The vast majority of guilty pleas are accepted.

Once the plea is accepted, all that remains is the sentencing. In almost every court, a defendant who pleads guilty can expect a more lenient sentence than one who is convicted as a result of trial.3 The reasons for this are both philosophical and pragmatic. The philosophical basis for this practice is the assumption that admission of guilt is the first step to rehabilitation; the pragmatic (and far more important) reason is that those who cooperate with the state in the rapid disposition of cases should be rewarded. This practice gives a defendant considerable inducement to plead guilty rather than risk a more severe sentence at a trial. Of course, the defendant will carefully consider his chances for acquittal, but where this seems less than promising, his decision can be influenced by the gravity of the sentence if he should be found guilty.4

The Supreme Court has brought guilty pleas within the umbrella of constitutional regulation by holding that they must be taken in accordance with due process of law. In *Boykin* v. *Alabama*, 395 U.S. 238 (1969), the Court ruled that a guilty plea is valid only if it appears on the record that it was made voluntarily and understandingly. This was not the first case that required guilty pleas to be competently made and voluntary; but *Boykin* marked the first time that the legitimacy of the plea had to appear as a matter of record. There is a world of difference between requiring that the validity of a guilty plea appear as a matter of record and requiring a defendant who challenges his own guilty plea to bear the burden of proving that it was coerced, unlawfully induced, or made without an intelligent understanding of its consequences.

It is not certain from *Boykin* precisely how the record must reflect the validity of a guilty plea, although the Court said that due process requires ". . . the utmost solicitude of which courts are capable in canvassing the matter with the accused to make sure he has a full understanding of what the plea connotes and of its consequences." (395 U.S. at 243-44.) Even before *Boykin* the federal courts were required to undertake such measures, and perhaps the provisions of Rule 11 of the Federal Rules of Criminal Procedure will be held to define the scope of the due process requirements of *Boykin*. Rule 11 provides that the court:

... may refuse to accept a plea of guilty, and shall not accept such plea . . . without first addressing the defendant personally and determining that the plea is made voluntarily with understanding of the nature of the charge and the consequences of the plea. . . . The court shall not enter a judgment upon a plea of guilty unless it is satisfied that there is a factual basis for the plea.5

Customarily federal courts comply with Rule 11 by asking the defendant, in open court, whether anyone has promised him any consideration of any kind for his plea of guilty, or has told him what sentence would be imposed. The court will also make sure that the defendant understands the nature of the charges contained in the indictment or information, and will expressly ask the defendant if he did the things alleged therein. Finally, the court will tell the defendant what possible sentence may be imposed, so that he fully understands the consequences of his plea.

PLEA BARGAINING: ITS NATURE AND RAISON D'ETRE

Prosecutors are well aware of the conclusion reached by Professor Donald Newman of the University of Wisconsin: that "compared to the typically long, costly and complex trial, the guilty plea is a model of efficiency, assuring conviction of defendants at small cost to all involved."6 Faced with the fact that our busy courts have time to try about only one defendant in ten, prosecutors know that to convict most of those they believe to be guilty they must rely on a high percentage of guilty pleas. Professor Newman notes that "prosecutors' offices are staffed, court calendars planned, and correctional facilities built in anticipation of this."7

Since judges almost universally dispense lighter sentences to those who plead guilty, prosecutors have taken advantage of defendants' fear of severe punishment to bargain explicitly with them, for assurance of more lenient treatment in return for a guilty plea. This process of plea negotiation was decribed by Michigan law professor Arnold Enker:

In what is probably the best known form, the "plea bargain" consists of an arrangement between the prosecutor and the defendant or his lawyer, whereby in return for a plea of guilty by the defendant, the prosecutor agrees to press a charge less serious than that warranted by the facts which he could prove at the trial. "Less serious" in this context usually means an offense which carries a lower potential maximum sentence.8

Prosecutors may also offer leniency by threatening multiple charges and then offering to drop the added counts in a multiple-count indictment. In other cases, the prosecutor may simply request the judge to be lenient, a request that is usually honored. Nearly every prosecutor must engage in these practices "since he is under extreme administrative pressure from an overwhelming caseload."9

The primary danger in plea bargaining is that the results of criminal proceedings may be anything but just. Before considering such dangers, however, it would be well to examine the reasons why this practice is considered valuable. One reason is that it permits judges and prosecutors to mitigate the harshness of a law, as when an offense carries a minimum sentence which is viewed as unfairly harsh for a particular offender. But, of course, the bargaining system is not necessary in such a case: a prosecutor has the option of lowering charges at his discretion and need not bargain the defendant into a guilty plea.

Other reasons are that an admission of guilt is a necessary first step to rehabilitation, and that persons who cooperate with the state should be rewarded. With respect to rehabilitation, it is probable that more guilty pleas arise from the defendants' desire for a minimum penalty than from true repentance. And rewards usually go only to those who are good negotiators. The process works best for the professional criminal, who knows the system well and is able to manipulate it to "cop a plea." The man who freely admits his guilt without seeking to strike a bargain throws away his negotiating power; though he is likely to be sincerely repentant, he will be given a harsher sentence, and thus is less likely to be helped in the long run.10

For the guilty defendant, plea bargaining can be extremely attractive. As a prominent defense attorney explains:

> If a man is guilty, and the prosecution has a good case, there is little satisfaction to the lawyer or his client in trying conclusions and getting the maximum punishment. A great deal of good can be done in the plodding everyday routine of the defense lawyer by mitigating punishment in this manner. Anyone who has spent a day in prison and experienced even vicariously the indignity and suffering that incarceration entails realizes full well that the difference between a three-year sentence and a five-year sentence is tremendous.11

For the defense lawyer, bargaining can be a satisfying conclusion to a hopeless case. However, there is some doubt as to the fairness of such advantages when those who are unfamiliar with court practices admit their guilt without demanding the aid of counsel. The fact that bargaining bears little relationship to a particular defendant's background and correctional needs makes the process tailor-made for the professional criminal, and extremely difficult to justify on juridical grounds.

Another reason for the bargaining system, of course, is that the administration of justice would collapse without it. The courts would be unable to handle them if all defendants demanded a jury trial.[12] It is generally assumed that defendants are naturally reluctant to admit their guilt and that the inducement of a lower penalty is necessary to assure a steady flow of guilty pleas. But that assumption may not be justified: other nations, which operate without plea bargaining, also have a high ratio of defendants who plead guilty.

It may even be that the strong reluctance of defendants to plead guilty is the precise function of the bargaining system. As a recent study concluded: "The strong reluctance of defendants to admit criminal liability, especially to serious charges . . . may be more a function of the negotiated plea system than a justification for it. It may well be that the long standing practice of granting concessions for guilty pleas has created the general impression that leniency is the quid pro quo for not standing trial."[13]

Thus guilty pleas are essential but the bargaining process may not be necessary to obtain them. But even if the number of guilty pleas induced by bargaining is not measurable, there is a strong likelihood that it helps. If only one out of nine would otherwise plead not guilty and require a trial, the system would have to process twice as many criminal trials.

But even if the plea process is necessary for efficient administration, that alone cannot justify it. Accuracy and fairness should be the primary concerns in a process which determines whether or not a man is imprisoned. As Professor Newman writes: "No matter how administratively efficient, unless the guilty plea process is accurate in its task, and fair in its application, it is less than an adequate means of adjudication."[14] Indeed, the loose and informal procedures which characterize the process pose serious risks.

THE DANGERS OF PLEA BARGAINING

The primary danger in plea bargaining rests in the prosecutor's ability to influence the defendant's decision. Nontrial adjudication rests primarily on the consent of the defendant rather than on the evidence. Unfair pressures which may coerce a defendant's consent must therefore be avoided at all costs. Yet the prosecution's ability to apply pressure of varying degree introduces precisely these sorts of unfair influence.

This is not a situation in which evil-minded prosecutors are out to "get" everyone they can. Rather, it is a function of the strong pressures on the prosecutor to maximize the number of guilty pleas. As Abraham Blumberg says: "All district attorneys' offices have bureaucratic characteristics similar to those of the police commitments to maximize production, the cult of efficiency, the ever-present batting average. And these are characteristics which depersonalize defendants."[15]

Prosecutors under such bureaucratic pressure, yet unhampered by personal involvement with the defendants' welfare, exercise enormous power over the accused; they decide who will or will not be prosecuted. If a defendant is uncooperative, they can threaten to increase the severity of the charges or bring multiple charges for a single act. They can influence the court's decision to grant bail, threatening the defendant with prolonged pretrial imprisonment. For those in jail while awaiting trial, they can threaten to prolong the wait. Professor Blumberg notes that the prosecutor's greatest threat may lie in his "rather awesome advantage in exercising his prerogative of 'calendaring'—making sure that certain cases go before certain judges." It is this power, he says, which "is often the critical factor in how a defendant fares."[16]

In addition to these powers the prosecutor usually has a strong advantage in terms of evidence. At the pleading stage, the defendant is faced with the full weight of the prosecutor's evidence, often amassed at substantial expense through the vast investigative and scientific resources of the state—"a circumstance that makes plea bargaining inevitable, if not mandatory, for most defendants."[17] Few defendants have the financial resources to match this investigative effort, and even those few are frequently intimidated by the apparent strength of the evidence against them.

The first and most obvious danger arising from these pressures is the possibility of inaccurate pleas. Faced with the threat of years of additional imprisonment, or even death, a defendant who acts out of fear may even plead guilty to a crime he did not commit, or to a charge more serious than is warranted by the facts. As Professor Enker writes: "The possibility that innocent defendants might be induced to plead guilty in order to avoid the possibility of a harsh sentence should they be convicted after trial is obviously cause for concern. . . . The truth is that we just don't know how common such a situation is."[18]

Though an accurate count is lacking, the danger is obvious. Hurried prosecutors apply the same plea procedure to all defendants, and after the decision is made to arrest and prosecute, no systematic attempt is made to determine guilt until after the pressure for a guilty plea is applied. Thus, according to Blumberg, the system "propels almost everyone caught up in it, innocent and guilty alike, toward a guilty plea."[19]

It might be argued in defense of this system that innocent defendants are occasionally convicted even in a trial. While that is a possibility, the danger is far greater in the plea process. The trial is a relatively fair, hard-fought debate on the merits of the evidence, but plea bargaining is not a contest—the defendant who accepts the bargain offers no defense. And the biased pressures of plea bargaining are not a factor in a trial.

Moreover, there are occasions on which the prosecutor with a weak case will redouble his efforts to obtain a guilty plea. Many prosecutors tend to apply greater pressure to those against whom their case is weakest.[20] Professor Newman cites a number of cases in Wisconsin where probation officers conducting presentence investigations came to doubt the guilt of the convicted offenders.[21] They concluded that the innocent defendant who pleads guilty is probably rare, but that often the facts did not warrant conviction for the crime charged. Newman says that in many cases "reports cast doubt on the appropriateness of the specific charges, to which the defendants have pleaded guilty, and in other cases the reports have indicated certain defenses or mitigating circumstances that could have been raised at trial."[22]

One cause of pleading guilty to excessive charges may be the pressure applied by a careless prosecutor. More frequent is the defendant's ignorance of his potential bargaining power. A recent study found that "prosecutors occasionally charge a more serious offense than is supported by the evidence in order to gain a more favorable bargaining position."[23] This might be legitimate if bargaining always occurred. Unfortunately, "the defendant or his counsel must explicitly trade the plea of guilty for a reduced charge or sentence."[24] Thus ignorant defendants simply plead guilty and are sentenced on the basis of an overly strict charge.

Failure to seek such a bargain, whether through ignorance, apathy, or intimidation, permits the defendant to be convicted of a more serious offense and receive a more serious sentence than is deemed just by society. A judge in Wisconsin, one of the few who investigates guilty pleas, discovered that "several times a year" a post-plea hearing reveals that defendants could not have been convicted at trial for the offenses to which they plead guilty. Thus, he concludes, the chance of error in a guilty plea is much higher than at a trial.[25]

This constant "overcharging" gives an advantage to those who know the system, usually because they have been convicted on previous occasions, while it penalizes first offenders who are ignorant of their bargaining power and are most easily intimidated by official pressure.

The problem of securing adequate and fair pleas can be largely overcome by a skilled, hard-working defense attorney. He will be able to accurately assess the strength of the state's case and the possibility of acquittal. He will easily recognize an unprovable charge. Such knowledge, in turn, dissuades prosecutors from attempting to try defendants on excessive charges.

There are, of course, limits to even a fine lawyer's value. He cannot make the defendant's choice between a plea of guilty or the risk of a severe sentence; for him this poses problems that even the best legal advice cannot solve. In some cases, even a good lawyer will see the wisdom of pleading an innocent man guilty.26 For example, it may do less harm to an individual's reputation to plead guilty to a disorderly conduct charge than to win acquittal on a morals charge in open court. And in some cases a lawyer may believe that the prosecution's case is so strong that his client stands little chance of acquittal.

A good lawyer cannot guarantee that an innocent man will not go to jail, but he can assess the chance of conviction at trial and thereby improve the fairness and accuracy of the plea bargaining process. Sadly, such assistance is available to too few defendants, the majority of whom are poor and lack both the means to hire a lawyer and a clear understanding of the legal system. Indeed, over 70 percent of all defendants are indigent.27 Although they have the legal right to counsel, Professor Newman states: "Defendants observed in practice apparently interpret the question of whether they want a lawyer to be another way of asking how they intend to plead. If guilty, they waive counsel. Judges typically do not explain to defendants that they may have counsel even if they want to enter a guilty plea."28 As a result, the majority of those who enter guilty pleas are not represented by counsel.29

Unfortunately, those who obtain legal aid may not be any better off, due to the poor quality of the aid available to them. Professor Blumberg notes: "It is the impersonal elements involving the economics of time, labor and expense, together with his commitment to the court organization, that win all the allegiance of most defense attorneys."30 As a consequence, according to a recent article in the *Harvard Law Review*, "the value of such [guilty] pleas to the defense counsel occasionally leads them to enter pleas which are not in the best interests of their client."31 Professor Newman concurs: "In current administration counsel seldom make an adequate effort to ensure that their clients fully understand the guilty plea process."32

An added problem is that many lawyers are incapable of assisting guilty plea defendants due to their own lack of knowledge. According to Newman's study: "The problem is that most lawyers lack the knowledge and skills to really make effective contributions to their clients . . . in the guilty plea system."33

In cases where he is of little positive value, the lawyer can actually be a liability. The blind faith that a confused defendant puts in a lawyer's advice is a severe liability when the latter knows as little as his client about the situation. The extent to which that faith can go was highlighted by a case that Newman found in California.

> A defendant who was being arraigned along with a group of others responded when his name was called and pleaded guilty to a charge of statutory rape. Before he left the courtroom, it was discovered that he was in fact charged with grand theft and that another defendant, who happened to have the same name, was charged with rape. When asked why he pleaded guilty to the rape charge, knowing all along that his offense was theft, the defendant replied, "Well, I thought maybe my attorney had made a deal for me."34

Another disadvantage occurs when a defendant appeals on the grounds that he did not understand the charges or that he was pressured and his plea was therefore involuntary. Though the poor quality of much of the legal assistance available to him makes this a possibility, courts are extremely reluctant to invalidate the pleas of counseled defendants.35

It therefore appears that the right to counsel has been a mixed blessing in assuring the fairness and accuracy of guilty pleas. Ideally, counsel can evaluate a defendant's options accurately and put him on an equal footing with the prosecutor, but few defendants avail themselves of the opportunity for counsel, and those who do find that such aid falls far short of the ideal.

The informality of the proceeding, the standardized sentencing, and the failure of counsel to fully explain the situation to defendants create serious problems later, when prison and correction authorities attempt to deal with convicts. Just as it is difficult to make any sentence beneficial for an innocent man, a convict's claim of innocence is doubly difficult to handle. A man seeking early parole, who insists on his innocence, deserves leniency if he is telling the truth; but if he is lying, his treatment should be different. Correctional authorities admit that there are probably a number of people in every prison who appear to be innocent, or at least not convictable by trial standards,36 and they pose a serious problem. How does one rehabilitate an innocent man?

In addition, the informality of the process creates confusion in a defendant's mind, plus a strong impression that the system works best for whoever manipulates it best. As studies have indicated: "If a defendant comes through the conviction process confused, not fully aware of what happened to him, or embittered and convinced that he could have beaten the rap if only he had had advantages equal to the prosecution's, rehabilitation is very difficult, if possible at all."37

Some have argued that plea bargaining is valuable for correctional purposes in that it allows defendants to believe they have a voice in their sentences.38 In fact, however, most view their own participation as little more than knuckling under to superior force. Professor Newman writes: "Common complaints of prisoners relate not so much to unequal treatment in society at large as to disadvantage with the police, prosecutor, and the judge. Offenders often claim that they did not know what they were doing, what was happening to them, or that so much officialdom was stacked against them that their voice was never heard and their side of the story never understood."39

Extremely serious problems also result from the discriminatory sentencing that can result from plea bargaining, especially for those who don't know enough to bargain and consequently receive much harsher treatment. Often they are first offenders, who are quickly and justifiably embittered at the unduly harsh treatment they receive. Newman's conclusion is that "it is extremely difficult to convince a man who has been sentenced to ten years imprisonment for a certain crime that he has been fairly treated and should bend his efforts to rehabilitation when other inmates, guilty of the same offense . . . are serving two year maximum terms."40

In nearly every instance the primary source of serious problems is the lack of attention that is given to the circumstances of a particular defendant's case. Solutions to the resulting problems, both of accuracy and of appropriateness in conviction and sentencing, are available, but greater effort is required. Above all, it is essential that steps be taken to end the mass production of convicts that all too often is the only result of "criminal justice." Defense attorneys and government officials alike must pay careful attention to each individual's problems.

APPELLATE SUPERVISION OF PLEA BARGAINING

Up to this point the plea bargaining system has been viewed at the operating level of defendant-prosecutor relations—the negotiating process itself. There are, of course, definite in-court standards which must be met, and definite means of appeal if they are not. The effectiveness of court supervision of guilty pleas is the primary check upon their accuracy and fairness.

These checks, however, are limited. It would seem, on the basis of court decisions in related areas, that plea bargaining would be difficult to uphold on constitutional grounds. No less than four possible grounds for rejecting the practice present themselves.

In the first place such pleas may be subject to coercion. Professor Enker of Michigan Law School writes: "Both at common law and pursuant to recent Supreme Court decisions, a confession is deemed coerced and hence inadmissible if it was induced by any promises or threats. A typical inducement invalidating a confession is the proffer of leniency."[41] Thus it could easily be argued, in parallel, that the offer of leniency in exchange for a guilty plea constitutes coercion.

In recent cases in which the government demanded information from its employees on penalty of discharge, the courts held that such action was illegal. *Garrity* v. *New Jersey* involved an employee who had testified under such a threat and the court held that his statements were inadmissible as evidence.[42] In a related case, *Spevak* v. *Klein*, the court held that an attorney could not be disbarred for refusing to testify under such a threat.[43] In both cases it held that the government cannot impose a penalty on the exercise of the right against self-incrimination, and this reasoning could be applied to plea bargaining. The government's implied threat of additional years in prison can readily be viewed as a penalty for exercising one's right against self-incrimination by means of a guilty plea.

In 1968 *United States* v. *Jackson* invalidated the provision of the Lindbergh Act that provided a maximum sentence of life imprisonment if the defendant pleaded guilty or waived his right to a jury trial, but it allowed the death penalty if the defendant demanded a jury trial.[44] The law was reversed because of the danger that the defendant's fear of the death penalty would pressure him to forego his constitutional right to a plea of not guilty and a jury trial. The court ruled that the chilling effect on the exercise of those rights is in itself unconstitutional.[45] The threat of the death penalty in a murder case would have an identical effect, inducing a defendant to forego his right to a jury trial and to plead guilty in exchange for a promise of leniency.

In 1969 *North Carolina* v. *Pearce* held it unconstitutional for a state to punish defendants who appeal their convictions by following "an announced policy of imposing a heavier sentence on every reconvicted defendant."[46] It also held that courts may not impose differential sentences on the basis of noncorrectional factors. The desire of a defendant to prove his innocence at trial can hardly be considered a correctional factor, justifying a heavier penalty. It has been argued, of course, that a defendant who admits his guilt has taken the first step toward rehabilita-tation. But the primary reason for the courts' leniency is, admittedly, to reward the defendant for easing the states' burden of cases.47 Thus plea bargaining involves the higher sentences for noncorrectional factors which *Pearce* bans. If this practice cannot be used to deter defendants from contesting their convictions on appeal, why is it allowed to deter them from contesting their guilt at trial?

Supreme Court decisions thus offer a number of arguments for the unconstitutionality of plea bargaining, as it is presently practiced. But the court has chosen not to apply them. Plea bargaining has been held constitutional in a number of cases, and most recently in the fall of 1970.48 The court has held that the only constitutional requirement is that the plea be voluntarily entered by a competent defendant who has been fully informed of the charges against him and the penalties involved. In 1970, the court held that an offer of leniency does not necessarily divest a plea of its voluntary nature. Even the possibility of the death penalty does not necessarily do that. The logic is that the defendant must be aware of the consequences of his plea; but the mere fact that a plea involves a more severe sentence does not mean that this decision is coerced.

Of course, this is not to say that every threat or promise is legitimate. The standard of voluntariness can be violated by an overenthusiastic district attorney, as was established in *Machibroda* v. *United States*, in which the court held: "A guilty plea, if induced by promises or threats which deprive it of the character of a voluntary act, is void."49 Of course this standard, while permitting the overturning of an involuntary guilty plea, leaves the most important question unresolved. What kinds of promises or threats divest a guilty plea of its voluntary nature? The judgment can be made only on a case-by-case basis. Insecure or unin-telligent persons will be intimidated far more easily than most, and ac-tions that are normally permissible might deprive their decisions of their voluntary character.

In practice, a threat of severe punishment if a trial is demanded has been held improper, but pleas made pursuant to a promise of leniency will be upheld. For example, a man who is charged with armed robbery may be legitimately offered a chance to plead guilty to a charge of un-armed robbery. If the prosecutor demands a guilty plea to the lesser charge upon penalty of prosecution and sentencing under the more seri-ous charge if the defendant demands a trial, the plea is not considered voluntary.

If this distinction seems a bit hard to follow, it is because it does little more than dictate the grammatical form the prosecutor's threat must take. It might be possible for the courts to determine the severity of the threats or promises if the precise form in which they were presented were available, but usually there is no record of the conversations between prosecutor and defendant or defense attorney; so there is no way of judging the degree of coercion.

The voluntariness standard is still of great importance as the basis upon which an inaccurate plea can be appealed. That a defendant is innocent, as a matter of uncontested fact, is not a legitimate ground for appealing a conviction following a guilty plea. It is a matter of evidence, and the plea itself, if voluntary, is considered proof of guilt. Thus the accuracy of the plea is irrelevant to its validity.

This was illustrated in a case before the Michigan supreme court, in which a man without counsel had pleaded guilty to a charge of rape. He appealed his conviction on the ground that he was innocent, and in support of his appeal he offered an affidavit by the woman in question denying that the defendant had raped her. The court ruled that the fact that the crime had not occurred was not relevant; only the voluntariness of the plea was at issue. As the majority concluded: "The record satisfactorily shows that the defendant's plea was voluntarily made. There was no abuse of discretion in denying defendant's motion."[50] There are instances in which courts have overturned voluntary guilty pleas because they were inaccurate, but they are not required to do so.

The problem of appeal, and even the basis of voluntariness, is difficult. The lack of records poses even greater problems for the appellate court than it did for the original trial court. And this problem is aggravated by the fact that the defendant must, in order to present his plea, swear that his plea has not been induced by threats or promises.[51] Everyone involved knows that this is an outright lie, that bargains are the rule, not the exception. But the defendant must swear to the contrary, and later try to convince an appellate body that he was coerced—with no evidence but his own word and in the face of his sworn statement that there was no coercion.

The defendant's plight if he tries to claim that he did not understand the charge is similar. Courts are usually required to explain the charge to him, and in the absence of a transcript there is no hard evidence that this was not done. Again, a condition for the acceptance of the plea is the defendant's statement that he fully understands the nature of the charges to which he pleads.

Thus the primary flaw of the appeals process in guilty plea cases is that "the record of guilty plea convictions is so sparse and contains so little information that it is virtually useless to appellate courts . . . when they are later confronted with the defendant's allegations of unfair or otherwise improper conviction proceedings."52

At the appellate level, this problem is primarily due to the lack of information at the plea hearing. No evidence is required, and although federal courts and some state courts are required to make an inquiry into the factual bases of pleas, these inquiries are usually perfunctory and generally ignored.53 Thus the accuracy of a plea is seldom investigated in the courts.

Nor is sentencing especially appropriate. The same lack of information, combined with the usual acceptance of the prosecutor's negotiated agreement, means that penalties have little to do with correctional factors. Rehabilitation, and even consistent and fair sentencing, are sacrificed for the sake of administrative efficiency.

ALTERNATIVES WITHIN THE SYSTEM

Throughout the criminal justice system administrative needs are primary; the accuracy and appropriateness of penalties are distinctly of second priority. The need for more provisions to assure justice is clear. Short of the drastic step of outlawing plea bargaining, several steps could be taken to improve the situation.

Much of the problem in the appellate process could be resolved if the bargaining were formalized, with a court officer, perhaps a judge different from the one who heard the trial, presiding over it. Also bargaining sessions could be regularly scheduled before the trials, and held in the open with accurate records.

Such an approach would ease the difficulties associated with the appeals process, and also ease the inequities imposed on those who lack the knowledge to bargain effectively. The correctional problems that result from the inequity and from the confusion generated by informal practices would be alleviated by a procedure in which the defendant's position was clearly explained to him and to his attorney by an officer of the court. And the very presence of the attorney and the court officer, plus the knowledge that a record is being kept, would deter prosecutors from subjecting defendants to overly harsh pressures.

Second, the investigation into the factual situation behind a plea should be substantially expanded into a thorough examination of the circumstances of the crime. This requires more than a perfunctory statement of the evidence, since the prosecutor will have a prima facie case in all but the weakest cases. Only if the evidence is challenged by the defendant, or by a thorough investigation by the court or a staff responsible to the court, will flaws in the case appear and mitigating circumstances and legitimate defenses be found. If this were done well, the expense would be substantial, but much less than the costs of a full trial.

A careful investigation of the facts would ease several problems. It would help balance the early advantage of the prosecutor. It would reveal facts upon which mitigating circumstances or legitimate defenses might be founded. It would reveal flaws in the prosecution's case that are not apparent before trial, thus reducing the likelihood that a man could be compelled to plead guilty when a trial would acquit him. Overly serious charges would be revealed, and defense attorneys, even those unfamiliar with the negotiating process, would be able to advise their clients with clear knowledge of the situation.

Another valuable though less practical reform would require a defense attorney to be present at all bargaining sessions to assure fairness and a sound evaluation of the situation. The practical limit, in this instance, is the limited number of experienced lawyers who are qualified to give such advice. A requirement like this, however, would maximize the use of qualified persons. And a formal procedure, with rules and procedural safeguards, would increase the number of qualified lawyers who have the knowledge to be of value in such situations.

The final, drastic solution is the prohibition of plea bargaining; but this might not be as impractical as it appears. As indicated earlier, there is no evidence that the number of guilty pleas would be substantially reduced without bargaining. More critically, as the *Harvard Law Review* recently noted, "much of the harm threatened by the abolition of plea bargaining can be avoided by providing the additional resources necessary for more trials."[54] If the increase in the number of trials is not massive, the additional cost will be trifling.

As indicated in part II, the criminal-court system could easily be expanded if we were willing to pay the cost. The issue, then, is a value judgment. Currently, it seems that accuracy and fairness are less important than a relatively small amount of money. Surely, even in so materialistic a society as we have become, that judgment is open to severe criticism.

9 Juvenile Courts

To imprison adolescents or children for their wrongdoings or youthful excesses has always seemed fundamentally incorrect. For youths who are simply confused by the process of growing up, or are simply immature, to be confined with hardened criminals would guarantee the most counterproductive solution possible. It would ensure that the antisocial attitudes which led to their incarceration would be strengthened, leading to still more violent conflicts with society.

At the beginning of the twentieth century legal reformers became especially concerned about the welfare of young criminals, who might easily be reformed with proper handling. Convinced that one youthful mistake should not be permitted to ruin a life and propel an individual toward a career of crime, they sought to create a separate court system in which the problems of young persons could be discovered and corrected without subjecting them to a criminal proceeding. Thus by the mid-1930s virtually every state had established a juvenile court system that was dedicated to benevolent treatment rather than punishment.[55]

The very fact of separation of young offenders from cynical and callous criminals is of great importance. Keeping their court records confidential is an allied benefit; it protects them from job discrimination and other kinds of informal retribution later in life. For many, such protection is essential to establish the confidence necessary for successful rehabilitation, rather than automatic punishment, because many youths are arrested for offenses which they may not consider serious. For some, the mere fact of arrest may dramatize the seriousness of their antisocial conduct, but punishment may easily embitter them, turning them permanently against the system and society in general. Many young criminals are rebelling against intolerable treatment or negligent parents, or suffering from a social or psychological disturbance, and often the need is for psychiatric care or a better environment. Referral to welfare or counseling agencies can help provide them a better future—at least this is the theory.

In practice, the juvenile courts have been failures in almost every respect, primarily because of the way they have operated. Informal hearings were substituted for trials and heavy reliance was placed on the investigations of social workers and probation officers. The right to counsel was denied and most procedural safeguards were eliminated on the grounds that they would produce an adversary system in which there could not be frank and open discussions.

All this, of course, was well intentioned, and with sufficient resources and personnel might have succeeded. However, Americans have never been partial to spending money to "coddle criminals," and the idea of establishing an elaborate system to aid juvenile delinquents and "young hoodlums" was unpopular. As a result, the juvenile courts suffered: the staffing and other necessary resources were not forthcoming. Skilled personnel to provide counseling on an individual basis could not be hired and juvenile-court judges were not provided the proper sort of rehabilitation facilities.

Thus the informality of the juvenile proceeding became its greatest liability instead of a potential strength. Under the pressure of heavy calendars and understaffing, the envisioned hearings to inquire into a child's welfare degenerated into perfunctory trials in which guilt was presumed. The spirit of cooperation with which the system was supposed to operate was transformed into pressure on juvenile offenders to confess their guilt. Those who maintained they were innocent were presumed to be incorrigible and received long periods of imprisonment. Unchallenged hearsay, even the unproved allegations of a spiteful neighbor, became grounds for removing children from their parents in favor of a correctional school which resembled a prison. The immense discretion of the judge to define delinquency, though intended to allow him to protect those who had committed no offense but were living in a deleterious environment, became grounds for jailing children for "being in danger of falling into habits of vice." The absence of procedural safeguards became the source of arbitrary and unlimited control of young people's lives by a juvenile-court judge.

In short, the system attempted to implement a fine idea in an ill-funded and ill-equipped manner. The inadequate resources and staff, combined with excessive discretion, have made the juvenile courts little more than institutes of injustice.

JUVENILE OFFENDERS

The primary source of danger in the juvenile court system is the range of its authority. Not only lawbreakers but all "wayward" children can be brought before these courts. The court can legally deal with any youth who is deemed delinquent, and delinquency can mean virtually anything the court decides—not only violations of the law but such offenses as "associating with bad companions," "willful disobedience of parents," "being in pool rooms or other bad places," "swearing," "smoking," and "being in danger of falling into habits of vice."[56] The purpose of such statutes is to permit the court to deal with all who transgress in whatever minor way, and even those who are considered in danger of transgressing.[57] Delinquency is whatever behavior officials choose to define it as, and the statutes are written accordingly. In New Jersey, for example, the statutory definition of delinquency is "incorrigibility, immorality, or growing up in idleness or delinquency."[58] Tautological, to say the least.

Some have argued that such discretion is necessary to deal with the rise in juvenile crime in recent years. As J. Edgar Hoover notes, juvenile crime is the fastest-growing portion of serious crimes: "Between 1960 and 1967, the arrests of juveniles for serious crimes increased 57 percent, while the juvenile population increased only 22 percent."[59] And commenting on crime statistics for 1970, Harvard criminologist Lloyd E. Olin noted that teenagers have been largely responsible for the rapid rise in the crime rate.[60]

But the existence of a crime problem hardly justifies the arbitrary action that stems from unbridled police discretion. In adult crime, the number of crimes has never been a sufficient rationale for the arbitrary denial of a man's freedom. It is no more justifiable to impose such treatment on the young, but this has been done to a considerable degree. The very existence of such statistics on juvenile crime should be evidence that the system is not working well.

Most important, however, is the fact that the discretion made possible by vague laws does not operate against serious offenders, though it is used to arrest and jail vast numbers of adolescents who are not guilty of serious offenses. If young people were receiving the benevolent treatment envisioned in the law, this discretion might be acceptable; but they are not.

Each year, thousands of youths whose actions fall far short of any definition of criminal behavior are imprisoned. F.B.I. statistics reveal that 1.5 million juveniles are taken before juvenile courts every year,[61] and among them are thousands who would be found completely innocent in the regular criminal courts. However, their chances of being sent to correctional schools are higher than the chances of imprisonment for those who have violated major laws. As the *Pennsylvania Law Review* observed: "According to national juvenile court records, children alleged to have violated laws that apply only to juveniles, such as curfew regulations, and children variously designated as 'ungovernable,' 'incorrigible,' or 'in need of supervision,' account for 25 percent of the total number of juveniles brought before the courts and for 30 percent of the population of state institutions for delinquent children."[62]

The vast discretion permitted the police and court officials in the determination of delinquency and the subsequent handling of delinquents presents another vast potential for abuse which can be found at all levels. Although the functions of police, judge, and court investigators frequently overlap, the following sections will use the divisions employed by the Supreme Court in the case of *in re Gault:*[63] pre-judicial, adjudicative, and post-adjudicative.

Pre-Judicial Procedures

The wide latitude given to officials in defining juvenile crimes means that this kind of pretrial investigation is governed by much less formality than normal criminal cases. In practice, this means more frequent abuses and fewer rights. As the President's Commission on Law Enforcement and the Administration of Justice observed: "Statutes often define juvenile delinquency so broadly as to make virtually all youngsters delinquent."[64]

The police do not, of course, arrest all youths who could be brought before a juvenile court, but the decision is based on a number of subjective criteria that make the system unfair and discriminatory. Whether a youth is arrested for "growing up in idleness," "being in a pool hall," or "in bad company" depends very much upon how he acts in the presence of the police. Arrogance, assertion of one's rights, or even acting unflustered by the experience is sufficient to brand a youth as incorrigible.[65] And the likelihood of arrest for petty actions skyrockets for those who live in slums. Police assume that young black ghetto residents will be antisocial, and this attitude quickly becomes self-fulfilling. Inner-city children learn to anticipate a hostile and unfair attitude on the part of the police, and such hostility leads to arrests. It is common for them to be arrested for activities that are unnoticed in the white suburbs.

Similar discrimination exists in determining which juveniles will be referred to the courts for further action. The approximately 50 percent who are arrested but are released without referral to the courts[66] are, for the most part, those who appear humble and contrite or frightened by the experience. Those who resist or deny their guilt, and even those who show no fear, are almost invariably sent to court. In effect, youths are punished for failing to cringe before authority. Such juveniles are often held in custody, sometimes in jails with adults, during the period before they appear in court.

The investigation of a juvenile case is seldom a taxing matter for the police because the circumstances leading to an arrest are generally sufficient to justify bringing the youth before the court. In court, findings are almost universally based on a combination of evidence from two sources: the youth's confession and the report of the probation officer or social worker.

The number of cases in which juveniles admit their guilt is almost unbelievable: by the end of the court hearing nearly all juvenile offenders have confessed. Moreover, a large proportion of these confessions are involuntary[67] because of the strong pressure applied by the welfare worker or the police. And because the entire system is focused on assisting wayward youths, most officials assume that all the youths they deal with are wayward. Therefore confession is seen as a good thing for the youth, representing the first step to rehabilitation.[68] Attempts to deny guilt, on the other hand, are automatically viewed as evidence of incorrigibility, never as signs of innocence.

Most youths quickly learn how this process works, and many are told that things will be much better for them if they admit their guilt. Whether this sort of pressure creates fear or trust probably varies with the individual, but studies have indicated that it is effective in obtaining confessions. However, the nature of the interrogation and the susceptibility of the accused cast strong doubt upon their accuracy.

The validity of these confessions is a matter of peculiar importance, since they are used to justify lengthy sentences in juvenile detention homes. However, every citizen is supposed to be protected against such involuntary self-incrimination; no one may be compelled to testify against himself, and since the 1966 decision in *Miranda* v. *Arizona*, police have been required to advise all suspects of that right.[69] However, the rule that confessions obtained in the absence of such warnings cannot be used as evidence has not been applied to juvenile courts. Police may interrogate juveniles freely, and confessions gained in this way can be used to prove delinquency.

Because juvenile court proceedings are considered to be civil rather than criminal, none of the normal criminal procedural safeguards are applied to juvenile trials.70 But the *Gault* case (cited earlier), which is the first break in this wall, held that juveniles have the right of freedom from involuntary self-incrimination at the adjudication stage. But as *Gault* also stated that the special circumstances prior to adjudication merit different treatment, the Supreme Court refused to extend the right against self-incrimination to pre-judicial situations. As a consequence, protection from coerced confessions before a juvenile gets to court is almost nonexistent. For those who are sent to the criminal courts, protection is only slightly better.

There have been cases in which the confessions of juveniles were invalidated on grounds of coercion. But proof of coercion is difficult to establish. The Supreme Court held in *Gallegos* v. *Colorado* that a confession to robbery and murder, obtained from a 14-year-old boy after a five-day detention period in which he was permitted to see neither a lawyer nor his parents, was invalid.71 Yet the Court noted that it was only the excessive period of detention, not the denial of counsel, which convinced the Court that coercion was involved. Normally, any seemingly voluntary confession by a juvenile will be admitted in criminal courts. Thus the danger of a coerced or involuntary confession is substantial.

The second major source of evidence is usually an investigative officer of the court. He will issue recommendations based on his findings about a youth's background, findings that may contain all sorts of hearsay allegations relevant to the youth's tendencies and prospects. This information is almost never traced to the original sources or examined in the trial, yet these investigations can seriously prejudice the juvenile's case in court. In many instances the results of the investigatory officer's report are known to the judge prior to his determination of the case;72 thus the rules of procedure that are supposed to be followed in the trial may be rendered useless by the knowledge. If any of the controls applied to adjudication are to be useful, they must be extended to the pre-judicial stage, which is all too often prejudicial as well.

It is on these two primary evidentiary sources, coerced confessions and investigatory conclusions, that the case is put before a judge for adjudication.

Adjudicative Procedures

A number of serious problems also exist at the adjudication level, or the trial before the juvenile court, in addition to the possibility of pretrial prejudice. One of these is the vagueness of the charges that most juveniles face. Some 30 percent of the juveniles who have been institutionalized were found guilty of such indefinable offenses as "being in need of supervision." A clear finding of fact in such instances must await a clear statement of the law.

Unreasonable vagueness has been deemed by the Supreme Court to be grounds for invalidating a law, in civil as well as criminal proceedings.[73] As the court wrote: "A statute which forbids or requires the doing of an act in terms so vague that men of common intelligence must necessarily guess at its meaning and differ as to its application violates the first essential of due process."[74] *Gault* applied this to juvenile courts, to an extent, by holding that these courts are "required to set forth the alleged misconduct with particularity."[75] It is not certain, however, that this means anything more than a clear statement of the language of the law violated and the acts of the accused because the court has not used this requirement to strike down vague statutes.

This was clearly demonstrated in the case of a 17-year-old Connecticut girl who was incarcerated in 1966 under a statute which allowed the state to assume responsibility for girls between ages of sixteen and twenty-one who are "in danger of falling into habits of vice." The girl was also convicted on a second, equally explicit charge of "walking with a lascivious carriage."[76] Her lawyer appealed on the grounds that the law was unconstitutionally vague, but both the Connecticut and the United States supreme courts refused to overturn the conviction. The girl remained in a correctional institute, though the conditions therein almost guaranteed even greater danger of falling into habits of vice.

A second major problem in the adjudication stage stems from the low quality of the judicial personnel, both judges and staff. If the juvenile courts are to fulfill their intended role of examining a child's needs and providing proper treatment, skilled and experienced personnel are essential. Unfortunately, as Justice Fortas lamented in the *Gault* decision, though good will, compassion, and similar virtues are prevalent throughout the system, expertise, the keystone of the process, is lacking.[77] As *Christian Science Monitor* correspondent Howard James wrote: "A recent study of juvenile court judges shows that half had no undergraduate degree. A fifth had no college education at all. A fifth were not lawyers. And nearly three fourths of them spent less than one quarter of their time handling juvenile and family matters. Most admitted they really didn't know if they were doing a good job."[78]

Juvenile proceedings, though established as informal hearings so as to provide special care, are hampered by the absence of the necessary skills, which means that the supposed beneficiaries have neither legal protection nor regular care and are tried and disposed at the whim of the least educated and least qualified judges in our country.[79] Again, according to Justice Fortas, "the child receives the worst of both worlds: he gets neither the protection accorded to adults nor the solicitous care and regenerative treatment postulated for children."[80]

In response to this situation and the serious injustices which could arise in the absence of legal rights or procedural safeguards, the Supreme Court decided, in *Gault*, to extend certain rights to juveniles. Gerald Gault had been sentenced to a correctional school for up to six years for making an obscene phone call, but the court had a number of reasons for rejecting this conviction. The neighbor upon whose complaint he was convicted had not appeared in court to testify, Gault had been denied a lawyer, and neither he nor his parents had been informed of the precise charge against him.

The court rejected the traditional position that the rights available in criminal cases are not necessary in juvenile hearings. Recognizing that the system was not the benevolent process it was intended to be, the court held that where an individual's freedom may be curtailed for a period of years, certain rights must be observed. Specifically, the court required: (1) notice to both parents and child sufficiently in advance of the hearing; (2) notice of the alleged misconduct, stated with particularity; (3) notification to both parents and child of the right to counsel, with one to be appointed by the court if they are unable to afford one; (4) the right against self-incrimination; and (5) the right of confrontation and cross-examination of witnesses.

While this decision will do much to protect juveniles, three important reservations remain. The first, of course, is that *Gault*'s provisions apply only to the trial, not to the pretrial investigation, wherein much injustice and discrimination occurs. The second is that confessions are still permitted in the absence of counsel. This is a serious limitation, since judges often pressure juveniles into confessions of guilt. As the court noted in the Gallegos case, notice of the right to counsel may not be of much value. "A 14-year-old youth, no matter how sophisticated, is unlikely to have any conception of what is happening to him."[81] His parents are also notified, but studies indicate that most delinquents come from broken homes, and parental neglect is a frequent cause of the problem. Parents often do not even appear at the hearing.[82]

The third limitation concerns the admissibility of hearsay or second-hand evidence. *Gault* demands that witnesses appear and be subject to cross-examination but does not prohibit witnesses from relating hearsay. Since the primary witness is usually the probation officer, and much of his testimony is based on hearsay, a good deal of evidence is beyond scrutiny. The court took an additional step in 1970 in the case of *in re*

Winship,[83] which required proof beyond a reasonable doubt that the child had committed the act of which he was accused. But the decision does not specify the means by which that proof must be established. It does, however, suggest the beginning of a more substantive requirement for juvenile courts by following the rules of evidence that are required in criminal trials.

Use of the Jury

As the Supreme Court has begun to require juvenile court hearings to be accurate finders of fact, there has been increasing interest in the use of jury trials in juvenile cases. Currently, juries are put to extremely limited use in juvenile proceedings. No state utilizes them for the initial hearing, although a few allow juries to hear appeals. But it is clear that the states have the authority to make greater use of the jury if they so choose.[84]

However, the Supreme Court has decided that trial by jury is not constitutionally required in the adjudicative phase of state juvenile court proceedings.[85] Chief Justice Burger and Justices Stewart, White, and Blackman viewed the jury as an unnecessary component of accurate fact-finding and so not a prerequisite of "fundamental fairness"—the test for due process of law. They feared that requiring trial by jury would convert juvenile proceedings into fully adversary processes, thereby ending the "idealistic prospect of an intimate, informal protective proceeding." Justice Brennan concurred with the majority, believing that jury trials in juvenile proceedings were unnecessary if another aspect of the process (for example, the right to a public trial) protected the offender's interests. Justice Harlan voted with the majority on the ground that the Sixth and Fourteenth Amendments do not even require trial by jury in adult criminal cases.

If the goal of current court decisions is to improve the fact-finding accuracy of the juvenile procedure, extension of the right to trial by jury may be of considerable value in several respects. The *Indiana Law Journal* enumerates them:

> A number of factors attest to the need of the right to a jury trial in the juvenile system. First, if a juvenile court judge is expert, it is not in fact-finding but in determining what care and treatment is needed for each individual defendant. Second, as both *Gault* and *Kent* indicate, the dangers of judicial arbitrariness in juvenile proceedings are real. The jury system is an essential safeguard against arbitrariness because it assures that the decision will not be influenced by the impact which similar past cases may have

on the mind of a judge trying the facts. Third, it prevents decisions being made by a single individual, the judge, who frequently has access to or has participated in preparing facts prior to the adjudication stage which may be prejudicial to the youth. Fourth, the function of a jury to evaluate the credibility of each witness regardless of how often he has appeared in court, or how well known he may be to judge, is particularly desirable in the juvenile court system where the probation officer who is the official arm of the juvenile judge appears as a witness to support the case against the youth.[87]

It seems apparent, in light of these conclusions, that the adjudication stage is the best-regulated part of the juvenile process. Court decisions have regarded the constitutional procedures of the criminal trial essential to a juvenile trial as well. They have prompted a substantial number of states to initiate statutory reforms to improve the fact-finding accuracy of the juvenile system, to ensure that all who receive rehabilitation are in need of it. Finally, the extension of the right to a jury trial may offer a means of furthering the accuracy of the process.

Post-Adjudicative Problems

The manner in which juvenile courts have disposed of the young people brought before them leaves much to be desired. While, in theory, they are supposed to be given guidance and corrective treatment, the courts must generally choose between releasing them or punishing them with imprisonment.[88] In fact, the many thousands who are sent to state correctional schools receive no more assistance than they would in a penitentiary.[89] And in most cases, those who misbehave may be transferred to regular prisons, even if they have not committed a crime. Wisconsin law professor Seymour Hallett notes: "As our juvenile institutions become more crowded, the number of 'unmanageable' delinquents transferred to reformatories or prisons is rapidly increasing."[90] John F. X. Irving, executive director of the National Council of Juvenile Court Judges, estimates some 100,000 juveniles are placed in adult prisons each year.[91]

A second major injustice in the disposition of these cases is the harshness of the sentences. While juveniles' offenses are frequently petty, short sentences are rare.[92] Mere children are often sent to state institutions until their eighteenth or twentieth birthday—in effect a sentence of several years for offenses that would carry a light sentence in criminal court. Gerald Gault received two years for making an obscene phone call, whereas an adult would get a maximum sentence of two months upon conviction. The girl in Connecticut, who was convicted of "walking with a lascivious carriage," was sent to the reformatory at age seventeen, to remain there until she was twenty-one. The maximum sentence an adult could have received for soliciting for prostitution is one month—not the four years she ultimately served.

In one respect the *Gault* decision may have helped the rehabilitative efforts. The studies cited in the decision claimed that the informality of the fact-finding procedure, far from creating the trust and cooperation that was intended, was creating hostility in juveniles by implanting the conviction that they were being arbitrarily dealt with and betrayed by the system. As the President's commission noted in 1967: "Efforts to help and heal and trust, if they are to have any chance of success, must be based on an accurate determination of facts."93

NEGLECTED CHILDREN

One of the great difficulties of the juvenile courts is that they deal with neglected children and juvenile delinquents in virtually identical fashion. Two serious problems arise from this treatment. First, many states treat the two categories in precisely the same type of hearing. Neglected children, unwanted and ignored by their families, are hauled before the court and disposed of as if they had committed an offense. That is unjust in itself, since the fault, if any, is the parents'. And it is grossly compounded by the institutional treatment they are subjected to.

The second problem is the lack of control over the parents of such children. Often the products of broken homes, these children become the responsibility of a juvenile court which has but limited knowledge of the parents and no control over them, though they are the source of the problem. As Howard James notes:

> In almost any city in the nation, a single family may be involved in hearings in several different courts. A juvenile court passes on a charge of delinquency involving the children . . . a divorce court entertains a suit for divorce, alimony, and custody . . . a court of civil jurisdiction entertains an action for goods furnished to an abandoned wife by a grocer . . . and a criminal or domestic relations court deals with charges of desertion and non-support.94

Clearly, all of those actions should be settled in a consistent manner by a court that has jurisdiction over the entire family. This would reduce the need for institutionalizing children who are merely neglected, as opposed to actual delinquents. In this respect, the system of justice for juveniles would be drastically improved.

10 First Amendment Rights

Few values are as important, or fragile, as those embodied in the First Amendment to the Constitution, wherein is secured the freedom of thought, expression, and association necessary for individual fulfillment in a free society. The amendment is short and direct: "Congress shall make no law respecting an establishment of religion, or prohibiting the free exercise thereof, or abridging the freedom of speech, or of the press, or the right of the people to peaceably assemble and to petition the government for a redress of grievances."[95] Yet the interpretation of this brief command has provoked a long and often bitter controversy, in which divergent conceptions of American life have struggled for preeminence.

This chapter will examine the relationship between trial by jury and the First Amendment. It will treat the broad question of establishing standards for distinguishing behavior protected by this amendment from that subject to social control. The related but narrower issue of the appropriate roles of judges and juries in First Amendment cases will also be considered. Crucial to a comprehension of both inquiries is familiarity with the specific justifications for prohibiting the abridgment of thought, expression, and association.

VALUES OF FREE SPEECH

Philosophical Background

The roots of free speech doctrine reach to the birthplace of Western philosophy. Plato's dialogue, *The Apology*, relates the argument of

Socrates for his right to think and teach as he pleased. More recently, the thread of libertarian thought ran through the philosophy of Francis Bacon, John Milton, Benedict de Spinoza, and John Locke. It emerged most forcefully in the polemics of eighteenth-century English radicals and the writings of Jeffersonian politicians, and found its most eloquent expression in John Stuart Mill's essay *On Liberty*. In the twentieth century in the United States, the doctrine of free expression has been elucidated by philosophers, legal scholars, journalists, sociologists, psychologists and, most importantly, the justices of the Supreme Court.

Mental Development

The values of free speech, as elaborated over the years, relate to both the individual and the community. Each person should be able to realize his potential for reasoned thought, imagination, insight, and knowledge. None of these capacities can properly develop if beliefs are strictly concerned and thought is directed along proper paths. Critical thinking and creativity are stifled unless the mind is free to explore alternative modes of cognition and consciousness. The foundation of intellect, however, requires more than the sanction of unmolested thought. The individual must be free to express his ideas and to consider the opinions of others. Dialogue with the self can serve to sharpen the mind and test new hypotheses. In general, however, mental facilities are extended and concepts refined when one is exposed to critical comment and fresh perspective. Thought patterns congeal and creativity shrivels when the individual cannot perceive multiple models of experience. Most insidious is the fact that convictions molded by the selective import of ideas and information often appears to be the result of discriminating intelligence. Unless freedom of expression is preserved, true mental autonomy may dissolve into a false affirmation of liberty.

Psychological Well-being

As the physical well-being of modern man has been enhanced, his psychological health has been jeopardized, and the most trenchant analysis of this trend is offered by psychologist Erich Fromm. Discarding Freud's static conception of man and society, Fromm believes that the two are in constant interaction, each serving to shape the other. Thus Fromm states that the constituents of industrial society have dramatically altered our psychological status. Modern man is no longer in unison with nature, or integrated into a structured, homogeneous society, or joined by a common religion. Yet the freedom that resulted from severing these bonds entails new torments. Alienated from the economic forces that now dominate his existence and overwhelmed by the vastness and complexity of his world, the individual lacks security. Facing the world as an isolated entity, he feels "powerless and alone, anxious and insecure."[96]

Seeking to relieve these tensions, many have forfeited their freedom. They have sought security by submitting to authority, by destroying those who seem threatening, and by mechanically following the trend of common opinion. They have resolved the dilemma of freedom by forging new chains to bind themselves. These tendencies are apparent in Richard Nixon's so-called silent majority: submission to presidential authority; uncritically supporting presidential aims and actions; blind patriotism, which submerges the self in devotion to country; violent reaction to hippies, Black Panthers, peace marchers, and others who challenge such mechanisms. None of these, however, satisfactorily resolves the problems of isolation. Not only do they cripple spontaneity and compassion, they fail to bring tranquillity; and doubt and anxiety remain.[97]

Freedom of speech alone will not counteract these self-destructive attempts to "escape from freedom." Only by preserving such liberty can the trend toward authoritarianism, destructiveness, and conformity be combatted. Curtailment of dissent would give unrestrained momentum to those forces that seek to compel uniformity. Moreover, a productive and healthy solution of individual detachment demands freedom of expression, and such a resolution involves the spontaneous activity of man's true self. "Spontaneous activity is the one way in which man can overcome the terror of aloneness without sacrificing the integrity of his self; for in the spontaneous realization of the self man unites himself anew with the world—with man, nature, and himself."[98] Clearly, such spontaneity could not develop in a society where thought, expression, and association are controlled by external authority.

Search for Truth

Facilitating the quest for knowledge is an important function of the good society. Truth not only heralds technological advance, it provides guidelines for public policy and our private lives, and is a legitimate end in itself. But the pursuit of truth is crippled by the limitation of thought and expression. Even slight restrictions on free speech may silence the one man who has a new insight.[99] Truth is best sought in an atmosphere conducive to the clash of ideas. All judgments must be subject to comment, revision, and rejection; all lines of inquiry must be open.

Even if an issue seems settled beyond reasonable doubt, free inquiry and discussion must continue. The most final, deeply rooted tenets of past ages have been proved false (e.g., that the earth is the center of the universe) or have been found to be partial truths (e.g., Newtonian physics). Man's wisdom is limited, and must always be subject to question.100

A philosopher and holy man once asked: "What does it mean when people say that Truth goes all over the world?" and he answered: "It means that Truth is driven out of one place after another, and must wander on and on."101 As this saying indicates, truth will not spontaneously germinate and take root. Guaranteeing freedom of speech is one means of furnishing the conditions and cultivation it requires.

Vitalizing Doctrine

Even if dissenting opinion is false, its articulation is valuable. If correct opinion is not vigorously contested, it loses its potency and may deteriorate into platitude or prejudice. On the one hand, it has little or no effect on our thought or behavior; on the other hand, it is applied in a reflexive, nonrational way. This has happened to many vital ideas of our democracy: they have become sterile recitations or, even worse, the blind prejudices of ignorant, unthinking people.

Moreover, the meaning of a doctrine can be lost unless it is challenged and debated. A once lively opinion can become "enfeebled and deprived of its vital effect on character and conduct, the dogma becoming a mere formal profession, inefficacious for good, but cumbering the ground and preventing the growth of any real and heartfelt conviction from reason or personal experience."102 Our beliefs about communism, for example, have suffered from this degeneration; founded in a different historical context and generally exempted from dispute, they have become meaningless dogma, unrelated to current realities.

Promotion of Change

The collective volition of society is no more perfect than individual judgments. Even when the ends of public policy are not in dispute, the chosen means may be hotly contested. Majority approval alone is not the touchstone of valid decision. Moreover, rarely does policy emanate from the common will; it is shaped by small, self-serving groups with special access to the various levels of power. Thus societal decisions may fail to promote the general welfare, and may even degrade human dignity.

Unfettered criticism of the existing order is the first-line remedy for misguided policy. Change induced by open debate is deeper and more lasting than that engineered by coercion or deception. Such progress involves true conversion rather than a reaction to pressure, and it is legitimized by broad participation in the decision process. Under ideal conditions, free speech preserves a delicate balance between stability and constructive change.

Suppression of thought, expression, and association forces dissent into patterns of cunning and compulsion. If critics cannot pursue progress through argument and petition, they must resort, even for minor innovations, to violence or intrigue. Not only is change provoked in this manner inherently unstable, but the process itself has costly side effects.

Maintenance of Democracy

This point need not be elaborated. Although common opinion often produces less than optimal policy, the process of majority rule, tempered by minority safeguards, is still the best way that has yet been devised to resolve societal conflict. Clearly, the efficacy of this process depends upon free expression. Democracy is an illusion unless people are free to form opinions and make them available to others. Furthermore, as was previously mentioned, dysfunction often develops even in a soundly conceived democracy when inordinate power is seized by private factions. Under these circumstances, sufficient guarantees of expression are most important; otherwise, elite groups will exert maximum pressure for controlled conformity.

A Dissenting View

Conservative spokesmen have not directly disputed the values of free expression; instead, they have sidestepped the issue by asserting the need to balance freedom of speech against other societal demands. Left-wing critics, however, most notably Herbert Marcuse, have frontally assaulted the utility of tolerance in all but ideal communities.

Marcues argues that American society is controlled by a ruling establishment whose interests conflict with the fundamental values of peace,

211

security, and individual development. This group, through its preeminence, so tightly regulates public opinion that people are duped into accepting its goals as just and desirable. Under these circumstances, he argues, freedom of expression cannot promote constructive change. In fact, it can be a regressive force, for the existence of free speech lulls the public into believing that it actually shapes its own destiny. The belief that the destructive, self-serving practices of the ruling class stem from common consent and promote the societal welfare can derive only from toleration of the evil forces that currently dominate society.103

Marcuse would grant free expression only to groups that strive for progressive change. The criteria for this allocation of tolerance, he argues, need not rest on a value judgment but can be empirically determined. Defining progress as the "reduction of cruelty, misery, and suppression," Marcuse contends that it is possible to "identify policies, opinions, and movements" which advance these goals and those which do not. The historical record reveals, he says, that progress stems only from the activities of oppressed classes and from revolution conducted on their behalf and in their interest. "Liberty, tolerance, then, would mean intolerance against movements from the Right and toleration of movements from the Left."104

Marcuse's contention that formal guarantees of free expression fail to generate genuine dissent when communication and education are administered by a repressive establishment has great merit. However, he exaggerates the monolithic quality of American leadership and overestimates its capacity for thought control. American men of power, while they can be located within a broad ideological rubric, manifest sufficient diversity to offer alternative policy models, some of which serve to advance the goal of combatting "cruelty, misery, and suppression." Moreover, attempts to mold attitudes are not as effective as Marcuse would have us believe. The human mind is not well understood and human behavior is often unpredictable, so that mental conditioning frequently backfires: witness the carefully nurtured children of America's middle class who inexplicably rebel against society. But given these two qualifications, we can accept the proposition that elite control of important institutions vitiates the virtues of free speech.

Marcuse's arguments for the application of "liberating tolerance" are less persuasive. First, as Marcuse himself admits, his proposal can never pass from theory to reality.105 He demands, in effect, that the state voluntarily destroy itself. Marcuse is not really propounding a free speech dogma, he is calling for revolution.

Second—even assuming that Marcuse's criteria of tolerance are correct—they are still subject to dispute. Critics can challenge both his ideal of progress and his historical analysis. Given different criteria, selective tolerance could be employed in justification of any opposition viewpoint. Imagine Hitler as the advocate of "liberating tolerance" and the Aryan race as the guardian of progress.

Third, after the leaders of Marcuse's "oppressed groups" have obviated the free expression and association of their former masters and seized control, there is scant likelihood that they will simultaneously convert to libertarianism and relinquish their dictatorial powers. The substitution of Soviet-style communism for American-style democracy would be, at best, a mixed blessing.

Marcuse's analysis of modern democracy calls not for selective freedom but for the greatest possible extension of civil liberties. Freedom of expression must be scrupulously preserved so the establishment cannot patch up the chinks in its armor of thought control by the suppression of dissidence. Moreover, the import of opposition views should be enhanced through positive actions, such as expansion of local educational television, community participation in education and public safety, government financing of political campaigns, etc. Free speech doctrine should give dissenting opinion wide scope for persuasion; it should not discriminate on the basis of political values.

HISTORY OF FREE EXPRESSION

Despite the remarkable prescience we generally grant the founding fathers, they apparently had little comprehension of the implications of the First Amendment. Nevertheless, our information indicates that their ideas did not differ significantly from the common law notion that free speech means the absence of prior restraints on expression, but not the curtailment of civil and criminal sanctions for the written or verbal dissemination of licentious or seditious matter.

It was only in reaction to the Alien and Sedition Acts of 1798 that American statesmen originated a broad theory of freedom of expression. Promulgated during the administration of Federalist John Adams, these acts were regarded by opposition Jeffersonians as political measures designed to suppress antiadministration criticism and ensure a Federalist victory in the elections of 1800. The libertarian theory developed by writers of the Jefferson party included many of the warrants for free speech discussed above, and extended it well beyond the notion of "no previous restraint." Guidelines were suggested which protected utterances from subsequent prosecution as well as prior censorship. The most expansive of these tests would punish not speech but only "overt acts."106

For over one hundred years after the Alien and Sedition Acts, the federal government generally eschewed attempts to regulate expression. Matters pertaining to speech were left to the states, which were not subject to First Amendment restrictions. But states' power only loosely restrained expression. With some notable exceptions, the nineteenth century witnessed relatively little curtailment of civil liberties.107

Important limitations of civil liberties developed during the conflict over slavery, and the "peculiar institution" itself represented the ultimate repression. Slaves were deprived of all basic liberties, including those set forth in the First Amendment. White Southerners, however, clung fiercely to their degraded social system. Their dread of abolition often crossing the borders of paranoia, Southern legislatures formally prohibited all discussion of the slavery question. For a time (1836-1844), they even succeeded in establishing a congressional "gag rule" which required all antislavery petitions submitted to Congress to be indefinitely tabled without being read.108 But the South was not unique in its race prejudice; many Northern states and localities also adopted racial legislation restricting the civil liberties of free blacks.109

When the dispute over slavery culminated in rebellion and war, individual rights were jeopardized by the executive's assumption of wartime emergency powers. Some newspapers were suppressed or suspended and some individuals were prosecuted for advocacy, but, overall, limitations of expression were relatively mild during the Civil War. The key concern was arbitrary arrest and suspension of habeas corpus rather than abridgment of substantive rights.110

The most serious governmental infringement on civil liberties during the late nineteenth century was the interference with labor's freedom of association. Through injunctions, police harassment, restraint of trade and conspiracy prosecutions, and enforcement of contracts which forbade participation in unions, the state and federal governments helped stifle union development.111

The activities of private groups and individuals also limited civil liberties during the nineteenth century and the early twentieth century. In the antebellum South, proponents of abolition risked maiming or death, and, in the North, anti-Negro elements instigated race riots, destroyed abolitionist newspapers, and physically intimidated opponents of slavery. After the war, personal violence was directed primarily against union members and radicals. Bosses hired spies and thugs who harassed and threatened recalcitrant employees. Strikes were crushed by calculated violence, and sometimes murder. Radical leaders and union organizers were threatened and assaulted.112

Until World War I (with the exception of cases involving religious freedom), First Amendment matters were not adjudicated by the Supreme Court (or any federal court). During the last fifty years, however, a wealth of precedent has been created by the Supreme Court vis-à-vis free expression as the court extended application of First Amendment guarantees to the state governments, formulated general rules for distinguishing constitutionally acceptable speech, and established guidelines in a large number of specific areas relevant to the First Amendment.

Because the history of freedom of expression in the twentieth century is best examined in the context of Supreme Court decisions, the following pages will discuss particular issues arising under the First Amendment and then consider some overall theories of First Amendment application.

Religious Liberty

In *Reynolds* v. *United States* (98 U.S. 145, 1878) the Supreme Court set forth an interpretation of religious liberty that guided the legal system for over eighty years. Speaking for the majority, Chief Justice Waite declared that while religious beliefs are inviolable, action taken in pursuit of those tenets is subject to state regulation. No limitation was placed upon this governmental power by the court.113

The *Reynolds* precedent was not rejected until 1962. In rejecting the plenary power of the state to control behavior whether or not it stems from religious motives, the court declared, in *Sherbert* v. *Weiner* (374 U.S. 398, 1962), that "it is basic that no showing merely of a rational relationship to some colorable state interest would suffice; in the highly sensitive constitutional area, only the gravest abuse, endangering paramount interests, gives occasion for permissible limitation." Thus the courts are now required, in cases involving religious practices, to balance any curtailment of religious freedom against the need for governmental regulation. The state no longer has carte blanche power in controlling religiously motivated behavior.114

Obscenity

All levels of government in the United States have promulgated laws designed to protect the public from the dissemination of immoral or depraved matter. These acts encompass both administrative regulation and criminal prohibition. In reviewing cases arising out of such anti-obscenity statutes, the courts (with few exceptions) were long guided by the British precedent in *Queen* v. *Hicklin*. Lord Chief Justice Cockburn noted in that case that the test for obscenity was "whether the tendency of the matter charged as obscenity is to deprave and corrupt those whose minds are open to such immoral influences, and into whose hands a publication of this sort might fall." This standard, basing societal guidelines upon the most corruptible, is so broad that it renders First Amendment rights virtually inapplicable in obscenity cases.[115]

It was not until 1957, in *Roth* v. *United States* (354 U.S. 476, 1957), that the Supreme Court began to establish more sophisticated criteria for identifying obscenity. In that case Justice Brennan articulated for the majority that expression is obscene if "to the average person, applying contemporary community standards, the dominant theme of the material taken as a whole appeals to prurient interests."[116] Thus obscenity was no longer to be appraised with respect to the most susceptible, but rather to the average, member of society.

The guideline, however, remained vague, and in later years the court sought to explicate it. In *Manual Enterprises* v. *Day* (370 U.S. 478, 1962) it held that obscene matter must not only cater to prurient interests, it must be "patently offensive" as well. In *Jocabellis* v. *Ohio* (378 U.S. 184, 1964) it further ruled that expression which has literary or scientific or any other form of social importance may not be branded as obscene. An additional criterion for determining obscenity was announced in *Ginzburg* v. *United States* (383 U.S. 463, 1966). In evaluating the claims of the publisher of *Eros* and other erotic literature to First Amendment protection, the court introduced the notion of intent, stating that "where the purveyors' sole emphasis is on the sexually provocative aspects of his publications, that fact may be decisive in the determination of obscenity."

Although the court has properly sought to confine the scope of anti-obscenity legislation, current efforts are unsuccessful in clarifying poetic license; they compel jurists to enter the thicket of literary criticism. Judges are asked to consider questions of taste and artistic merit that have baffled critics for centuries. The most profound philosophers of art have foundered whenever they attempted to abstract the essence of good art. The contribution of the Supreme Court to this endeavor has been a collection of empty generalities that offer scant guidance in difficult cases.

Once sex is recognized as a valid aspect of artistic expression, it becomes virtually impossible to draw lines. Other nations have eliminated censorship legislation for adults, and the United States should do the same.

In its obscenity discussions the Supreme Court has also acted to shield the individual from the actions of administrative censorship agencies. In *Freedman* v. *Maryland* (380 U.S. 51, 1965) it held that only a judicial tribunal has the power to exercise final restraint on free expression. Thus provision must be made for judicial review of administrative decisions in First Amendment cases.[117]

Symbolic Speech

"Symbolic speech" involves the communication of an idea through conduct rather than words, and the concept was first applied, although not explicitly, to peaceful picketing. *Thornhill* v. *Alabama* (310 U.S. 88, 1940) first embraced peaceful picketing as protected expression. Subsequent decisions, however, have held that because picketing comprises elements both of speech and of action, it may be more strictly regulated than speech. Thus an ad hoc rule of reason has been established for control of peaceful picketing.

The Supreme Court has also dealt with more applications of symbolic speech. *O'Brien* v. *United States* (391 U.S. 367) rejected the notion that draft card burning was constitutionally sanctioned as free speech: "We cannot accept the view that an apparently limitless variety of conduct can be labelled speech whenever the person engaging in the conduct intends thereby to express an idea. . . . When 'speech' and 'non-speech' elements are combined in the same course of conduct, a sufficiently important governmental interest in regulating the non-speech element can justify incidental limitations on First Amendment freedoms."

In 1969, however, the court limited state regulation in order to safeguard symbolic speech. *Tinker* v. *Des Moines Independent Community School District* (393 U.S. 503, 1969) reversed the suspension of high school students for wearing black armbands as a war protest, viewing the armbands as protected public expression. Thus the Supreme Court has recognized that conduct designed to express ideas may be classified as speech, but has been particularly solicitous of state interests in checking its non-speech activities.

Freedom of Assembly

American courts have ruled that public places may be utilized for peaceful assembly and communication but that this right must be subject to reasonable state regulation, designed to ensure public safety and convenience. Thus the Supreme Court has sustained the practice of requiring a permit for large gatherings, but has invalidated statutes vesting licensing discretion in public officials or discriminating against particular groups.118

First Amendment rights to demonstrate or declaim in public may also clash with a governmental interest in preventing breaches of the peace. The court faced this problem in *Feiner* v. *New York* (340 U.S. 315, 1961), in which it enunciated a general rule that gave broad discretion to the police: "It is one thing to say that the police cannot be used as an instrument for the suppression of unpopular views, and another to say that when, as here, the speaker passes the bounds of argument or persuasion and undertakes incitement to riot, they are powerless to prevent a breach of the peace." In a series of cases stemming from the civil rights demonstrations of the 1960s, the court sharply narrowed the discretion implied in *Feiner*, reversing several state breach-of-the-peace convictions on constitutional grounds. Continuing this trend, the court in 1971 invalidated a state loitering statute forbidding gatherings of three or more individuals.119 The interface between public expression and breach of the peace, however, remains hazy, with no clear guidelines available to police or courts.

Loyalty Tests

The public's obsession with subversion that accompanied the cold war spawned a variety of statutes withholding privileges from those who failed to satisfy various criteria of loyalty. These criteria included loyalty oaths and security investigations for government employees and restriction of the public and private activities of members of certain political organizations. The opinions of the Supreme Court have curtailed, but not eliminated, most of such practices.

On the state level, legislatures have sought to weed out dangerous employees by demanding formal affirmations of fealty, sometimes including affidavits disclaiming membership in allegedly subversive organizations. Initially, the Supreme Court upheld such oaths, holding that there is no constitutional right to state employment and that evidence of dangerous beliefs or associations is relevant to fitness. The only significant restriction imposed by the Supreme Court was that loyalty statutes must distinguish between knowing and innocent membership in subversive groups.120 Recently, however, it has acted to limit the application of loyalty oaths. In a set of rulings commencing in 1966, the court embraced the principle that civil disabilities are important enough to warrant the requirement imposed in criminal prosecutions—that a specific intent to further the illegal actions of an organization must be demonstrated if an individual is to be denied employment or other privileges. In practice, these decisions have rendered meaningless the loyalty oaths disclaiming affiliation with condemned groups, and thus attempts to establish guilt by association are now prohibited.121 The possibility is not precluded, however, that carefully drawn loyalty oaths may be constitutional.

In addition to oaths, the national government has instituted an interlocking set of investigatory procedures designed to identify potential subversives and bar them from federal employment, particularly in defense areas. Begun by President Truman, the loyalty-security program was extended by President Eisenhower to the point where it was possible to discharge an employee if, after a hearing, it was found that his retention "may not be consistent with the interests of national security." In 1961 the federal loyalty program was circumscribed to the extent that the Attorney General could no longer compile a list of subversive organizations in which membership constituted grounds for dismissal. Other procedural safeguards have been established, but thus far the Supreme Court has not directly confronted the constitutional issues involved in loyalty dismissals.122

The most sweeping civil disabilities imposed upon association and expression are embodied in the Internal Security Act of 1950, also known as the McCarran Act. This act requires all Communist-front and Communist-action organizations to register with the federal government. Such registration entails a loss of various privileges, such as organizational mailing procedures. After more than ten years of litigation, the registration provision was so hedged with restrictions that, although not formally voided, it had become inoperable. Basically, the compulsory registration was seen as a violation of the Fifth Amendment prohibition against self-incrimination. Thus the court held that a member of the Communist Party could not be compelled to register, either for himself or his organization. Nonetheless, the government has succeeded in imposing civil disabilities via the Communist Control Act of 1954, principally the elimination of Communist candidates from election ballots.123

The federal government has also sought to deny, on security grounds, the right of Communists to secure passports and union privileges by invoking the prohibitions of the National Labor Relations Act. Section 91 (h) of the 1947 Taft-Hartley Act denied labor unions the protection of the National Labor Relations Board (which guarantees collective bargaining) unless their officers filed affidavits affirming that they are not

Communists and neither belong to nor believe in nor support any organization advocating the overthrow of the government by force. In *American Communications Association* v. *Douds* (339 U.S. 94, 1950) the court upheld this section, arguing that it was intended to prevent political strikes which might be called by Communist officers, and that any incidental restriction on free expression was too slight to justify voiding it on constitutional grounds. The provision, however, proved ineffective, and was replaced in 1959 by a stipulation that imposed criminal sanctions on a member of the Communist party who served as an officer or employee of a labor union.[124] In *United States* v. *Brown* (381 U.S. 437, 1965), the court struck down this new provision.

With respect to the denial of passports to Communists, the court first decreed, in *Aptheker* v. *Secretary of State* (378 U.S. 500, 1964), that a provision of the Smith Act (denying passports to Communists and fellow travelers) was too broad a curtailment of travel in that it failed to distinguish harmless excursions from those related to national security. Subsequent decisions attempted to clarify which types of travel could be restricted. In *Zemel* v. *Rusk* (381 U.S. 1, 1965) the court upheld the government's refusal to issue a passport for trips to Cuba, maintaining that valid foreign policy commitments sanctioned this practice. *Zemel*, however, was modified by an unappealed ruling of the District of Columbia Court of Appeals, which in December 1967 held that the State Department could not refuse passports to persons who sought to enter forbidden areas. The appeals court stated that the government did not have the statutory authority to control travel, but could only extract the promise that travelers would not use their passports for trips to restricted zones.[125]

Legislative Investigations

Since the 1930s, Congress has also lashed out against radicalism with its investigatory committees. Principally through the House Un-American Activities Committee, the legislature has sought to expose subversives to the glare of national publicity. Dominated by conservative Southerners, the committee, now called the House Internal Security Subcommittee, has set out "after reds, pinkos, blacks, foreigners, beatniks," and subjected individuals to harassment and public ostracism for their beliefs and expressions. In the course of this twisted crusade, the committee has frequently collided with the First Amendment.[126]

The actions of the committee were first subjected to judicial scrutiny in 1957 in *Watkins* v. *United States* (354 U.S. 178, 1957). The court recognized the principle that congressional investigations cannot infringe on First Amendment rights and that this question is reviewable by the judiciary. The rule laid down in *Watkins*, however, was merely procedural: a committee must establish, in advance, that the questions it puts are pertinent to the subject of the investigation. In *Barenblatt* v. *United States* (360 U.S. 109, 1959) the court retreated from its initial stand and gave the committee carte blanche for wide-ranging inquiry, and in a companion case extended the same power to state committees. In later decisions it returned to the stricter standards of *Watkins* in reversing contempt of Congress convictions. It has not, however, made a clear statement on the scope of congressional investigatory power when First Amendment rights are at stake.[127] Recent controversy over the committee has cooled as it has turned its attention to radicals who revel in public exposure rather than to persons who seek to preserve their private lives (e.g., Abbie Hoffman versus Alger Hiss).

Right to Privacy

Issues centering on the right to privacy are particularly difficult to resolve. This right, kindred in spirit to those specifically outlined in the First Amendment, is a requisite for intellectual refinement, spiritual development, and psychological health. In fact, the right to privacy has been inferred from the First Amendment guarantees of free speech and association. Yet the right to be left alone clashes at key junctures with liberty of expression. At what point should public comment be circumscribed in the interests of personal seclusion?

Open discussion may impinge upon privacy if it intrudes into one's personal affairs, impairing his human dignity and disturbing his internal tranquillity, or if it "subjects him to ridicule, hatred, or contempt, and thereby injures him in his business, profession or vocation."[128] Infringements of the latter type have a venerable legal history and are encompassed by the law of libel and slander.

Until recently, defamation of individuals was held to be outside the scope of the First Amendment; civil libel was strictly under the aegis of state tort laws. Defamation may also be punished criminally, but it is usually the subject of a civil suit. Though left primarily to the states, various rules had been elaborated to restrain the promiscuous assertion of libel claims.[129]

An absolute privilege of unrestricted comment has been extended to legislators and participants in court proceedings. A qualified privilege extends to "publications on matters of public concern . . . to relieve the publisher from the strict liability which applies to non-privileged publi-cations."130 In such instances the plaintiff must usually prove actual malice in order to recover; but in some jurisdictions this qualified priv-ilege is forfeited if the libelous statement is one of fact rather than opinion. Truth is usually a sufficient defense against alleged defamation; but some states add the additional requirement that the statement must be made with good motives and for justifiable ends.131

In 1964 the Supreme Court brought the law of libel within the First Amendment. *New York Times* v. *Sullivan* (376 U.S. 254, 1964) held that the Constitution protects false expressions of fact, subject to narrow exceptions, where they refer to public officials in the context of discourse on public affairs. Such speech, the court said, is libelous only if the plain-tiff can demonstrate "calculated falsehood or reckless disregard for the truth." In reaching this decision the court observed: "We consider this case against the background of a profound national commitment to the principle that debate on public issues should be uninhibited, robust, and wide-open, and that it may well include vehement, caustic and sometimes unpleasantly sharp attacks on government and public officials."

The *New York Times* decision was elaborated in a series of subsequent cases. In a set of three decisions, although the court did not establish clear doctrine, a majority indicated that the *New York Times* rule can be extended to the publication of any matter that is fit subject for public debate.132 And in 1971 the court specifically applied the standard to comment upon public officials, no matter how far removed from the con-duct of public affairs the comment may be.133

Intrusions into strictly private affairs through media discussion have for the most part been regulated by state laws and decisions, and few cases have been litigated to the Supreme Court. The issue has not yet been resolved, but the Supreme Court has indicated that, insofar as newspapers are concerned, the *New York Times* test may be the guiding principle.134

A far more serious threat to the sanctity of private life is posed by electronic surveillance and data processing. We now are able to tap a man's phone, record the number he dials, install hidden listening devices in his home, his car, his clothing, and follow his every movement through high-powered lenses. The results of these efforts, along with the vast quantity of other information available about individuals in this society, can be stored and processed by high-speed electronic computers. The data can be retrieved almost instantaneously and universally dissem-inated; it can even be used to simulate a person's thought and behavior patterns. Few legal safeguards insulate the individual from electronic scrutiny of his intimate affairs, particularly when the snoop is the government.135 The American government is one of the most prolific scanners and recorders of individual activities in the history of the world. A body of substantive law must soon be created in this area if personal privacy is not to become a forlorn memory.

GENERAL THEORIES OF THE FIRST AMENDMENT

Having examined the impact of the First Amendment in several specific areas, we may now attempt to formulate general standards for determining the permissible limits of free expression. Because these guidelines seek to distinguish that speech which forfeits constitutional protection, they cut across the special cases previously discussed and seek to define the extent to which any dissenting opinion may be controlled.

Bad-Tendency Test

The Supreme Court initially propounded a First Amendment philosophy in the context of World War I indictments for disloyal and dangerous advocacy. These prosecutions, the first of their kind in over a century, were based on the Espionage Acts of 1917 and 1918. These statutes proscribed a wide variety of expression that was deemed inimical to the war effort. In their final form, the Espionage Acts prohibited (among other things)

> false reports or false statements with intent to interfere with the operation or success of the military or naval forces of the United States or to promote the success of its enemies . . . attempts to cause insubordination, disloyalty, mutiny, or refusal of duty in the military or naval forces . . . attempts to obstruct the recruiting or enlistment services . . . saying or doing anything with intent to obstruct the sale of United States bonds . . . uttering scurrilous or abusive language, or language intended to cause contempt, scorn, contumely, or disrepute as regards the form of government of the U.S.; or the Constitution; or the flag; or the uniform of the Army or Navy . . . words or acts supporting or favoring the cause of any country at war with us, or opposing the cause of the U.S.

Under this umbrella legislation a motley collection of war protestors and radicals were prosecuted, almost none of whom posed the slightest danger to the war effort. Some of the prosecutions rivaled the theater of the absurd. Mrs. Rose Pastor Stokes was indicted and convicted for declaring in a letter that "I am for the people and the government is for the profiteers." A farmer was imprisoned for using blasphemous and unpatriotic language at his dinner table in the presence of two guests. Others were convicted for expressing pacifist views, for questioning the constitutionality of the draft, for profanity uttered in the heat of argument, for criticizing the Y.M.C.A. and the Red Cross, and (under state law) for discouraging women from knitting socks for the troops.[136]

The standard employed by the Supreme Court for distinguishing constitutional utterances from those subject to the Espionage Act was the bad-tendency test. Under this doctrine, any speech which has a tendency, however remote, to provoke substantial evil forfeits its constitutional protection. As the previous illustrations suggest, the bad-tendency test is so broad that it virtually repeals the First Amendment. The standard was not rejected in the calm of normalcy, and was used to evaluate state laws against subversive expressions in the 1920s and 1930s. It was not until 1937, with the decision in *Herndon* v. *Lowry* (301 U.S. 242, 1937), that the bad-tendency test was superseded by the clear-and present-danger rule.[137]

Clear-and-Present-Danger Test

The clear-and-present-danger standard was first enunciated by Justice Oliver Wendell Holmes in *Schenk* v. *United States* (249 U.S. 47, 1919), one of the World War I Espionage Act cases: "The question in every case is whether the words are used in such circumstances and are of such a nature as to create a clear and present danger that they will bring about the substantive evils that Congress has a right to prevent." This guideline, however, was not long lived; by the early 1950s it had been tacitly abandoned in favor of the ad hoc balancing test.[138]

The clear-and-present-danger rule represents an improvement over the bad-tendency test in that it requires the state to justify the restriction of freedom of speech by establishing a far more direct link between utterance and illegal or dangerous conduct. Yet it is hardly a potent instrument for safeguarding free speech.[139] First, it fails to recognize that expression, even when it poses a clear and present danger of substantive evil, may merit protection. Free expression is bound to conflict with societal interests, and should not automatically be forced into a subordinate position in view of its vital importance. Second, the test is too vague. "Clear and present danger" is subject to a variety of interpretations, and each word affords wide latitude for subjective judgment. In difficult cases this standard forces judges to rely on intuition. Third, to effectively implement the test there must be a factual determination of a sort normally beyond the scope of judicial inquiry. It requires the prediction of individual and mass behavior, a difficult and sometimes impossible task that involves the sophisticated manipulation of a vast quantity of unreliable data.

Balancing Test

At its fringes, the clear-and-present-danger rule touches upon another test which explicitly rejects any attempt at an a priori classification of speech. This is the ad hoc balancing test, which in each instance involves a weighing of the value of the expression the government seeks to restrict against the social objective preserved through such regulation. Justice Felix Frankfurter was the foremost advocate of the balancing standard, and it has been employed most frequently in cases involving the indirect infringement of free speech.

The balancing test also has several serious defects. First, it entails even more difficult factual investigations than the clear-and-present-danger test, as both sides of the balance must be appraised. Second, the standard biases judicial judgment in favor of the legislative decision, as Justice Frankfurter's opinions in First Amendment cases would indicate. First Amendment rights are generally asserted by the poor and minorities, while control is based upon the broad social interest in law and order. Yet the protection of such minorities from the tyranny of the majority is a major goal of the Constitution.

Third, the rule fails to specify the standards that should form the balancing procedure. Should the scales tip but a feather's weight in favor of the government to justify abridgment of speech or must the state satisfy a more stringent requirement? Fourth, the standard makes the protection of free speech almost wholly dependent upon the attitudes of judges. If the present Administration retains power, and its new Supreme Court appointees mirror the anti-libertarian perspective of Justices Burger and Blackmun, First Amendment guarantees could be balanced into oblivion. Fifth, the test confronts the judicial system with a difficult dilemma. Legitimate balancing would have to consider the possibility that the state could achieve its objectives through less restrictive means;

yet it is extremely hard for the courts to discuss such potential legislation without encroaching upon the legislature's prerogatives or rendering advisory opinions.140 Sixth, the balancing standard cannot afford police, prosecutors, other government officials, or private citizens adequate advance notice of which rights must be protected and which may be overruled.

Incitement Test

The most popular free speech standard today is the incitement test. As expressed in *Brandenburg* v. *Ohio* (395 U.S. 444 at 447, 1969), "the constitutional guarantees of free speech and free press do not permit a state to forbid or proscribe advocacy of the use of force or of law violations except where such advocacy is directed to inciting or producing imminent lawless action and is likely to incite or produce such action." The incitement standard is, in effect, a narrower and more precise restatement of the clear-and-present-danger rule. As such, it is probably the best guideline yet employed by the court. *Brandenburg* offers the most extensive protection to date of individual rights against state and local prosecution. Nonetheless, it suffers from all the defects of the original doctrine, at least to some degree.

Absolute Test

An absolute test has never been an accepted standard as promulgated by a majority of the Supreme Court. Primarily advocated by Justices Black and Douglas, absolutist doctrine is still in an ill-defined state. It is based upon the premise that the founding fathers literally meant that the freedom of speech must not be abridged at all. Thus it seeks to distinguish protected speech by "defining" rather than by "balancing." Certain types of expression, it argues, can be termed "speech" under the meaning of the First Amendment, and cannot be abridged. Other expression, however, may be termed "action" and thereby be subjected to some type of balancing test.

Thomas I. Emerson has extended and refined this formulation in an effort to devise a First Amendment theory based upon the difference between speech and action, the definition of the words "law" and "abridge," and the delineation of "those sectors of social activity which fall outside the area in which, under the basic theory, freedom of expression must be maintained."141 Emerson undertakes a lengthy and elaborate analysis of the way in which application of these principles would alter the practical application of First Amendment guarantees.

Admittedly, Emerson's ideas bring the interpretation of the First Amendment into a new context, that of classification. Nevertheless, they do not guide this process adequately. Nothing in his theory prevents the same considerations which underlie a balancing approach from determining the distinction between speech and action, the definition of law and abridge, and delineation of the areas in which usual rights of expression do not operate. For example, suppression of the Communist Party could be justified on the grounds that the organization and operation of a political party constitutes action rather than speech. Although Emerson's concretization of his ideology advances civil liberties in specific instances, the same process, if undertaken by a scholar with different intuitions, might yield opposite results.

A Rationality Standard

The following paragraphs suggest a new theory of free speech, one that is libertarian enough to permit wide scope for expression and sufficiently demanding to foreclose attrition by interpretation. The suggested doctrine is that all advocacy warrants unqualified protection unless it is presented in such a context that the listener does not have an opportunity to rationally decide whether to heed the speaker's appeal. Although this test adequately applies to the straightforward assertion of unpopular or subversive opinions, it does not cover all types of advocacy, such as (1) speech that is an integral part of a criminal act, (2) speech that conflicts with other provisions of the Bill of Rights, and (3) speech that includes a substantial amount of conduct.

Condition 1 poses no serious problems. Crimes may involve the use of speech or other forms of communication: orders may be given, plans laid, gunmen hired, etc.; or expression may be used to bribe or defraud or swindle. Current doctrine recognizes that such communications may be proscribed, and few difficult cases arise.[142]

Condition 2 relates to the interface between privacy and free expression: two absolute rights cannot simultaneously exist. Some regulation of expression is necessary to maintain the sanctity of our personal lives. The tradeoff between privacy and free speech is so complex that general standards can hardly be given, except to note that there is now a far greater need to shield privacy from the government than from private individuals.

Condition 3 pertains to the indirect regulation of symbolic speech. Clearly, the government cannot give free rein to all forms of symbolic speech regardless of the conduct involved. This issue would need resolution by some type of balancing test.

All three conditions are simply an admission that not all free speech issues can be encompassed in a single comprehensive standard. Other special cases include freedom of religion, indirect controls on speech, and the regulation of public facilities.

The general standard (discussed above) is premised on the libertarian arguments set forth at the beginning of this chapter. Society, in order to promote its long-term welfare and provide for individual fulfillment, should allow maximum scope for expression. It simultaneously recognizes that the community must protect itself from direct encroachment on its security. Given this dialect, the only restriction of speech that can be tolerated is that which, because of its content and the circumstances of its delivery, provides the listener no opportunity to rationally evaluate the speaker's words. Such expression may constitute a direct threat to law and order, and at the same time be of virtually no value for the development of the individual, the search for truth, or the preservation of democracy. It relates, to some extent, to the promotion of change, but only insofar as it sparks violence; and when the forces of change operate at this level, society has the right and the responsibility to defend itself. If a man advocates violence and an individual decides to heed such advice, the crime is clearly the responsibility of the listener. Only if the listener is unable to control himself, if he is moved to violence by forces beyond his control (such as a mob or riot), is the responsibility properly placed upon the speaker.

The suggested rule is sufficiently narrow to avoid the wide-ranging interpretations that reflect the prejudice of judges. Under its guidance, the rationale for limiting speech is not an assessment of public danger, which leaves great room for subjective opinion, but simply whether or not the nature and context of the speech preclude rational consideration. This is strictly a question of fact; value judgments do not intrude. The judgment it requires is admittedly difficult, but it should be recalled that the only question is whether the listener has a reasonable opportunity to react rationally—not whether, in fact, he did react rationally. Moreover, through expert testimony and the evolution of precedent, specific guidelines could be developed. Broadly conceived, the doctrine would do no more than prohibit incitement in a situation so emotionally charged that it would be unreasonable to expect a rational response from listeners. Aside from such special cases, individuals would be free to express any opinion, however noxious. Thus society would allow the advocacy of revolution but would draw the line at the actual sparking of violence.

The rationality standard is far more libertarian than those that are currently employed. It would mandate the repeal of virtually all statutes that punish expression. These include the Smith Act, which makes it illegal for any person to (1) knowingly or willfully advocate or teach the overthrow or destruction of any government in the United States by force or violence; (2) print, publish, or disseminate written matter advocating such overthrow; (3) participate in the organization of any group dedicated to such purposes; and (4) acquire and hold membership in such a group with knowledge of its purposes. Also subject to repeal would be the McCarran Act, the act prohibiting counselling young men to resist the draft, the National Anti-Riot Act, and the numerous state statutes proscribing allegedly dangerous advocacy. Thus the range of First Amendment cases that could be brought before a jury would be substantially curtailed. Moreover, if a narrowly written law should survive judicial review, and cases be presented before juries, the jury would have to base its verdict in part on whether the conduct fits the factual context of the rationality test.

The guidelines would also prohibit civil disabilities based upon expression. It would require the repeal of the Communist Control Act, loyalty oaths, and loyalty investigations into First Amendment activities.

The need for such a broadened interpretation of the First Amendment is not based solely upon theoretical considerations; it derives as well from an analysis of our society, from an atmosphere of repression. America's often hysterical fear of radical upheaval and her distrust of strange ideas and practices has become institutionalized in a vast, impersonal bureaucracy that is armed with the most modern intrusive technology. Moreover, the intolerance latent in the general public is constantly churned by politicians seeking an easy means of election. Given this situation, the countervailing force of legal safeguards becomes especially important.

A major manifestation of our society's incursion into the rights of individuals is the surveillance and recording of our daily lives. The efficacy of modern snooping devices and computers has already been described and examples of the use of this technology by governmental agencies have recently surfaced in the media. Most spectacular was the disclosure that the military intelligence agencies had been spying on civilians, ranging from Jerry Rubin to Adlai Stevenson III.[143] The compiled information, with copies forwarded to the army's intelligence center at Fort Holabird, Maryland, was used to "predict political behavior, voting patterns, political alliances, and political activities of the men investigated," said Senator Sam Ervin. "Individuals closely watched by the surveillance unit are of such eminent citizenship that no charge of political extremism can possibly be made." Ervin further declared that, "apparently, anyone who in the Army's definition was left of center was a prospective candidate for political surveillance."[144] Following these disclosures, the President ordered such operations to cease;[145] but the military establishment's intractability is such that the command may prove ineffective.[146]

Other examples of surveillance include the compilation of individual data banks by the Departments of Justice and H.E.W., and by other governmental agencies which document our sexual behavior, political activity, business affairs, credit records, and religious affiliations.[147] The F.B.I. observes minority organizations, left-wing political groups, college students and professors,[148] and attempts are made by investigative subcommittees to examine the records of newsmen.[149] The following minor incident indicates the scope of governmental knowledge of our lives and the uses to which it is put. T.W.A. board chairman Charles Tillinghast received a letter from F.B.I. director J. Edgar Hoover complaining about Donald Cook, a T.W.A. pilot who had criticized the F.B.I.'s handling of a hijacking attempt. The letter included confidential information from Cook's air force file detailing difficulties he had experienced with the military.[150]

Surveillance, in itself, restricts civil liberties. If people believe that they are under observation, they will hesitate to exercise their right of expression. This danger was articulated by Senator Ervin, chairman of the Subcommittee on Constitutional Rights: "When people fear surveillance, whether it exists or not, when they grow afraid to speak their minds and hearts freely to their Government or anyone else, then we shall have ceased to be a free society."[151] Moreover, the government is building a vast storehouse of information that can be employed in First Amendment prosecutions, as happened in the case of the Chicago Seven. Thus it is particularly important to circumscribe the scope of such prosecutions.

Equally appalling is the willingness of the government to abandon law and justice in its pursuit of subversion. Investigations of the response to demonstrations at the 1968 Democratic convention in Chicago reveal that the police force rioted, ruthlessly suppressing the protestors with tactics rivaling those of professional gangsters.[152] More recently, in forestalling disruptions by antiwar protestors in Washington, D.C., the police abandoned legally ordained procedures in favor of illegal mass arrest and detention. Hordes of people, including many bystanders, were swept off the street, herded into makeshift jails, and held without charges for almost a day. (Most of these arrests were invalidated by the courts.) 153 In its abandonment of law to secure order, the government forfeits its legitimacy and becomes a mob, distinguished from its adversaries only by superior technology, manpower, and organization.

Most destructive of our liberties, however, is the fact that the American public has been conditioned to tolerate severe limitations of long-cherished rights. A 1964 study by political scientist Herbert McCloskey revealed that a majority of the American people believed that "freedom doesn't entail the right to teach foreign ideas."154 Most revealing is a survey of 80,000 persons under the age of thirty-five by the Educational Commission of the States. The commission found that 68 percent of adults from twenty-six to thirty-five years of age would refuse to permit radio or television to air such statements as "Russia is better than the United States," "Some races of people are better than others," or "It is not necessary to believe in God." It also discovered that 79 percent of 17-year-olds would likewise refuse to allow such broadcasts. Its conclusions: "Young people lack any consistent understanding or conviction about the exercise of free speech."

This combination of government's violations of our rights and individuals' disdain for free speech poses a grave threat to the future of liberty in this country. The broadest possible interpretation of the First Amendment is necessary to counter this trend.

Having suggested a new theory of the First Amendment and sketched its implications, we may now examine some alterations that might be made in the present laws relating to free speech. Some of these changes would be mandated by the new standard; others would require specific legislation.

CHANGES IN CURRENT DOCTRINE

First Amendment Conspiracy

In addition to punishing certain types of expression, the government has prohibited agreements to commit illegal advocacy. An indictable conspiracy exists under current law if individuals band together to perform an illegal act or to pursue lawful ends by unlawful means. Such association is deemed criminal because it increases the likelihood that criminal objectives will be successfully pursued, and because it creates general tension and anxiety in society.155

Many of the criminal prosecutions involving free speech in the areas previously alluded to arose from conspiracies. During World War I, Americans were prosecuted for conspiracy to advocate draft evasion and for opposition to our military efforts. The anti-Communist paranoia of the 1950s spawned conspiracy indictments against party leaders, and over the past few years new-left radicals have borne the brunt of these charges. Dr. Benjamin Spock and four others have been prosecuted for counselling young men to avoid the draft and violate the draft laws, and several prominent radicals involved in protesting the 1968 Democratic national convention have been charged, tried, and convicted for conspiracy to cross state lines with intent to incite a riot. Although many of these cases have produced vigorous doctrinal controversy, the Supreme Court has not yet restricted the application of conspiracy laws to First Amendment matters.156

Despite the silence of the court, efforts to prosecute First Amendment conspiracies are not only unjustified but are detrimental to civil liberties. First, the rationale for conspiracy prosecutions does not apply to agreements of advocacy rather than action. As mentioned above, arrangements to undertake criminal activity can be considered criminal because they increase the likelihood that crimes will be successfully carried through. For example, a group might band together to rob a bank: one man drives the getaway car and another serves as lookout while gunmen enter the bank and demand its cash. Through such concerted action the desperadoes are far more likely to succeed (and to attempt to duplicate their success elsewhere) than if each had acted alone. Thus if the gang is apprehended in the planning stage, the members could be tried for conspiracy, even if no overt action has yet been taken. However, when the object of a pact is expression, its formulation does not render such speech more probable. Unlike a bank robbery, words cannot be halted in the attempt stage. A long-recognized constitutional principle is that there can be no prior restraint on expression. Everyone is free to say what he wishes, so long as he is willing to risk subsequent prosecution.

The only warrant for prohibiting First Amendment conspiracies is that, by coordinating their efforts, speakers can better assure that the violence they seek will occur as a result of their advocacy. The illegal acts they conspire to commit, however, are not the fruits of their incitement but the incitement itself. The violence is, in fact, twice removed from the conspiracy; violence occurs as a result of incitement, which occurs as a result of conspiracy.

Such a conspiracy could be controlled under a general-danger theory

—that indirect results tend to undermine societal objectives.[157] The general-danger theory is a catch-all rule, similar to the bad-tendency rule, that enables the state to punish men for the results of their acts— no matter how remote. In the sensitive area of free speech, where every idea is an incitement, such doctrine must be eschewed.

Also, prosecutions for First Amendment conspiracies have a thoroughly chilling effect on freedom of expression. Given the fact that speech must be analyzed in its context if its legality is to be assessed, it is impossible to determine at the agreement stage whether such contemplated advocacy is unlawful. Thus if a conspiracy prosecution is instituted before the expression is effectuated, it constitutes an a priori restraint on speech and should be disallowed.[158]

Even if prosecution takes place after the words have been spoken, it still curtails civil liberties substantially. And the criteria for establishing conspiracies are very broad: "An accused might be found in a net of conspiracy by reason of the relation of his acts to the acts of others, the significance of which he may not have appreciated, and which may result from the application of criteria more delicate than those which determine guilt as to the usual substantive offense."[159] A defendant may be guilty of conspiracy when he is indirectly party to an agreement to commit illegal advocacy, even though he never commits such advocacy himself. When these standards are combined with the difficulty of predetermining illegal speech, it is clear that a defendant may become implicated in a conspiracy without being aware of it. In fact, merely by associating with others who undertake unlawful conduct or expression, an individual could find himself accused of conspiracy.[160] The prospect of such unfair prosecution may very well deter people from associating with dissident groups or putting forth dissenting opinions of their own.

Finally, a conspiracy trial relaxes the normal rules of criminal procedure to the detriment of the defendants. Hearsay declarations by one co-conspirator are admissible against all co-conspirators. Testimony given against one defendant may be used against all of them. "[The] existence of a conspiracy may be inferred by the jury from the similarity of the purpose suggested by the overt acts of the defendants . . . the defendants need not have met in advance to plan their crime, nor have known each other personally, nor need their arrangements have been made in secret." The jury may even infer a conspiracy from the fact that the defendants are being tried together.[161] When First Amendment freedoms are at stake, such lax standards should not be tolerated.

The procedures for outlawing First Amendment conspiracies must be carefully designed so that they foreclose indictments for conspiracy to perform illegal acts with speech serving as the evidence. They must forbid use of "constitutionally protected public expression as evidence either of an overt act or an individual's specific intent. The chilling effect caused by the use of the protected expression as evidence in a conspiracy trial is the same as that which flows from prosecuting an individual for the speech itself."162

Anti-Riot Act

While First Amendment conspiracies punish agreements twice removed from the evils the state wishes to prevent, the Federal Anti-Riot Act of 1968 punishes intentions twice removed from such evils. The Anti-Riot Act warps legal theory to open a wedgelike pretext for federal prosecution of disruptive demonstrations. The statute, in fact, violates a basic element of due process: that intent to commit a crime and the crime itself must be contemporaneous. Under the Anti-Riot Act, an individual may be indicted months or years after he has traveled interstate, even though in the interval he may have changed his mind or developed a fresh intent.163

There are ample state laws against rioting or inciting a riot, and they rest on much more stable ground than the state of mind of an individual at the moment he crosses a state line. Moreover, they render federal action unnecessary. The federal government has, of course, duplicated local statutes, but this has been limited to areas with which state or local authorities have been unable to deal effectively (e.g., kidnaping or racial violence). Advocates perform their illegal function in the public domain and can easily be identified and prosecuted. And if they escape and flee the state, they can be pursued by federal agents under the Fugitive Felon Law.164

Not only does the act unnecessarily infringe upon state and local jurisdictions while violating due process, it significantly restricts freedom of expression. First, the definitions of incitement and riot are so vague that an individual may not be able to determine whether he is subject to the law. The terms "promote," "encourage," and "carry on" are so ambiguous that one cannot know whether a speech he makes at any demonstration will place him in violation of the law. The term "act of violence" is not defined, and may apply to any violent or criminal act by a group of three or more, whether or not it resembles a civil disorder or a defendant knowingly approved of such conduct. Unable to discover their liability under the law, individuals may be discouraged from traveling interstate to take part in demonstrations or other dissident political activities.165

Even if the terms were clearly defined, the act would deter free speech. Not only does it punish men for their thoughts, which should be inviolate, but—no matter how carefully its terms are defined—it could not provide the individual adequate predictability. The legality of speech cannot be determined prior to its circumstances. Thus at the point an individual crosses a state line and becomes subject to the act, he has no way of assessing his culpability.

Several burning issues in the realm of freedom of conscience have arisen from the Vietnam war and center about the means by which an individual may obtain exemption from conscription on conscientious grounds. First, what are the standards for validating conscientious objection to war in general? Second, what body is to apply these standards? Third, can a potential draftee seek deferment from military service in a particular war?

With respect to the first problem, doctrine has evolved through statutory rather than constitutional construction; the Supreme Court has never resolved the question of whether the Constitution mandates military deferments for conscientious objection to war. The Universal Training and Military Service Act of 1948 nonetheless granted conscientious objector status "by reason of religious training and belief . . . in relation to a Supreme Being involving duties superior to those arising from human relation, but [not including] political, sociological, or philosophical views, or merely a personal moral code." Until the Vietnam war, most conscientious objectors were religious pacifists from established denominations, such as Quakers, Mennonites, or Jehovah's Witnesses. Vietnam, however, has spawned large numbers of young men whose abhorrence of war is unrelated to organized religion.166

Once conscientious objection is separated from adherence to traditional religious dogma, extremely difficult problems of definition arise. What is the meaning of "religious training and belief"? Does it involve submission to established ritual and dogma? Must it involve a Judaic-Christian God, or are nontheistic religions, such as Buddhism and Unitarianism, included? Is it constitutional for Selective Service boards to exclude social, political, and philosophical beliefs? How can it be judged whether a belief is conscientious? Is the standard to be psychological, or does it relate to subject matter or action in pursuit of ideas?

The Supreme Court has consistently moved toward a standard which permits beliefs of any type to qualify for exemption so long as they are genuinely sincere. In *Seeger* v. *United States* (380 U.S. 163, 1965) the defendant claimed that he was opposed to war in any form on the basis of religious belief but that this opposition did not stem from any belief in a God; it was a "belief in and devotion to goodness and virtue for their own sake and a religious faith in a purely ethical creed." The court sidestepped the constitutional issue in the litigation and based its decision solely on the statutory interpretation. It construed belief in a Supreme Being as one that occupies "the same place in the life of the objector as an orthodox belief in God holds in the life of one clearly qualified for exemption." In response to this decision, Congress deleted "Supreme Being" from the Selective Service Act of 1967, but retained all other restrictions.[167]

The *Seeger* ruling was broadened in *Welsh* v. *United States* (398 U.S. 333, 1970). The defendant had crossed out the words "religious training" on the conscientious objector form to demonstrate that his opposition to war was based upon political, sociological, and philosophical principles. Speaking for four of the five majority justices, Justice Black declared that "essentially political or sociological or philosophical" views can be held strongly enough to be religious in the eyes of the law. In a separate concurrence, Justice Harlan stated that to deny Welsh's claim would violate the First Amendment prohibition against the establishment of religion. The key element in assessing conscientious objector applications is thus becoming the sincerity of the individuals' beliefs. Such beliefs must be composed of conscientious opposition to participation in *all* war. In *Gillette* v. *United States* (401 U.S. 437, 1971), the Supreme Court held that classification as a conscientious objector is not warranted where the registrant is opposed only to participation in a particular war, such as the one in Vietnam, even if such objection is religious in character.

Judgment of the sincerity of a belief rests upon psychological criteria— at best an inexact standard in view of the plethora of competing theories of psychology. Depending upon which school of thought is drawn upon, the definition of sincerity will vary widely from case to case. Inevitably, the question of motivation will be decided upon subjective grounds unless some arbitrary standards are institutionalized.[168]

If appraisals of sincerity are to be retained, however, the jury must become the fact finder of final determination. At present, local draft boards judge an individual's sincerity, and on that basis assign him a draft classification. This classification is not reviewable by a jury if an individual who has been refused conscientious objector status fails to report for induction and is prosecuted. "[The] courts are not to weigh the evidence to determine whether or not the classifications made by the local board were justified. The decisions of the local boards made in conformity with the regulations are final even though they be erroneous." The court further stated that such decisions can be voided only if they "have no basis in fact."[169] Thus judicial tribunals cannot duplicate the weighing process pursued by administrative boards to determine a defendant's sincerity, but could overrule a selective service judgment only if it had utterly no factual basis.

This ruling, in effect, deprives the individual of his constitutional right to a jury trial. Many other determinations are made by administrative boards, and their errors are considered susceptible to the system of laws, but the case of a conscientious objector is a special one. First, he is basing his appeal upon a commitment superior to all laws and, unlike the utility that is turned down in its request for a rate increase, he cannot be expected to accept administrative errors as an unavoidable consequence of submitting to society's laws.[170] Second, if the board erroneously classifies a sincere objector, it in effect consigns him either to jail or exile. The individual's only other alternative is to deny his conscience and submit to induction.

The current administrative procedures also deny the individual the right to counsel that is guaranteed in jury trials.[171] Such assistance is particularly important when the petitioner is uneducated or inarticulate. Thus the law discriminates against those who lack intellectual or verbal virtuosity. By not guaranteeing a court-appointed attorney it also discriminates against those too poor to afford consultation with a private attorney prior to the administrative hearing.

Finally, the draft board is a particularly inappropriate agency for determining conscientious objector pleas. Board members, who tend to be conservative and literal-minded, are not fair samples of the population. Moreover, they have a vested interest in minimizing the number of persons who are exempt from the draft. The Selective Service system often establishes general policy lines of leniency or strictness, rather than considering each case carefully.[172]

By both statute and judicial decree the right of conscientious objection to a particular war has been denied. Yet sound arguments can be adduced for granting such exemptions. First, opposition to a particular war may be no less crucial to the individual than opposition to all wars. Witness, for example, the many young men who have resigned themselves to jail or exile as a result of their opposition to the Vietnam war. Second, the individual who refuses to participate in a given war may simply be unwilling to generalize his beliefs to all circumstances. But an existentialist morality is no less valid than an absolutist one. In fact, the position of objectors to particular wars is often such that they would not be willing to participate in any conflict that is likely to develop.173

The impact of the changes in conscientious objection implied in the previous paragraphs would be substantial: thousands of young men would be spared the agonizing choice between violating their consciences or facing jail or exile.

Several arguments may be raised against this broadening of the scope of conscientious objection. First, a lenient standard, it is said, would encourage cheaters, persons who seek to avoid military service on non-conscientious bases yet claim to be C.O.s. Second, it is feared that such a development would endanger the state by creating a shortage of military manpower. Third, there is the danger that if we allow selective objection it would create a precedent for granting exemptions to those selectively opposed to other social decisions, such as paying taxes.174

The first argument is undercut by the fact that C.O.s can be required to perform two years in alternative service. But anyone who seeks to avoid military duty for selfish reasons would hardly opt for two years' alternative service; he would probably pursue total exemption on grounds of physical or mental unfitness. With respect to the second argument, many who are unable to attain conscientious-objector status under the current laws and procedures do not serve; they leave the country, or go to jail, or trump up medical deferments. If, however, the situation should pose a direct threat to national survival, ample manpower would be available; but if the vast majority of young men refuse to participate in a war, this should be a good indication that our involvement is misguided and should cease.175 Finally, military duty deserves a status apart from other social obligations; it demands that an individual place his life in jeopardy and take the lives of others. Should he be asked to undertake such an obligation for a cause he believes unjust or meaningless?176

Good-Faith Belief Defense

It has been suggested, in a different context, that an individual accused of criminal advocacy be permitted to offer the jury a good-faith belief defense, based on his belief that the conduct he advocates is legally or constitutionally protected. If he could establish the sincerity of such a belief to the satisfaction of the jury, he would be acquitted.177

The case for a good-faith belief defense is based on several considerations.178 First, such a defense is deemed necessary to safeguard draft counsellors. Selective Service laws are complicated and ambiguous, and a counsellor may often advise action which, upon litigation, proves to be illegal. Without a good-faith defense, he could be punished for criminal advocacy.179 Second, such a defense would blunt the effect of advocacy statutes on free speech. As previously mentioned, it is extremely difficult to determine in advance whether controversial expression will be deemed illegal; thus individuals may be deterred from putting forth dissident views. If they could offer a good-faith defense, the deterrent effect would be curtailed.

The major objection to such a good-faith defense is that an advocate could claim such a defense and render the incitement laws virtually inoperable. Yet a good-faith defense would be subject to jury scrutiny, and would not necessarily be granted every defendant. Blatant cases of prohibited speech would still be punished, but in borderline cases it would be desirable to tip the balance in favor of the accused. Moreover, juries tend to be prejudiced against defendants in First Amendment cases and a good-faith defense would be a salubrious countervailing influence.

Summary Imprisonment

Section 2 of the McCarran Act, the Internal Security Act of 1950, provides for the detention without trial in time of "war, invasion or insurrection" of those who could reasonably be expected to engage in espionage or sabotage. In essence, this provision authorizes the creation of concentration camps: places of internment into which a citizen could be thrust without jury trial, solely on the basis of his associations, speech, or politics. Not only is the legislation contrary to the ethos of our democracy, it appears to be blatantly unconstitutional, contradicting the First, Fifth and Sixth Amendments. Yet it has never been ruled unconstitutional in the courts, and previous precedent makes it consistent with legality. These precedents, which condoned the World War II exclusion of Japanese-Americans from constitutional protection, are among the most reprehensible events in American history.

In 1942 the combination of wartime hysteria and deep-seated racial prejudice spawned the internment of Japanese-Americans. In the name of military necessity, over 100,000 West Coast Japanese, including 70,000 United States citizens, were taken from their homes and placed in prison camps. The sole basis for this detention was the untested assumption that people of Japanese blood were likely to perform acts of sabotage. The Japanese were arrested and incarcerated without jury trial, without any inquiry. Yet there was no immediate emergency: the courts were open and functioning, and Hawaii, with more than twenty times as many Japanese in relation to its population, never felt the need for such Draconian measures. In fact, no Japanese-American in Hawaii was convicted of sabotage or espionage throughout the war.180

Three years after the initial arrests, 70,000 Japanese were still imprisoned. Not only did they suffer an enormous loss of freedom, many suffered irreparable property losses as well.181 The tragedy of the Japanese internment was summarized by Eugene V. Rostow, dean of the Yale Law School:

> Our wartime treatment of Japanese aliens and citizens of Japanese descent on the West Coast was hasty, unnecessary, and mistaken. The course of action which we undertook was in no way justified or required by the circumstances of war. It was calculated to produce both individual injustice and deep-seated social maladjustments of a cumulative and sinister nature.182

When litigation arising from the internments finally reached the Supreme Court, it did not issue a ringing declaration that the Constitution applied to these citizens as well as to the rest of society. In *Hirabayashi* and *Korematsu*, bowing to the military establishment and without reviewing its evidential foundation (nonexistent), the Court accepted the army's contention that "residents having ethnic affiliations with an invading force may be a greater source of danger than those of different ancestry" and that, in wartime, they could be dealt with in summary fashion.183 The Supreme Court thus sanctioned the rejection of our most precious rights on a slight possibility of military necessity. The word of the generals was taken on faith; they were given the power to repeal, by fiat, two hundred years of American democracy.

Given the broad phraseology of the McCarran Act and the precedent of the Japanese internments, many arguments might suffice to seize and intern individuals once the law is invoked. Membership in certain political organizations, allegedly disloyal speeches, participation in demonstrations are no more tenuous grounds for imprisonment than ancestry. Moreover, the act does not require a declaration of war to be invoked; a presidential declaration of emergency would suffice.

If the McCarran Act is tested judicially, the court may reverse the *Hirabayashi* and *Korematsu* precedents, especially considering the almost universal denunciation of these decisions. Yet cases may not reach the Supreme Court for months or even years after the initial imprisonment—the first Supreme Court test of the Japanese internments came three years after Pearl Harbor. Moreover, given the tendency of the court to defer to military pressure, such reversals may be a forlorn hope. Steps should be taken immediately to safeguard the constitutional rights of all Americans in time of war and emergency.

Section 2 of the McCarran Act should be repealed, and the rule established one hundred years ago in *ex parte Milligan*, that there can be no summary arrest and detention when civilian courts are open and operating, should be restored.[184] So long as juries can be convened and trials conducted, no one should be denied his constitutional rights to a trial by jury. None of our wars has shown this need for police-state measures. Rather than serving an essential purpose of pursuing war or quelling insurrection, such procedures provide only an opportunity for cashiering groups of individuals whose political opinions or racial background offend the military or executive establishments. The target in World War II was a despised racial group; but under present laws, any of us may be subject to the horrors of summary detention.

THE ROLE OF THE JURY

Prosecutions involving First Amendment issues are particularly sensitive. First, they entail extraordinarily difficult questions of fact. If the defendant claims that his actions are constitutionally sanctioned, the tribunal must determine whether they fit the appropriate standard for First Amendment protection. If this test involves balancing state needs and individual liberty or evaluating the danger of expression, as do all current rules, then enormously complex issues develop. Second, an abuse of criminal prohibition could substantially undermine the freedom of thought, association, and expression upon which our society rests. This point is particularly important in light of the fact that First Amendment prosecutions often involve detested members of society, such as Abbie Hoffman, Jerry Rubin, and H. Rap Brown.

Which fact finder, then, the judge or the jury, is best equipped to weigh the complicated matters arising in freedom of speech cases and to afford maximum protection to the accused? At first glance, the verdict seems divided. Judges, because of their legal background and training, are better able to apply First Amendment doctrine, while the jury is considered to be more protective of the individual.

Although, in most types of cases, juries may be more lenient than judges, this is not true of First Amendment trials. Defendants in such proceedings tend to be unpopular advocates of minority positions of which a jury is not likely to be tolerant. Some critics have argued that judges, "by virtue of their training and occupation . . . are more inclined to realize the importance of first amendment value."185 Combining this view with the judge's expertise in applying free speech doctrine, such critics have sought to narrow the role of the jury in First Amendment cases. They have proposed rules under which the issues juries may scrutinize are sharply limited. In some civil cases, the jury is entirely eliminated.186

Other critics, nonetheless, have stressed the importance of the jury in free speech cases. They maintain there is no conclusive evidence that, under current conditions, either the judge or the jury is more favorably inclined toward dissident defendants. But, they assert, if the government should attempt to trample on community mores, the jury could again serve as a valuable buffer against the state. Moreover, the jury performs a key ritualistic function in America: it helps legitimize criminal penalties by subjecting them to community judgments.187

At present, the best of both worlds may be realized, to a limited extent. Prior to the submission of the facts to a jury, a judge may decide whether the defendant's conduct is protected by the First Amendment. If he decides that it is, he can dismiss the charges. If he reaches a contrary judgment, he may or may not invite the jury to ponder the same issue.188 It is unlikely, however, that he would frequently grant the jury such power, and it is equally unlikely that a jury would overrule a judge in a constitutional matter. Thus a further procedure is necessary.

This procedure should establish formal consideration by both the judge and the jury of constitutional issues in First Amendment prosecutions. When it is found that a trial involves substantial First Amendment considerations, the defendant should first receive a jury trial in which all the issues are scrutinized. If the accused is convicted, he could then appeal to the judge to determine, on his own, whether his constitutional rights are being infringed upon, and the judge would have the power to void the verdict. In addition, prior to empaneling the jury, the judge could rule whether on its face the charge or claim should be dismissed on constitutional grounds.

It could be argued that appellate courts could validly perform the review function outlined above, but appellate bodies act on the basis of the record and seek only legal errors; they do not reach conclusions with respect to matters of fact. And, of course, the question of constitutional rights is often a matter of fact. Placing review powers in the hands of the trial judge ensures the defendant the benefit of both community and expert appraisal.

This safeguard, or at least the right to choose between judge and jury, should also be applied to petty offenses. Currently, trial by jury is reserved for serious offenses; it is not necessary in petty offenses, defined as those entailing a penalty of less than six months in jail. This exception is justified on the ground that while such punishment does not represent a severe hardship, bench trials help ease court congestion and thus expedite the trials of persons charged with serious crimes while conserving state resources.[189] Yet when First Amendment freedoms are at stake, prosecution for petty offenses can be critically important to both the individual and society in general:

> The social interest in protecting freedom of expression implicit in cases having a first amendment dimension is neither diminished nor attenuated by the consideration that the offense is petty. . . . Prosecutions for such low visibility crimes as breach of peace, obstructing passageways, and conducting a public meeting without a permit, to name but a few, may have serious deterrent effects upon the exercise of first amendment liberties, to say nothing of those instituted under statutes and ordinances which explicitly restrict speech and publication.[190]

Deprivation of the opportunity for jury trial places the accused at the mercy of the local legal system. He has no way of avoiding hostile judges or those who are the cronies of police and prosecutor. He can be arrested, charged, prosecuted, and convicted quickly and cheaply.

CONCLUSION

No one today questions the value of unfettered thought and expression. Yet the effectuation of these freedoms has been a slow, painful, and as yet uncompleted process. Most vexing has been the question of distinguishing constitutionally protected speech from that which is subject to curtailment.

This matter was first investigated by those who wrote in opposition to the Alien and Sedition Acts of 1798, but these laws soon disappeared and a lethargic government soon exerted little pressure on free speech during the nineteenth century. Only in 1917, when the government again began prosecuting expression, were free speech standards first articulated by the Supreme Court. Since that time continual governmental efforts to suppress various kinds of speech have spawned a substantial body of judicial precedent. Although the years between the bad tendency and incitement tests have witnessed much progress, free speech is not yet secure in this nation.

This chapter has suggested a new and more libertarian definition of free speech based upon the interaction between speaker and audience, and has offered specific reforms in the areas of conspiracy law, intended acts, freedom of conscience, summary detention, and petty offenses. The role of the jury in scrutinizing First Amendment matters has also been explored.

Given the repressive inclinations of the national government and the apathy or hostility of most American citizens, it is critical that judicial guarantees of free expression be substantially strengthened.

11 No-Fault Insurance

To assert that the personal injury and tort cases, which appear in droves in the civil courts, constitute a major problem is to assert the obvious. Delays of up to five years in settlement or final disposition are, regrettably, all too common. By far the primary source of such cases, and in the opinion of many the immense court backlogs, are automobile injury cases, leading to some two-thirds of all cases brought before juries in Massachusetts.[191] The figure for Michigan is 56 percent.[192] This chapter will therefore examine civil cases by way of a case study of the automobile personal injury claim and the means for its disposition.

Highway deaths are now running at an annual rate of well over 50,000, a plateau which was scaled five years ago. The 1 millionth victim of the slaughter on our highways died in 1954, and the 2 millionth victim will probably die by 1975.[193] Since 1964 the annual count of injuries caused by automobile accidents has exceeded 4 million.[194] Direct economic losses from these accidents were estimated in excess of $7.5 billion in 1963 alone.[195]

This carnage on the highways has been reflected in the civil courts which attempt to recompense the injured victims of highway accidents. As noted above, automobile accidents are a fruitful source of litigation; yet the attempt to aid the injured through the courts has been labeled "cumbersome, time-consuming, expensive, and almost ridiculously inaccurate" by the usually reserved Professor William L. Prosser of the Hastings College of Law.[196] Skyrocketing insurance premiums have aroused the public. And, of course, the claims of the 4 million victims must also be considered. In view of its magnitude, therefore, the problem of auto cases in the legal system deserves analysis.

This chapter will attempt to provide such an analysis by examining the apparatus of the automobile claims system, the conceptual formulation of the system, and the flaws which have appeared in practice. Attempts to reform the system while preserving its basic elements will also be considered. Finally, the prospect of entirely new systems of disposition of these claims will be discussed. The prospect of voluntary or compulsory arbitration of these claims, now used to a limited degree by the insurance companies among themselves, will be examined. So will a new system of auto insurance, one which replaces the adversary process with social insurance to all, regardless of fault. For purposes of illustration, the final section will explore in depth the "no fault" proposals advocated by Professors Robert Keeton and Jeffrey O'Connell, as their version is the most highly developed of a number of similar proposals.

While our analysis will focus primarily on automobile claims, it is of general validity. Many of the problems arising in automobile cases appear in virtually every other type of tort case before the courts. This largest single source of litigation, then, is typical of much of the rest.

THE FAULT SYSTEM OF COMPENSATION

The present system of compensating persons injured in traffic accidents operates upon a simple principle of fault: the person who was responsible for the accident assumes the burden of recompense for himself and for anyone he injured. This seemingly simple principle, however, has become hedged with exclusions which in many cases leave each party to the accident to his own devices. Even if insurance is carried, it often benefits neither party.

This situation occurs because the system operates on a principle of law that many consider to be outmoded: the old English common law of negligence.[197] Under this law, a person whose negligence is wholly responsible for injury to another is required to make good the loss.[198] It should be clear that, when applied to automobile claims, this "simple principle" becomes exceedingly complex. In the first place, a plaintiff in a civil action must show that he was injured as a direct result of the defendant's negligence; he must, in legal terms, establish that the negligence was the proximate cause of his injury. Often this requirement cannot be fulfilled. Many times there is no negligence by either driver— the accident "just happened."[199] Even if negligence was a factor, it may be hard to prove; the defendant is certain to deny it in court, and objective proof is rarely forthcoming. Finally, the plaintiff must show that his injury was a direct result of the accident.[200] The result, according to Prosser, is "a substantial number of cases . . . in which legal fault does not exist, or cannot be proven to exist."201 In these circumstances the injured party cannot recover anything for his injury.

Even where negligence can be proved there may be no recovery, for the law in most states imposes another restraint upon the plaintiff: he must be free of any negligence himself. If the plaintiff is guilty of contributory negligence, most states deny him any recovery.202 To illustrate: if the plaintiff, driving at 10 miles per hour above the speed limit, should be broadsided by a driver who has just run a red light, neither driver will recover. Both drivers were negligent, and the attitude of the law, in effect, is "a plague on both your negligent houses."

Finally, even where the plaintiff has satisfied the legal requirements of proof of injury, proof of defendant's negligence, and freedom from contributory negligence, what Keeton and O'Connell refer to as a "thicket of common law doctrines" may still bar recovery.203 Governmental agencies and charitable organizations are, for the most part, immune from suit, and most states do not allow recovery if the negligent driver is a member of the injured party's immediate family. Some states also retain guest statutes, by which a passenger may not recover from the driver of the car in which he was riding unless there had been gross or wanton negligence, such as drunk driving.204 Even in such extreme circumstances, the defendant may still plead that the plaintiff "assumed the risk" by accepting a ride with a drunken driver.205 Proof of fault, therefore, is far from the simple proposition that it seems to be on the surface.

The purpose of the fault system is, of course, basically laudable: to ensure that wrongdoers bear the burden of the wrongs and that their innocent victims do not.206 There is a basic appeal of equity in the common law which developed into the fault system. In view of the complexity of modern automobile negligence law, however, one may well ask how equitable the system is in practice. It is a question which will be discussed at length elsewhere in this chapter.

Another justification for the fault system has been offered: the claim that personal financial responsibility for accidents serves as an incentive for avoiding them. The president of the New York State Trial Lawyers Association, Abraham Markhoff, expressed that point of view in 1968:

> The community has a great stake in preventing accidents, but the granting of compensation without fault to all who seek it will eliminate this accident prevention incentive. Thus, the floodgates

would be open to the drunk driver, the reckless driver, the speeder, the chronic tailgater, and others who disregard basic rules of safety.207

Of course, if the fear of personal injury does not offer sufficient incentive to avoid accidents, one might well wonder if mere money provides more. Also, the prevalence of private insurance has in most cases removed personal financial responsibility from consideration in all but the most severe cases.208 Considerations such as these led insurance executive Harold S. Baile to conclude that "no significant deterrent of carelessness results from a system of reparations. . . . The real objective should be to relieve the economic loss that results from an accident."209 And, finally, it might be argued that even the drunk, the reckless driver, the speeder, and the chronic tailgater are worthy of societal assistance if they are injured. This is not to say, however, that there is no merit in retaining some financial responsibility. For large firms, such as trucking firms, imposing some financial responsibility might be an excellent method of promoting safety.

Recognizing the limited financial ability of most individuals to recompense their victims, the present system has developed an extensive program of private voluntary insurance. Automobile coverage is now available to cover not only damage to one's own vehicle and medical bills for the injuries of persons in one's own car, but also any damages to another for which the insured is legally liable. Thus liability insurance is the variety with which this section will be mainly concerned. However, liability coverage is *not* a blanket contract by one's insurance company to cover all losses arising from an accident; only those losses for which the insured is legally liable himself are covered. Hence the numerous requirements for proof, discussed previously, are not waived by virtue of insurance. The plaintiff must still fulfill his entire burden of proof in order to collect from a defendant's insurance carrier.

In most states such liability insurance is purely optional. Except in Massachusetts, New York, and North Carolina, where liability insurance is compulsory, motorists are under no legal compulsion to obtain any insurance at all; and many do not. The latest available figures (for 1960) show that some 11 million of the 73 million vehicles then on the road carried no insurance whatever.210 Tragically, these uninsured vehicles are usually the most likely to be involved in accidents. The lack of insurance indicates a driver with little money, or a driver who is not concerned about any damage he may do, or both. The result is that a disproportionate number of accidents is caused by uninsured drivers.211

248

A number of attempts have been made to provide for the financial responsibility of all drivers. The simplest of these is also the most widespread: a financial responsibility law. These laws provide that if an individual has an unsatisfied automobile judgment against him, he must furnish the state proof of his financial responsibility for any future accident. This proof might be in the form of cash, a bond, or a certificate of liability insurance. In their absence, the driver's license and vehicle registration are revoked.

These laws provide some protection, although the victim in the first instance has no recourse. More recent versions of these laws provide that anyone involved in an automobile accident must show proof of ability to satisfy a judgment arising from the accident, upon penalty of forfeiture of driving privileges.[212] This is some improvement, but all too often these laws are not enforced.

Other attempts to provide for financial responsibility include compulsory insurance (in three states) and an unsatisfied judgment fund (in six). Compulsory insurance is just that: motorists in Massachusetts, New York, and North Carolina are required to have minimum liability insurance as a condition for obtaining their driver's license. Insurance companies that do business in these states are required to provide minimum insurance protection to any driver who cannot obtain insurance through the normal channels. North Dakota and New Jersey have adopted the alternative of an unsatisfied judgment fund, which provides a taxpayers' fund to pay unsatisfied automobile judgments up to a specific maximum.[213] Florida, New Hampshire, South Carolina, and Virginia have adopted a variant of this idea by charging uninsured motorists a fee to establish such a fund.[214]

The insurance companies have also developed a measure of protection against financially irresponsible drivers: uninsured motorist coverage. For a nominal payment, the uninsured motorist will receive protection from any financially irresponsible driver who causes damage for which he would be liable in court. The insured person may collect, from his own insurance company, any judgment which he has obtained but is uncollectible due to the defendant's lack of funds. These policies are generally limited to $10,000 per person for any one accident, with an absolute maximum of $20,000 per accident.

However, these devices are all aimed at providing standard insurance to all motorists; they do not alter the nature of insurance. Thus the system retains the basic characteristics of the fault system, with all the proof requirements for negligence and injury discussed above.

Once the injured motorist establishes the liability of the defendant by means of these proof requirements, he may demand his actual damages in cash, but the determination of those damages is another area in which the criteria are unclear. Certain types of damages can be easily established with reasonable objectivity, such as the determination of lost wages, medical bills, and out-of-pocket expenses, and with some degree of accuracy. Even in such relatively clear instances, however, questions as to the need for specific types of medical treatment and the amount of time a plaintiff is unable to work due to an accident cloud the issue. Still more difficult to determine are the proper damages for disfigurement or scarring or from some type of permanent but partial disability. Finally, juries are also allowed to award damages for "pain and suffering," although determination of the proper monetary award is a process of no discernible objectivity.[215] A standard measure of pain and suffering in the insurance industry is three to five times the special damages (loss of wages, medical expenses, and out-of-pocket costs), depending on whether the victim has retained a lawyer; but this is merely an arbitrary agreement according to an arbitrary standard. Keeton and O'Connell conclude:

> How, for example, is one to measure the value of the loss of a leg— especially the pain and suffering accompanying the loss? How is one to translate such suffering—both past and future—into dollars and cents? The answer, of course . . . is that one cannot. And yet this measuring [of] the unmeasurable is precisely what the jury is asked to do. The result is that the matter of damages is turned over entirely to the jury's discretion with only the most permissive limits on its exercise. The result in turn is license to squander or stint through whim or bias . . . . This means that suing for an automobile accident injury is a gamble resulting sometimes in a spectacular award and sometimes in little or nothing."[216]

A final aspect of recovery is that the measure of an individual's damages is not affected by any insurance which he may carry. Thus even if a plaintiff's medical bills have been paid by his own medical coverage, he may demand, and receive, compensation from the defendant for those expenses. If he also carries a "blanket" health policy, he may, in addition, recover his medical expenses from that insurance company as well. Thus it is not unusual for a person to collect in full for the same medical expenses from three different insurance policies.

In fact, at least three interrelated problems have arisen from the requirement that a jury trial determine negligence. The present method for disposition of these civil cases is (1) costly in terms of insurance premiums, (2) time consuming with respect to the courts, and (3) inequitable in reimbursing the injured.

In the first place, the overhead charges of every insurance company mean that the system is extremely wasteful of the consumer's premium dollar, and a variety of factors, in turn, contribute to this huge overhead. The possibility of double or even triple recovery for the same expenses has already been discussed and this legal but inequitable method of collecting benefits necessarily costs money. Lawyers' fees, both for insurance companies and injured claimants, are high. Insurance companies pay their attorneys approximately 9 percent of their overall premiums, and add that cost to the cost of insurance.[217] Plaintiffs' attorneys, in turn, usually charge their clients on a contingent basis: a percentage of whatever damages are recovered. And because these contingency fees, of course, accrue only if the plaintiff wins in court, successful suits must pay for the failures. The result is that contingency fees are high, usually at least 30 percent and often as much as 50 percent.[218] A recent study in Michigan found hat 68 percent of those who recovered damages from the other party had to accept collection fees, which ranged up to 60 percent of the total recovery (the mean cost for cases in which such expenses were incurred was 32 percent).[219] Thus a substantial proportion of every recovery must be paid to the attorney who secured it, further reducing the money available to victims.

The award of damages for pain and suffering is the second "added cost" of the system. The rationality of the process by which pain and suffering is reduced to a cash payment has already been discussed, but the costs inherent in such an approach of course add to the cost of insurance. Walter Blum and University of Chicago law professor Harry Kalven estimate that approximately 15 percent of the total cost of insurance could be saved by eliminating awards for pain and suffering and removing most of these cases from the courts.[220]

When salesmen's commissions are also considered, the sum of overhead expenses becomes staggering. The Conard study, cited earlier, indicated that more than 50 percent of the premium dollar is absorbed in overhead expenses. In other words, less than half of the total paid to insurance companies in premiums is returned to the victims of auto accidents.[221] The inevitable trend, therefore, is high and ever rising premiums, which even now are "a real and serious obstacle to adequate coverage, or even any coverage at all, even on the part of those who want it."[222]

In fairness to the insurance companies, it must be noted that much of the rise in premiums has been beyond their control. The costs of medical care, of hospital and doctor fees, have skyrocketed. The cost of auto repairs has risen even faster. The result is that it now costs 31 percent more to settle a personal injury claim than it did in 1961, and property damage claims have risen 46 percent.[223]

But it would be erroneous to assert that the companies can do nothing at all about the high cost of auto insurance. Indeed, a number of suggestions have been made, of which the most important is simply a redefinition of insurance companies' accounting practices. Without delving too deeply into the mysteries of insurance accounting, it can be said that the companies are much more profitable than their accounting methods indicate; hence there is scope for lower premiums.

Because insurance companies calculate their underwriting profit or loss by subtracting their overhead costs and their payments to claimants from their total premium collections,[224] many companies show a loss on their underwriting business. What this accounting method fails to show, of course, is the huge profit made by insurance company investments. Premiums are paid in advance and the companies invest this money, usually at a handsome profit. This income, which also should be taken into account, makes insurance companies among the most profitable corporations in America. Thus a redefinition of accounting procedures that reflects investment income might well produce a substantial reduction in insurance costs when applied to the overhead costs encountered via legal fees, awards for pain and suffering, and duplicate coverage, which are substantial inefficiencies in the present system.

Inasmuch as the requirement that a jury trial settle large claims leads to lengthy court delays and court congestion, the fact that automobile injury cases constitute the major portion of all civil jury trials will again be recalled. The huge number of such cases, in the opinion of many, is a major reason for the delays which occur in trials. The average delay from the time of filing suit in an automobile injury case is thirty-one months.[325]

Thus the widespread belief that the automobile injury case is a major cause of courtroom congestion and the problems associated with such delays.

It is by no means certain, however, that auto cases are the primary cause of the delay. The fact that these cases are so prolonged may only reflect the higher priority given criminal cases, condemnation suits, and workmen's compensation claims.[226] Thus insurance executive James S. Kemper concludes: "It is doubtful if personal injury litigation is the principal or even a significant cause of court congestion."[227] It must be noted, however, that the most that can be said for this position is that auto cases do not create inequities for other classes of persons. The unfortunate individual who must wait two and a half years to settle his personal injury case may well be inequitably treated, and the process by which delayed justice becomes injustice will be considered shortly.

Various methods for reducing the time lags in trials have been discussed elsewhere in this volume and will not be repeated, but all of these reforms would reduce delay by increasing the capacity of the system. According to the influential magazine *Judicature:*

> The best way to reduce these pressures is to move forward with reforms, improvements and modernizations that will make the courts so advantageous an instrumentality that the demand for an alternative will disappear. In so doing, we may preserve for every claimant and every defendant the oldest and most important kind of basic protection—the rules of evidence, representation by counsel, and other elements of due process of law.[228]

Yet with respect to civil cases, as opposed to criminal cases, perfunctory attempts to increase the capacity of the system may be self-defeating. If more cases can be heard by the courts, it may well be that more auto injury cases will be tried before a jury. Indeed, only a small percentage of auto injury cases are eventually tried before a jury. As Keeton and O'Connell note: "If only modest improvements are achieved, more of the vast numbers of claims now settled and held back from litigation because of intolerable delays will be brought forward to overwhelm the courts still more."[229]

In any event, it seems clear that the major source of court congestion is the automobile personal injury claim. Especially with respect to traffic victims, therefore, the huge backlog of personal injury suits is a leading cause for the third major problem of the system: the inequity of the entire process.

Auto insurance, in short, does not compensate those who need compensation while it lavishly overpays those who do not. Moreover, the reason for this inequity is intrinsic to a fault system which places the parties in an adversary proceeding. In other words, the settlement of large claims is often delayed, to the detriment of the injured victim, but small claims are processed rapidly and generously to avoid suits over small amounts of money.

The seriously injured victim is all too often the victim of the insurance system as well, because he needs money quickly. Not only must he pay large hospital and doctor bills but, if he is a breadwinner, his earnings are temporarily cut off. Because most people do not have the financial resources to pay for a lengthy stay in a hospital, insurance companies often take advantage of this situation to offer inadequate but immediate settlements to injured victims. The latter, faced with the prospect of waiting three years for a judgment in their favor, all too often take the settlement, even if they are not fully compensated for their out-of-pocket expenses.

The most comprehensive study of this problem, made in 1932 by a Columbia University study group, found that in 47 percent of the cases of temporary injuries the parties recouped less than their out-of-pocket expenses, which did not include disability or loss of earnings. The figures were 56 percent for those with permanent injuries and 55 percent for those with fatal injuries.[230] This study, of course, is dated, but its central conclusions are still valid.

If anything, the situation has grown even worse in recent years. The Conard study in Michigan discovered that most persons who suffered a loss of $25,000 or more received less than 25 percent of their loss and *none* received more than 75 percent.[231] These are the net recovery figures, after attorney fees and collection expenses were deducted.

The lack of ready cash also poses immense difficulties for early rehabilitative work—despite the latter's probable effectiveness. Some plaintiffs foolishly attempt to build a larger claim by forgoing such services and remaining in the hospital that much longer. Others are simply unable to afford expensive rehabilitation. Nor are insurance companies likely to aid "the enemy" with advance payments; rather, in many instances, they try to withhold payments to force a quick, and cheap, settlement.[232]

But again in fairness to the insurance industry, it should be noted that various companies are experimenting with an advance payments plan under which an injured person may be given periodic payments by the adverse insurance company, which are deducted from the final settlement. This program, however, is only experimental, operates only at the option of the company, and is used only in cases in which liability is clear and the claimants forgo the services of an attorney.

In addition to seriously injured claimants who are forced to settle for less than their expenses by sheer economic necessity, others receive no settlement at all. The reason for this is the strict morality of the fault system: if there is contributory negligence, injured victims cannot recover in most states. Thus if both parties were negligent, neither has a legal right to recover.

This is not an insignificant problem. The Conard study showed that some 45 percent of all seriously injured victims received no settlement and had to rely on their own insurance and resources, if any.233 The figure was 63 percent among all injured persons.234 Thus nearly half of the seriously injured and nearly two-thirds of all injured persons received no compensation (except, possibly, from their own personal medical payments coverage). Other out-of-pocket expenses and the loss of earnings were not covered.

Paradoxically, the reverse is true with respect to small claims, where the bargaining positions are reversed: an insurance company is anxious to escape a costly trial and hence eager to overpay a small claim. In the Michigan survey, nearly two-thirds of the claimants with small losses (under $1,000) received substantially more than they had lost.235 Since there are many more small injuries than large ones, the process most readily benefits those who do not need compensation more or less at the expense of a few who need it desperately. Thus the conclusion of Keeton and O'Connell, that "our system of compensating traffic victims is inadequate—rife with undercompensation or complete lack of compensation of many victims, and overcompensation of others," is unfortunately borne out. 236

12 Arbitration, Mediation and No-Fault Alternatives

An alternative to the trial system that clogs our courts and mistreats the injured victims of automobile accidents is a system of either voluntary or compulsory arbitration of civil cases. In effect, this would substitute the judgment of a skilled arbitrator for that of a trial judge and jury. In considering the merits and disadvantages of such a scheme, therefore, it will be easiest to discuss it as merely one of a number of alternatives to the jury system.

There is no single ideal system of arbitration; hence a description of the process must necessarily be general. This general analysis will be supplemented, however, by an examination of the arbitration mechanism insurance companies use to settle property damage claims among themselves.

Arbitration is a substitute for trial. There is no judge per se, no jury, and very little of the procedural formality that characterizes a jury trial.[237] The functions of both judge and jury are performed by the arbitrator, who may be an individual or a panel of any size. Usually the hearing is carried on in adversary fashion, with both sides represented (if they choose) by counsel. Occasionally, however, a more informal bargaining process may take place, which might be more appropriately called mediation.

The hearing can resemble a trial in that both parties are present, evidence is heard, and arguments are presented. This is not necessary, however, and many arbitration processes use only written documents, which are submitted to them by each party. Appeal may be allowed, but it is generally restricted to procedural points; there would be little purpose in arbitration if its findings of fact were reviewable by a court of law.

An excellent example of arbitration is implicit in the Inter-Insurance Company Arbitration Agreement, to which most major insurance companies in the United States are signatories. It substitutes binding arbitration for a trial in disputed property damage claims. To understand the operation of the agreement, however, insurance will have to be more fully explained.

Many people carry automobile collision insurance which allows them to collect from their insurance company if their car is damaged in a collision. If a negligent driver collides with the insured vehicle, the owner has two methods of recourse: he can attempt to recover from the negligent driver or he can recover from his own insurance company. If he opts for the latter, his right of recovery from the other driver is transferred, or subrogated, to his insurance company. In effect, the latter has bought the rights to the policy owner's claim against the negligent driver. If this second driver has property damage insurance, he will notify his company and the dispute will be handled by the two insurance companies.

Prior to the arbitration agreement, disputed claims were settled by trial; this, however, proved inordinately expensive. Most property damage claims were relatively small (from the standpoint of insurance companies): a few thousand dollars at most. Thus it made little sense to spend $1,000 or $1,500 to try such cases before a jury when the maximum recovery might be less than $1,000. After the arbitration agreement was promulgated, each signatory company surrendered its right to file suit against any other member of the agreement. Instead, disputes would be settled by arbitration.

Decisions are usually rendered by one person, an insurance adjuster experienced in automobile law. For obvious reasons, he will not be connected with either company involved in an action. If the damage claim exceeds a specified maximum, either company may request that a three-man panel hear the case. Hearings are based on submitted documents only, and the decision of the arbitrator is final and binding. This system has been employed for several years, and the member companies are well satisfied with it.

It would not be strictly necessary, of course, to substitute arbitration for the entire trial—it might be possible to use the procedure to settle certain issues of fact and to refer other issues to trial. Or arbitration could be used to narrow the issues before the parties by determining which issues of fact will be the subject of the trial.

(In view of modern pretrial procedures, however, such a provision would seem to be useless because minor issues can easily be dispensed with by stipulation between the parties. Pretrial discovery processes quickly reveal which facts are in dispute, and most lawyers have no desire to waste time in trial; they are too busy, and hence are usually eager to settle minor issues in advance of trial. But this does not mean that they are in a hurry to get to court—merely that they do not waste time once they are in court.)

It is almost essential that any new system of arbitration be compulsory upon the parties. In the first place, voluntary arbitration can be, and is, used today, and if there is motivation for using an arbitrator there are mechanisms that can provide one. But such motivation is usually lacking. For voluntary arbitration to be useful, both parties must perceive that it benefits them. In civil cases, what benefits one party generally operates to the detriment of the other. Hence neither party is likely to agree to binding arbitration because each fears that to do so would provide an advantage to the other.

The success of the insurance arbitration agreement does not refute the above thesis; it is successful only because of the large number of cases each insurance company handles. To illustrate, it would be to the advantage of State Farm Mutual to force Allstate to sue for all its property damage claims against State Farm (the small claims would probably never be pressed), but State Farm has similar claims against Allstate and it knows that intransigence in settling Allstate's claims will lead to similar intransigence against itself. In an individual case, arbitration would benefit only one of the parties, but in the aggregate it can assist both. Such a happy result, however, can occur only if each company has many identical claims, which is rarely the case for the individual citizen. What is practicable for a giant insurance company is senseless for the common man.

Moreover, there are usually strong pressures against arbitration from both sides in a civil dispute. Plaintiffs' attorneys are fearful of independent, knowledgeable experts, so that the techniques that win large awards from juries are useless in front of an experienced and impartial legal expert. In the aggregate, a plaintiff's chances of collection are not improved and his chances of collecting a large settlement (if he collects at all) are lessened.

However, insurance companies are not especially eager to settle claims via arbitration, and precisely because such a process is assumed to be speedier than a court trial. Inasmuch as insurance companies use lengthy pretrial delays to force claimants to accept cheap settlements, the last thing they want is a method of speeding the disposition of lawsuits. Thus voluntary arbitration seems doomed to failure, and only compulsory arbitration will attract any volume of cases.

The primary advantage associated with arbitration proceedings is efficiency. Presumably, they take much less time and money than a full-scale jury trial. Also, the need for greater speed is obvious: if an individual has been injured by another it is only simple justice to right the wrong as soon as possible. Moreover, the lengthy delays associated with civil cases allow insurance companies to "bargain down" the claimant with an offer of an inadequate but immediate cash settlement. If the arbitration process can eliminate or reduce these delays, it should be well worthwhile.

On its face, arbitration will do just that because it eliminates the jury trial, which generally consumes about 40 percent more time than a trial before a judge alone.[238] Presumably, this saving in time would be increased by arbitration, which eliminates many of the time-consuming rules of evidence and procedure, and which often dispenses entirely with personal appearances.

Unfortunately, this potential time saving may not be realized in practice. Various types of arbitration hearings are presently conducted by numerous quasi-judicial administrative or regulatory agencies of the government, such as the Selective Service system, but these hearings have not proved to be models of efficiency. As the *Columbia Law Review* noted:

> The number of federal cases involving ten or more trial days has increased steadily over a recent ten-year period, 160 in 1955 to 228 in 1965. . . . But the length of judicial proceedings is dwarfed by the amount of time consumed in an administrative hearing. A survey of 20 agencies made in 1958, the last year in which these figures were compiled by the Office of Administrative Procedure, showed that the total time consumed from the moment when a case was assigned to a particular hearing examiner to the moment he announced his decision on the merits exceeded one year in 373 of the cases examined in 1958. In 1,222 cases, it exceeded six months.[239]

Of course, an analogy between these hearings and arbitration is not necessarily valid, nor are fourteen-year-old statistics the most reliable. Also, even these lengthy delays may be preferable to the more intolerable delays associated with the court system. But these data provide evidence that the arbitration process is not the instantly effective process that many of its advocates claim.

Even if the delays could be significantly reduced via an arbitration process, there is a question as to the long-term effectiveness of such a process. It will be recalled that the vast majority of lawsuits are settled out of court, but if the pretrial period is reduced substantially, more of these cases will be pressed to their conclusion, which might create the same conditions we now face. Thus expanding the capacity of the system may only expand the inundation of claims.

Finally, it may be asked whether, in fact, the arbitration process is necessary to achieve a substantial increase in the capacity of the system. Numerous other alternatives, such as the six-man jury, have been proposed, and it has been asserted that such a reduction in the size of the jury has done much to speed up the trial process.[240] Another possibility might be the establishment of firm dates for trial, with only one or two continuances allowed. Such a reform would not only speed up the trial process, but the pressure associated with a firm trial date might cause more cases to be settled and thereby be a double incentive to efficiency.[241] Thus there is substantial question as to both the effectiveness and the necessity of the arbitration process.

The problems associated with the transfer of civil court cases to an arbitration process are no more quantifiable than the advantages, inasmuch as the jury's role as fact finder cannot be proved to be essential, or even desirable. Lacking an absolute standard for determining truth, we cannot pass judgment on the jury's ability to accurately determine the facts of a given situation. However, that does not imply that the jury has no value as fact finder. In the public's eye, the jury is essential to an accurate factual determination, and thus decisions handed down by a jury are considered more legitimate than those given by a judge alone.[242] Tradition plays a very important role in American life, and the legitimizing function of a jury should not be overlooked.

It is enough, then, to say that people believe the jury is essential, and therefore its elimination would only damage faith in and respect for the law in general. Persons whose cases are settled by a jury verdict believe that they "had their day in court." They would not necessarily lose faith in the law if they received an adverse decision from an arbitrator, but there would be a loss of respect.

Another disadvantage associated with the arbitration process is the elimination of procedural rules. To the extent that these rules are valuable (and for the most part they are), arbitration will not yield as accurate a decision as a trial. Most procedural rules have a solid basis in experience and their elimination lessens the likelihood of accuracy in a decision. It is, of course, possible to retain these rules in arbitration, but only at the sacrifice of a main source of their efficiency.

In sum, while the problems generated by compulsory arbitration are not great, neither are the advantages associated with it. Arbitration would probably not do a great deal of harm, but it would not be especially valuable either. Perhaps the solution to the heavy civil court caseload is another alternative: elimination of the fault principle.

THE NO-FAULT ALTERNATIVE

The no-fault concept is not new, but it was recently given a major boost by the publication of the Keeton-O'Connell basic protection plan,[243] the most thoroughly documented and detailed proposal for reform that has yet been presented. It includes a model statute that would initiate the plan, plus a detailed analysis of its procedure (a variant was recently adopted in Massachusetts), and for these reasons the Keeton-O'Connell plan will serve as a model for discussion of the no-fault concept. Because it has flaws which are not generic to the no-fault concept, the focus of this section will be on its ability to avoid the difficulties encountered in the present system.

The Keeton-O'Connell plan eliminates the concept of fault from automobile accident settlements in most instances. It also requires compulsory, no-fault insurance for all motorists. In the event of an accident, an injured person is compensated by his own insurance company for his economic losses: medical expenses, loss of wages, and out-of-pocket expenses. Awards for pain and suffering are not allowed, except in cases in which the normal award for pain and suffering would exceed $5,000 and all damages exceed $10,000. If the injuries are so severe that these conditions are fulfilled, a normal negligence suit is allowed; otherwise every motorist is exempt from personal liability for personal injury. The initial proposal was confined to injuries but later versions include optional clauses to cover damage to automobiles as well.

The plan, in effect, is a type of workmen's compensation within the present systemic structure of insurance. All injury victims are compensated for their economic losses, regardless of who was at fault. Benefits are payable monthly to prevent the economic pressure which now forces many claimants to settle for less than their actual losses.[244] The plan contains a number of other clauses, but these are its essential features.

Keeton and O'Connell claim that their proposal will substantially reduce the costs of automobile insurance. While the proposal would provide an increase in benefits and (as drafted) the payment of attorneys' fees, it would also provide important savings. It would eliminate the double coverage of medical payments and policies against uninsured motorists; it would (hopefully) reduce the expenses of litigation; and it would not provide pain and suffering awards.[245] Insurance actuary Frank Harwayne estimates that the basic protection plan would reduce costs by about 25 percent.[246]

On the other hand, the additional cost factors inherent in the basic protection plan might cancel out these savings. The plan provides more benefits; that is its raison d'être. It also provides for the payment of legal fees in negotiating settlements. And because of the difficulty of determining actual economic losses, this provision would seem to invite costly and complicated legal battles. Thus Massachusetts chief actuary M. G. McDonald estimates that the plan would raise premiums from between 18 and 35 percent in Massachusetts.[247] Even if the plan should realize the full cost savings claimed for it, the rate reduction would be only on the order of a dollar or so per month for the average driver.[248]

The truth of the matter is that no one really knows, or can predict with any accuracy, the real cost of the plan.[249] Insurance company statistics are not organized so as to predict the effects of such a change, and the Massachusetts experience has not been helpful this way. Before the plan had been in effect for six months, the state supreme court ruled that a number of its rate-setting factors were unconstitutional.

The same factors that make cost savings problematical also cast doubt on the plan's ability to reduce court congestion, although Keeton and O'Connell claim a reduction of up to 75 percent in the time a court requires to administer the basic protection plan.[250] Presumably, this would be achieved by the cessation of tort suits, as everyone's economic loss would be covered up to $10,000. Nevertheless, two problems remain. First, negligence suits for more than $10,000 are common, and the plan's provision for legal fees is an incentive to file additional suits.[251] Second, the plan provides for court determination of economic loss, which would not seem to relieve the crowded court schedules. As Kemper concludes: "It seems highly probable that congestion in those few metropolitan court systems that now have the problem will be unrelieved or increased, and that congestion will become a problem in the far greater part of our judicial system which is now free of it."[252]

There is a precedent for such a gloomy conclusion when the analogy of basic protection in workmen's compensation is recalled, which has proved to be most productive of litigation. Disputes over the degree and cause of injuries and the amount of compensation are frequent and commonplace. As the Supreme Court observed, workmen's compensation has been "litigiously prolific."[253]

Arbitration boards might be of real value here if they could determine the proper amounts of settlement. However, this procedure is used in workmen's compensation cases and the results were indicated in the preceding paragraph. Thus it seems that the basic protection plan will not have much effect on crowded court calendars.

With respect to equity, however, the Keeton-O'Connell plan is encouraging, although critics attack it for the exclusion of damages for pain and suffering and for compensation of careless or dangerous drivers. Its exclusion of pain and suffering awards (except in severe cases) has been the most important objection by far, and the basis for the attack upon the constitutionality of the Massachusetts no-fault law. The Massachusetts supreme court heard arguments that the elimination of the pain and suffering award unconstitutionally deprives the individual of property without due process of law.[254] The critics' position is that pain and suffering is an integral element of damages and should be allowed.

Three comments are in order vis-à-vis pain and suffering. First, nothing in the no-fault concept excludes awards for pain and suffering by one's insurance company. Second, an award for pain and suffering is equivalent to an additional type of benefit from an insurance policy, which can be financed as such. In light of the objections to the cost of no-fault insurance, the exclusion of pain and suffering may very well be justified. Third, if a choice must be made of which benefits to forgo, it seems clear that everyone should recover his economic loss before additional money is spent for compensating such an intangible as pain and suffering. Cost apparently dictates the maximum level of total benefits, and therefore the division of benefits is the only real question. By any rational assessment, providing for the minimum needs of all traffic victims is superior to providing an additional benefit to some at the expense of others.

Other critics have charged that the no-fault concept would reward socially reprehensible behavior.[255] The theory is that drunks, speeders, etc., should not be compensated by society for injuries they suffer through their own negligence. The only rationally defensible principle behind this argument is that their inability to recover their economic losses will deter them from such antisocial behavior, but the principle is wrong. If an individual is not deterred from speeding or drunken driving by fear of injury, he will hardly be more receptive to financial pressure. And if withholding societal aid cannot deter them from antisocial conduct, its only function is retribution, which is unworthy of modern society.

The Keeton-O'Connell plan, therefore, would seem to accomplish its goal of providing a more equitable method of compensating traffic victims. In sum, the no-fault plan avoids the lengthy delays and inadequate settlements associated with the present system by promptly compensating all, regardless of fault, to the full extent of their economic loss. Although the plan may not succeed in its secondary aims of alleviating court congestion or lowering the cost of insurance, it promises to be a basically fairer system. It is therefore worthy of legislative consideration.

IV Assessment

13 Retrospect and Prospects

Every society, if it is to survive, must succeed in bringing violence under law and law in tune with justice. Bringing violence under law means that the state must have the monopoly on the legitimate use of force; true sovereignty cannot be shared, and various groups within a socially reprehensible behavior.255 The theory is that drunks, speeders, That exercise must be reserved for the government lest blood feuds, civil war, and myriad other violent acts destroy the order which can allow freedom to develop. This does not mean that an act of violence is pernicious to society's survival; it is only threatened by those perpetrators who claim the right to use force.

China could not survive as one nation with Mao Tse-tung controlling the countryside and Chiang Kai-shek the cities. Both armies could not claim to be the defender of the people and the protector against imperialism; a struggle for men's loyalties was inevitable. Before it ended, the fabric of Chinese society had been rent asunder; centuries-old traditions had been discredited; and millions of people had been brought into the political process for the first time. Chiang fled and Mao brought violence under law—his law.

The United States has done well in bringing violence under law. As the frontiersmen pushed west, settling new territory, they sought to establish some sort of protective order, but they could not rely on the nascent western governments. As a result, if a man was wronged by his neighbor he settled the score himself, in gunfights and family feuds. The next step in the development of western justice was for the aggrieved person to mobilize public opinion behind him when he was wronged and thus get help to even the score. This, after all, was a less risky and more effective way to get revenge, but it led to mob lynchings, vigilante groups, and tar and feathers, which marred the order of the United States in the nineteenth century. Finally, when government became installed in western society, revenge was taken out of the hands of ordinary citizens and given to specific governmental agencies. If a man committed a crime, the people could do nothing; the man would be arrested and brought to trial in a prescribed fashion.

However impressive the record of the United States has been, there have been occasions when violence has gone beyond the law and been used by those who felt they had the right to supplant the state in this, its almost definitional function. The Groveland case is one of the more infamous examples of force being taken from the government and turned into violence.

The increase of white violence against Negroes in the late 1950s and early 1960s is another example. While lynching had dwindled to only one case in 1947 and two in 1948, a new type of killing began. After the commencement of school integration in 1954, there were 530 cases of violence (mostly burnings and bombings) within four years. The black violence of 1965 to 1967 was in great part a reaction to this white violence. Thus the exercise of violence to obstruct compliance with the mandate of the state resulted in what can only be termed rebellion by 11 percent of the populace.

The recent attack on student demonstrators by construction workers again exemplifies the propensity of groups within a society to preempt the government's job of protection and punishment. Ironically, this confrontation occurred on Wall Street, the very epitome of the culture from which the students sought to "deliver" the workers, who did not care to be "saved."

In its attempt to monopolize the use of force, the government has taken steps to monopolize the means to carry on violence. It was easier to go next door and shoot your neighbor than to sue him in court, as long as you had a gun. Slowly, however, restrictions on firearms have grown and fewer guns are harbored in the homes of anxious citizens. While this has caused sudden acts of retributive violence to decline, it has not precluded such things as well-planned assassinations.

The process sought by the state is that of substitution. The violent reaction of the individual is replaced by the more reasoned response of the state. The success of this method depends on how quickly and effectively the state can step in and handle a situation. Indeed, not only must the state be able to do this, the people must have confidence that the state is ready and able to do this, if it is to deter them from acting on their own.

However, there are instances when this substitution process cannot be accomplished quickly enough to be effective, such as killing in self-defense. In the face of a physical attack by a hostile party, a citizen will not wait for government to come to his aid; he will inevitably resort to violence himself. The state allows for this contingency, and does not punish a person who has killed in self-defense.

In most cases, the state can fulfill its role and act with sufficient speed to satisfy the people. To engender faith in their ability to do this, many states make their police force highly visible, in addition to being well-trained and effective.

On balance, the United States has been fairly successful in construing the formula which seeks to link violence and justice. For the most part, violence has been brought under law. It is the task of bringing law in tune with justice that has proved the most elusive, and the focus of this volume has been on this very problem. The people will not defer the right to use violence unless they perceive that the state will exercise this right in accordance with the functions they seek to maximize. The function that society most often seeks to maximize is justice.

Hence all groups that perceive that the state does not use violence under law to bring about justice are prone to be mobilized for violence against the state. There are many such groups in our society; the Black Panthers and the Minutemen are but two. Similarly, there are always groups that feel there are basic flaws (ideological or inherently structural) in the system of government which preclude the attainment of justice. These people seek to overturn and change the system. There are other groups, however, that have no quarrel with the nature of the system but, instead, are disenchanted with its actual operation when compared to its potential. This gap between justice and the law grows wider as the system's operation worsens, and disenchanted groups become more and more alienated from the system.

This book has traced the development of the jury system from its inception to the present and has analyzed its deficiencies. The role of the free press in biasing juries has also been discussed. But the state cannot exercise its power justly if it cannot guarantee judgments that are rendered by honest, unpredisposed jurors. The activities of the press have made this a difficult guarantee; so to preserve its viability as a just governor the state must either silence the press or seek to circumvent its influence by changing the location of a trial, isolating the jurors, and the like. If this problem is ignored, it has the potential of alienating all classes of society, since anyone may be victimized by an unfair trial.

Next, the inability of military defendants to obtain justice was examined. These defendants are tried not by a jury of their peers but by officers who can more or less be coerced to do the bidding of the commanding officer. Inasmuch as officers are invariably concerned primarily with discipline, a minority of 3 million servicemen are often denied justice.

In addition, virtually all minorities are discriminated against, in one way or another, by the judicial system. The poor languish in prison, unable to make bail; blacks are judged by predominantly white juries, all too prone to convict them; the young and the radical political minorities are subjected to outrageous searches on campuses, streets, in their dormitories, and on our borders. Not even conversation is safe. In many cases not only is there unconscionable intrusion but, as a result of this intrusion, people are forced to spend years in prison, having been convicted by the evidence thus acquired. Thus many minorities are losing faith in the government's ability to enter into disputes and provide justice and order in place of chaos and anomie.

But transcending all these special evils is a massive, overriding problem: our badly overloaded courts. Any attempt to weed out biased jurors or exclude the findings of unconstitutional searches takes time, and aggravates the problem. Even the jury, society's best determinant of justice, whose power is superior to that of government officials, increases the length of trial. Meanwhile, helpless defendants, though presumed innocent, cannot make bail and languish in prison for perhaps several months awaiting their trials. Such incarceration costs the prisoner his job, often his mental balance, and sometimes his wife and family.

The law's delays and crudities in meting out justice has produced a mutation known as plea bargaining. As a result of this process, 95 percent of all defendants plead guilty, and hope for leniency in return, in large part, for permitting the court system to function in its decrepit fashion. However, this process is often coercive, and defendants have no safeguards, having waived the protections granted all who go to trial.

The problems of delay and plea bargaining affect all groups but they are especially pernicious for the poor, who, pleading innocent, face long months in jail, unable to make bail. As states assumed the powers of violence, they formalized the power to kill as a counterpart to the revenge killings they sought to eliminate. As society evolved, however, its need for killing virtually disappeared, although the state still has laws permitting the killing—which can be used by a repressive government in an anxious time.

Most of the disputes handled by the government have been classified as civil, but only 3 percent of them ever reach the court system; the rest are negotiated out of court. And well they might be, since the record of recovery through the courts shows that plaintiffs pay much of the cost of their misfortunes. Confidence in the government's ability to deal with these disputes is low among all classes. It takes too long to sue, and only rarely is satisfaction obtained.

Because of what has been shown about justice in the United States, it is no wonder that confidence in the government's ability to settle disputes is so low. Partly as a result, we witness record numbers of violent acts—crimes committed by people who do not think they will be caught and retributive acts by people and groups who will not rely on the government's substitute for their own quick, effective action. But the more that such acts are committed, the more overcrowded our inequitable system becomes. Thus confidence sinks ever lower.

As this tragedy unfolds, more and more people move from disenchantment to alienation. For the disenchanted, respect for law and the state is sufficient to keep them within the system. But as more and more people become totally alienated by the lapses of justice, the law becomes incapable of protecting society from violence by those who put justice before the law.

I Introduction to the Jury System

Notes

1 Trial by Jury

1. Maximus A. Lesser, *The Historical Development of the Jury System* (Rochester, N. Y.: New York Lawyer's Cooperative Publishing Co., 1884), p. 4.

2. George Grote, *Greece* (New York: Collier, 1889),pp. c,xlvi.

3. Lesser, op. cit., p. 15.

4. Ibid., pp. 26-27.

5. Sir Thomas Erskine Holland, *The Elements of Jurisprudence* (Oxford: Clarendon Press, 1880), ch. 2-3.

6. James B. Thayer, " 'Law and Fact' in Jury Trial," *Harvard Law Review*, 4:55.

7. William Carey Morey, *Outlines of Roman Law* (New York and London: Putnam, 1891), p. 390.

8. Lesser, op. cit., p. 35.

9. Morey, op. cit., pp. 86-87.

10. Lesser, op. cit., p. 37.

11. Morey, op. cit., pp. 87-88.

12. John Norton Pomeroy, *An Introduction to Municipal Law* (New York: Appleton, 1864), p. 785.

13. Lesser, op. cit., pp. 45-46.

14. Friedrich Karl von Savigny, *Geschichte Dei Romischen* (Heidelberg: J.C.B. Mohr, 1834), i.c.4. art.2.

15. Karl August Rogge, *Ueber Das Gerichtwesen Der Germanen* (Halle: Gebauer, 1820), ch. 3, sec. 14.

16. Savigny, op. cit., p. i.c.4.

17. Ibid., art.2.

18. Jakob Ludwig Karl Grimm, *Deutsche Rechts Alterthumer* (Gittingen: Dieterich, 1828), p. 786.

19. Ibid., p. 777.

20. Savigny, op. cit., p. i.c.4. art.2.

21. William Forsyth, *History of Trial by Jury* (London: Parkek, 1852), p. 39.

22. Ibid., p. 47.

23. Rogge, op. cit., ch. 4, sec. 28.

24. Forsyth, op. cit., pp. 52-53.

25. David Hume, *The History of England, from the Invasion of Julius Caesar to the Abdication of James the Second, 1688* (Boston: Phillips Sampson, 1849), p. c.I.

26. Lesser, op. cit., p. 57.

27. Hume, op. cit., p. c.I.

28. Ibid.

29. Forsyth, op. cit., p. 45.

30. Lesser, op. cit., p. 63.

31. Hume, op. cit., p. C.II.

32. Ibid., app. 1, p. 1.

33. Forsyth, op. cit., p. 56.

34. Ibid., pp. 57-58.

35. Pomeroy, op. cit., p. 368.

36. Thayer, op. cit., pp. 58-65.

37. John Reeves, *History of the English Law* (London: E. Brooke, 1787), 1:20.

38. Rogge, op. cit., p. c.8.

39. Pomeroy, op. cit., p. 980.

40. Lesser, op. cit., p. 83.

41. Hume, op. cit., app., p. 1.

42. Forsyth, op. cit., pp. 80-81.

43. Ibid., p. 83.

44. Thorieifr Gudmundson Repp, *Historical Treatise on Trial by Jury, Wager of Law, and Other Co-Ordinate Forensic Institutions Formerly in Use in Scandinavia and Iceland* (Edinburgh, 1832), p. 233.

45. Ibid., p. 167.
46. Lesser, op. cit., pp. 72-73.
47. Sir William Blackstone, *Commentaries on the Laws of England*, T. M. Cooley, ed. (Chicago: Callaghan, 1879), vol. 2, ch. 4.
48. Lesser, op. cit., p. 89.
49. Forsyth, op. cit., p. 93.
50. Reeves, op. cit., 1:30.
51. Forsyth, op. cit., p. 96.
52. Hume, op. cit., p. 653.
53. Lesser, op. cit., p. 93.
54. William Stubbs, *Selected Charters and Other Illustrations of English Constitutional History* (Oxford: Clarendon Press, 1874), p. 385.
55. James B. Thayer, "Ancient Modes of Trial," *Harvard Law Review*, 5:250.
56. Ibid., p. 251.
57. Hume, op. cit., app. 1.
58. Blackstone, op. cit., bk. 3, ch. 3.
59. Pomeroy, op. cit., sec. 125.
60. Stubbs, op. cit., ch. 12.
61. Lesser, op. cit., p. 106.
62. Fleta, *Ioannis Seldeni Ad Fletam* (Cambridge: Cambridge University Press, 1925), bk. 4, ch. 16.
63. Reeves, op. cit., p. c.II.
64. Ibid., p. 78.
65. Stubbs, op. cit., p. 545.
66. Forsyth, op. cit., pp. 140, 122.
67. Fleta, op. cit., bk. 4, ch. 14.
68. Forsyth, op. cit., p. 151.
69. Henry de Bracton, *Bracton De Legibus Et Consuetudinibus Angliae* (New Haven: Yale University Press, 1915), bk 4, ch. 34.
70. Ibid., p. 290.
71. Thomas Starkie, *On the Trial by Jury* (Boston: Little, Brown, 1880), p. 20-21.
72. Bushell's Case, Vaughn, 135,6, How. St. Tr. 999.
73. 4 Maule and S. 532.
74. Lesser, op. cit., p. 121.
75. Starkie, op. cit., pp. 38-39.
76. Ibid., p. 40.
77. Ibid.
78. Lesser, op. cit., p. 128.
79. Ibid., p. 151.
80. Forsyth, op. cit., pp. 340-341.
81. Ibid., p. 342.
82. Ibid., pp. 344-345.
83. Ibid., p. 421.
84. Ibid., p. 436.
85. Ibid., p. 429.

II Deficiencies of the Jury System

Notes

2 The Role of the Jury

1. Oliver Wendell Holmes, 10 *Harvard Law Review* 457 at 459 (1899).
2. Harry Kalven, Jr., and Hans Zeisel, *The American Jury*, p. 62.
3. Ibid., p. 59.
4. Ibid., p. 10.
5. 69 *Columbia Law Review* 422 (March 1969).
6. Ibid., p. 425.
7. Ibid., p. 421.
8. *Duncan* v. *Louisiana*, 391 U.S. 145 (1968).

3 Court Backlogs

9. Lloyd L. Wiehl, "The Six-Man Jury," 4 *Gonzaga Law Review* 35 (Fall 1968).
10. *Burton* v. *U.S.*, 391 U.S. 123 (1968).
11. *Duncan* v. *Louisiana*, 391 U.S. 145 (1968).
12. Task Force on the Administration of Justice, President's Commission on Law Enforcement and the Administration of Justice, *Task Force Report: The Courts* (1967), p. 31 (hereafter cited as *Task Force Report: The Courts*).
13. Ibid., p. 31.
14. J. Edgar Hoover, quoted in *Grand Rapids Press*, Aug. 13, 1969, p. 3.
15. John Mitchell, quoted in *Boston Globe*, Apr. 11, 1971, p. 25.
16. Nutter, "The Quality of Justice in Misdemeanor Arraignments Courts," 53 *Journal of Criminal Law, Criminology and Police Science*, 215 (1962).
17. *Task Force Report: The Courts*, p. 30.
18. Ibid., p. 143.
19. Ibid., p. 32.
20. Report of the Massachusetts Law Reform Institute, *Boston Globe*, May 27, 1971, p. 22.
21. *Task Force Report: The Courts*, p. 30.
22. Patricia M. Wald, "Poverty and Criminal Justice," in *Task Force Report: The Courts*, p. 144.
23. *Task Force Report: The Courts*, p. 29.
24. Sheridan, *Urban Justice*, p. 41.
25. *Task Force Report: The Courts*, p. 29.
26. Howard James, *Crisis in the Courts*, p. 45.
27. Walter McLaughlin, *Boston Globe*, Mar. 15, 1971, p. 4.
28. Howard James, op. cit., p. 22.
29. Donald Newman, *Conviction: The Determination of Guilt or Innocence without Trial*, p. 3.
30 McLaughlin, loc. cit.
31. *Annual Report of the Director of the Administrative Office of the U.S. Courts*, p. 261.
32. James, loc. cit.
33. *Report of the President's Crime Commission on the District of Columbia*, p. 984.
34. James, op. cit., p. 23.
35. *Task Force Report: The Courts*, p. 90.
36. Ramsey Clark, *Crime in America*, pp. 184-185.
37. James, op. cit., p. 29.
38. "Interview with Chief Justice Warren Burger," *U.S. News and World Report*, Dec. 14, 1970, p. 32.

39. Richard Ogilvie, "The Crisis in Our Courts," 58 *Illinois Bar Journal* 97 (Oct. 1969).

40. Ibid., p. 95.

41. "Interview with Chief Justice Warren Burger," loc. cit.

42. Clark, op. cit., pp. 191-192.

43. *Time,* Jan. 18, 1971.

44. "The Unconstitutionality of Plea Bargaining," 83 *Harvard Law Review* 1389 (1970).

45. James A. Myhre, 5 *Houston Law Review* 651 (Mar. 1968).

46. "The Unconstitutionality of Plea Bargaining," op. cit., p. 1388.

47. Richard M. Nixon, quoted in *New York Times,* Mar. 12, 1971, p. 180.

48. "Interview with Chief Justice Warren Burger," loc. cit.

49. *Task Force Report: The Courts,* p. 87.

50. Albert V. Bryan, "For a Swifter Criminal Appeal—To Protect the Public as Well as the Accused," 25 *Washington and Lee Law Review* 175 (Fall 1968).

51. *Task Force Report: The Courts,* p. 87.

52. Ibid.

53. ABA Committee on Appellate Delay in Criminal Cases, "A Report," 150 *American Criminal Law Quarterly* 151-152 (1964).

54. Gresham Sykes and Michael Isbell, "Court Congestion and Crash Programs," 44 *Denver Law Journal* 377 (Summer 1967).

55. *Task Force Report: The Courts,* p. 45.

56. "Interview with Chief Justice Warren Burger," loc. cit.

57. Ibid.

58. Clark, op. cit., p. 192.

59. *New York Times,* Mar. 12, 1971, p. C-43.

60. Benjamin Landis, "Jury Trials and the Delay of Justice," 56 *American Bar Association Journal* 950 (Oct. 1970).

61. *New York Times,* Mar. 17, 1971, p. 1.

62. McLaughlin, loc. cit.

63. James, op. cit., p. 23.

64. Ogilvie, op. cit., p. 98.

65. Clark, *op. cit.,* p. 179.

66. *Task Force Report: The Courts,* p. 81

67. *New York Times,* Feb. 21, 1971, p. 44.

68 *Task Force Report: The Courts,* p. 87.

69. Ibid., p. 46.

70. Ibid., p. 45.

71. Ibid., p. 99.

72. Sanford Kadish, "The Crisis of Overcriminalization," *The American Criminal Law Quarterly* 26 (Fall 1968).

4 Pretrial Publicity

73. Hodding Carter, "The Wave beneath the Froth," in Paul L. Fisher and Ralph Lowenstein, eds., *Race and the News Media.* p. 54 (cited hereafter by title).

74. *Wall Street Journal,* Apr. 7, 1971, p. 16.

75. *Time,* Apr. 12, 1971, pp. 14-15; *Newsweek.* Apr. 12, 1971, pp. 30-31.

76. *Time,* Apr. 12, 1971, p. 16.

77. Ibid.

78. Ibid.

79. Ibid.

80. Ibid.

81. *Pittsburgh Post-Gazette,* Nov. 27, 1969, p. 30.

82. *Northeastern News,* Apr. 30, 1971, p. 1.

83. Alfred Friendly and Ronald L. Goldfarb, *Crime and Publicity,* p. 4 (cited hereafter by title).

84. Ibid.

85. *Oberlin Evangelist,* Mar. 18, 1857, p. 46.

86. *Crime and Publicity,* loc. cit.

87. Marvin Summers, *Free Speech and Political Protest,* pp. 19-20.

88. *Crime and Publicity,* loc. cit.

89. *Boston Globe,* Mar. 19, 1971; the CBS report of criticism on "The Selling of the Pentagon," may be found in *Congressional Record,* Feb. 26-Mar. 24, 1971; also see *Boston Herald Traveller,* April 9, 1971, and *Boston Globe,* July 14, 1971.

90. *Crime and Publicity,* p. 5.

91. Ibid., p. 11.

92. Kalven and Zeisal, op. cit., p. 14.

93. "Fair Trial, Free Press," *Federal Rules and Decisions,* 38 (1966) 435-437. Also see *Free Press and Fair Trial.* S290, Parts I and II (Washington, D.C.: U.S. Government Printing Office).

94. *Crime and Publicity,* p. 56.

95. *Boston Globe.* Mar. 30, 1971, p. 1; for a complete description of the murders see Lawrence Schiller and Susan Atkins, *The Killing of Sharon Tate,* 1969.

96. *New York Times.* Mar. 31, 1969, p. 20.

97. Ibid.

98. Ibid.

99. *Boston Globe,* Mar. 30, 1971, p. 1. It should be noted, however, that Linda Kasabian's testimony contradicted that of the other women; she testified that Manson was the organizer of the entire affair.

100. *New York Times,* Mar. 31, 1971, p. 20.

101. *Washington Evening Star,* Aug. 5, 1970, p. A-6.

102. Ibid.

103. Ibid.

104. Ibid., p. A-18.

105. Ibid., p. A-6. However, Manson hardly deserves sympathy for the communication of Nixon's statement to the jury. It was Manson himself who held up the headline in court for the jurors to see; they were sequestered and might not have known of the incident were it not for Manson's unfortunate act.

106. *Boston Globe,* Apr. 4, 1971, p. 26.

107. Ibid., Feb. 25, 1971, pp. 1, 14.

108. Ibid., Mar. 30, 1971, p. 1.

109. Ibid., Apr. 4, 1971, p. 1.

110. Ibid., Apr. 5, 1971, p. 5.

111. *Chicago Tribune,* Apr. 2, 1971.

112. *New York Times,* Mar. 31, 1971, p. 4.

113. *Boston Globe,* Apr. 4, 1971, pp. 1, 20.

114. *New York Times,* Apr. 2, 1971.

115. *Boston Globe,* Apr. 11, 1971, p. 14.

115. *Boson Globe,* Apr. 11, 1971, p. 14.

116. Aubrey Daniel, *Boston Globe,* Apr. 7, 1971, p. 2.

117. *Time,* Apr. 19, 1971, p. 13.

118. *Newsweek,* Apr. 19, 1971, p. 29.

119. *Boston Globe,* Apr. 6, 1969, p. 18.

120. Ibid., Apr. 4, 1971, p. 1.

121. Ibid., Apr. 6, 1971, p. 18.

122. Ibid., Apr. 4, 1971, pp. 1, 20.

123. *Boston Herald Traveller,* Apr. 30, 1971, p. 12.

124. Ibid., p. 13.

125. *New York Times,* Apr. 10, 1971.

126. *Newsweek,* Apr. 19, 1971, p. 30.

127. Ibid.

128. *Time,* Apr. 19, 1971, p. 13.

129. Ibid., p. 14.

130. *Newsweek,* Apr. 19, 1971, p. 29.

131. *Boston Globe,* Apr. 29, 1971; *Washington Evening Star,* Apr. 29, 1971.

132. Ibid.

133. *Boston Herald Traveller,* Apr. 30, 1971, p. 2.
134. *Boston Globe,* Apr. 4, 1971, p. 60.
135. *Chicago Tribune,* Apr. 19, 1971.
136. *Boston Globe,* May 3, 1971, p. 1.
137. Ibid.
138. *New York Times,* Apr. 13, 1971.
139. *Chicago Daily News,* Apr. 11, 1971.
140. *New York Times,* Dec. 11, 1970, p. 32.
141. *Boston Globe,* Apr. 6, 1971, p. 14.
142. Ibid., Apr. 8, 1971, p. 17.
143. *Chicago Tribune,* Apr. 6, 1971.
144. Ibid.
145. *Boston Globe,* Apr. 1, 1971, p. 23.
146. *New York Times,* Nov. 27, 1969, pp. 1, 16.
147. Ibid.
148. "What's Wrong with the Press?" *Newsweek,* Nov. 29, 1965, p. 55.
149. Joseph L. Brechner, "Were Broadcasters Color-Blind?" in *Race and the News Media,* p. 101.
150. *Cleveland Plain Dealer,* Aug. 29, 1954, p. 6-B.
151. Ibid., Dec. 22, 1954, p. 10.
152. *Lorain Journal,* July 23, 1954.
153. *Cleveland Plain Dealer,* Dec. 16, 1954, p. 9.
154. *Cleveland Press,* Dec. 22, 1954, p. 10.
155. Ibid., Oct. 23, 1954, p. 2.
156. Ibid., Oct. 18, 1954, p. 2.
157. Ibid.
158. Ibid., Oct. 22, 1954, pp. 1, 19.
159. Ibid., Oct. 23, 1954, p. 2.
160. For Sheppard's view of his trial and retrial see Samuel H. Sheppard, *Endure and Conquer,* 1966.
161. *Cleveland Plain Dealer,* Aug. 28, 1954, p. 7.
162. *Cleveland Press,* July 17, 1954, p. 1.
163. *Lorain Journal,* Aug. 25, 1954, p. 1.
164. *Cleveland Plain Dealer,* Oct. 8, 1954, p. 1.
165. *Cleveland Press,* July 20, 1954, p. 1.
166. Ibid., Dec. 22, 1954, p. 11.
167. Ibid., Oct. 23, 1954, p. 1.
168. Ibid., July 30, 1954, p. 1.
169. Ibid., July 20, 1954, p. 1.
170. Ibid., July 30, 1954, p. 1.
171. Ibid., Nov. 5, 1954, p. 6.
172. Ibid., Oct. 22, 1954, p. 2.
173. Ibid., Nov. 3, 1954, p. 18.
174. Ibid., Dec. 8., 1954, p. 22.
175. Ibid., Nov. 23, 1954, p. 1.
176. Ibid., July 29, 1954, p. 10.
177. Ibid., July 9, 1954, p. 1.
178. *Cleveland Plain Dealer,* July 13, 1954, p. 1; *Cleveland Press,* July 13, 1954, p. 3.
179. *Cleveland Press,* July 13, 1954, p. 3.
180. Ibid., July 14, 1954, p. 6.
181. Ibid., July 23, 1954, p. 1.
182. *Lorain Journal,* July 24, 1954.
183. *Cleveland Plain Dealer,* July 23, 1954, p. 1.
184. Ibid., July 24, 1954, p. 1.
185. *Cleveland Press,* July 24, 1954, p. 1.
186. Ibid., July 24, 1954, p. 2.
187. *Lorain Journal,* July 26, 1954.
188. *Cleveland Press,* July 26, 1954, p. 1.
189. Ibid., July 27, 1954, pp. 1, 6.
190. *Lorain Journal,* July 28, 1954.

191. *Cleveland Press,* July 28, 1954, p. 1.
192. Ibid., Aug. 4, 1954, p. 1.
193. *Lorain Journal,* Aug. 5, 1954.
194. *Cleveland Press,* Aug. 5, 1954, p. 10.
195. 1bid., Aug. 18, 1954, p. 9.
196. *Cleveland Plain Dealer,* Dec. 2, 1954, p. 1.
197. *Cleveland Press,* Dec. 13, 1954, p. 1.
198. Ibid., July 6, 1954, p. 5.
199. Ibid., July 8, 1954, p. 1.
200. *Lorain Journal,* Aug. 4, 1954.
201. Ibid.
202. Ibid., July 10, 1954.
203. Paul Holmes, *The Sheppard Murder Case,* p. 210.
204. *Lorain Journal,* July 21, 1954.
205. Ibid.
206. *Cleveland Press,* July 21, 1954, p. 1.
207. *Cleveland Plain Dealer,* Aug. 28, 1954, p. 7.
208. *Cleveland Press,* Oct. 8, 1954, p. 1.
209. Ibid., July 8, 1954, p. 2.
210. Ibid.
211. Ibid., July 10, 1954, p. 1.
212. Ibid., July 21, 1954, p. 1.
213. *Lorain Journal,* Aug. 10, 1954.
214. *Cleveland Press,* July 29, 1954, p. 1.
215. Ibid., Oct. 15, 1954, p. 1.
216. Ibid., Aug. 16, 1954, p. 1.
217. Ibid., Sept. 7, 1954.
218. *Lorain Journal,* Aug. 18, 1954.
219. *Cleveland Press,* Aug. 27, 1954, p. 1.
220. Ibid., Aug. 27, 1954, pp. 12-13.
221. Ibid., Oct. 18, 1954, p. 6.
222. Ibid., Oct. 19, 1954, p. 6.
223. 36 *Notre Dame Lawyer* 77 (1960).
224. *Cleveland Press,* Oct. 25, 1954, p. 1.
225. Ibid., p. 6.
226. Ibid.
227. Ibid., Nov. 26, 1954, p. 8.
228. Ibid.
229. *Cleveland Plain Dealer,* Nov. 3, 1954, p. 1.
230. *Cleveland Press,* Dec. 22, 1954, p. 11.
231. Ibid.
232. Holmes, op. cit., p. 161.
233. *Elyria Chronicle-Telegram,* Feb. 14, 1963, p. 23.
234. Holmes, op. cit., p. 158.
235. *Cleveland Press,* Dec. 24, 1954, p. 3.
236. Ibid.
237. Ibid.
238. Holmes, op. cit., p. 159.
239. Ibid.
240. Ibid., p. 160.
241. Ibid., p. 164.
242. Ibid., p. 163.
243. Ibid., p. 164.
244. Ibid., p. 165.
245. Ibid., p. 173
246. Ibid., p. 174.
247. Ibid., p. 179.
248. Ibid., p. 192.
249. Ibid.
250. Ibid., p. 193.
251. Ibid.
252. Ibid.

253. Ibid., p. 199.
254. Ibid., p. 205.
255. Ibid., pp. 205-206.
256. Ibid., p. 211.
257. Ibid., pp. 210-211.
258. Ibid., pp. 214-215.
259. Ibid., p. 215.
260. Ibid.
261. Ibid.
262. Ibid., p. 217.
263. Ibid.
264. Ibid., pp. 219-220.
265. Ibid., p. 243.
266. *Cleveland Press,* Oct. 20. 1966.
267. *Cleveland Plain Dealer,* Sept. 25, 1966, p. 4-A.
268. Entry from U.S. District Court, Southern District of Ohio, Eastern Division, received by the clerk of Common Pleas Court of Cuyahoga County, July 18, 1966.
269. *Elyria Chronicle-Telegram,* Oct. 12, 1966.
270. *Cleveland Press,* Oct. 20, 1966.
271. Ibid.
272. *Elyria Chronicle-Telegram,* Oct. 13, 1966, p. 3.
273. *Cleveland Plain Dealer,* Oct. 25, 1966, p. 8.
274. Ibid., Oct. 28, 1966.
275. Ibid., Oct. 29, 1966.
276. Journal entry in the Court of Common Pleas, Nov. 16, 1966.
277. *Cleveland Plain Dealer,* Nov. 18, 1966, p. 4.
278. *Sheppard v. Maxwell,* 384 U.S. 333 (1966).
279. *Elyria Chronicle-Telegram,* Nov. 7, 1964.
280. *Time,* Mar. 22, 1971, p. 13.
281. 333 U.S. 257 (1948).
282. 33 *Rocky Mountain Law Review* 5 (1960).
283. 35 *New York University Law Review* 874 (1960).
284. See *Roth* v. *U.S.,* 354 U.S. 476 (1956); *Dennis* v. *U.S.,* 341 U.S. 494 (1951); *Champlinsky* v. *New Hampshire,* 315 U.S. 568 (1942).
285. *Pennekamp* v. *Florida,* 328 U.S. 331 (1945).
286. *Crime and Publicity,* p. 57.
287. *Sherbert* v. *Verner,* 374 U.S. 398 (1963).
288. 41 *St. John's Law Review* 439 (1967).
289. 314 U.S. 252 (1941).
290. *Irvin* v. *Doud,* 366 U.S. 717 at 728 (1961).
291. 36 *New York University Law Review* 810 (1961).
292. *Marshall* v. *U.S.,* 360 U.S. 310 (1959).
293. *Irvin* v. *Doud,* loc. cit.
294. *New York Daily News,* Jan. 5, 1970, p. C-13.
295. *Strobe* v. *California,* 343 U.S. 181 at 191-192 (1952).
296. Ibid., at 193.
297. *Irvin* v. *Doud,* loc. cit.
298. *Estes* v. *Texas,* 381 U.S. 532 at 541 (1965).
299. Ibid., at 544.
300. 360 U.S. 312 (1959).
301. 373 U.S. 723 at 727 (1963).
302. 379 U.S. 466 (1965).
303. *Estes* v. *Texas,* 381 U.S. 532 (1965).
304. Ibid. at 544.
305. *New York Times,* Apr. 14, 1971. In the case of the CBS production "The Selling of the Pentagon," Congress feels that further action is necessary and has attempted to subpoena all film used in making the controversial documentary. On July 13, however, the House declined to press charges against CBS despite its defiance of a Congressional subpoena for unused film and tapes in the documentary.
306. *Sheppard* v. *Maxwell,* 384 U.S. 352 (1966).

307. Ibid. at 358-363.

308. 41 *St. John's Law Review* 443 (1967).

309. On May 1, 1971, the *Boston Globe* reported that more than 400 students from Harvard Law School signed a petition asking Congress to begin impeachment proceedings against the President for conducting an unconstitutional war. The petition, which outlines legal arguments against the war, was also signed by three Harvard Law School professors.

310. *Sheppard* v. *Maxwell*, 384 U.S. 352 at 362 (1966).

311. *New York Times*, Mar. 12, 1971, p. 18.

312. *Report of the President's Commission on the Assassination of President Kennedy* (1964), p. 242.

313. Paul C. Reardon, "The Fair Trial-Free Press Standards," 54 *American Bar Association Journal* 343 (1968). Also see American Bar Association, *Trial by Jury* (Washington, D.C.: Institute of Judicial Administration, 1968).

314. Clark, op. cit., pp. 175-176. On July 5, 1971, Chief Justice Warren E. Burger warned the American Bar Association that the legal profession must impose "more stringent discipline" on unruly or dishonest lawyers or outside forces will take over the job of policing lawyers' ethics. Mr. Burger spoke out against courtroom "incivility" by some lawyers, according to the *New York Times* on July 6, 1971.

315. David L. Shapiro, 22 *Oklahoma Law Review* 128 (1969).

316. 54 *American Bar Association Journal* 348-351 (1968).

317. *Boston Globe*, May 22, 1971, p. 9.

318. Ibid.

319. Ibid.

320. Clarence Darrow, quoted in Perry, "The Courts, the Press and the Public," 30 *Michigan Law Review* 234 (1931).

321. John Lofton, *Justice and the Press*, p. xi.

322. *Report of the Warren Commission*, pp. 216-224.

323. David L. Grey, *The Supreme Court and the News Media*, p. 3.

324. For excerpts from Agnew's attacks on the news media consult the *New York Times*, May 19, 1971.

325. Ibid., p. 30, *Boston Globe*, May 19, 1971, p. 7.

325. Ibid., p. 30. *Boston Globe*, May 19, 1971, p. 7.

326. Ibid., p. 28.

327. Ibid.

328. *Boston Globe*, May 11, 1971, p. 3.

329. *Cleveland Plain Dealer*, Apr. 27, 1963.

330. *Elyria Chronicle-Telegram*, Nov. 19, 1964.

331. *Vital Speeches*, Feb. 1, 1970, p. 234.

5 Justice, the Poor, and Minority Groups

332. *Nation*, Mar. 24, 1967, p. 33.

333. Senator Joseph Tydings, *Hearings of the Subcommittee on Constitutional Rights*, Jan. 21, 1969, p. 76 (amendments to the Bail Reform Act).

334. *Newsweek*, Mar. 8, 1971, p. 28.

335. Ronald Goldfarb, *Ransom* (New York: Harper Row, 1965).

336. Harold Greene (chief judge of D.C. Court of General Sessions), *Hearings of the Subcommittee on Constitutional Rights*, p. 35.

337. Senator Roman Hruska, *Hearings*, op. cit., p. 3.

338. *The Challenge of Crime in a Free Society*, report of the President's Commission on Law Enforcement and the Administration of Justice (1967), p. 131.

339. *Bail in the U.S.: 1964*, report of the National Commission on Bail and the Administration of Justice (Washington, D.C., 1965), p. 40.

340. *Challenge,* p. 131.
341. 155 *Cornell Law Review* 367 (Jan. 1970).
342. Pauline Morris, Committee of Political and Economic Planning, *Prisoners and Their Families* (New York: Hart, 1965), p. 281.
343. *Bail in the U.S.,* p. 46.
344. Ibid.
345. Ibid.
346. Ibid., p. 52.
347. Judge Hart, *Hearings,* p. 10.
348. *Newsweek,* Mar. 8, 1971, p. 39.
349. Hart, *Hearings,* p. 24.
350. Patricia Wald, *Hearings,* p. 136.
351. Ibid., p. 143.
352. Goldfarb, *Ransom,* p. 156.
353. Ibid., p. 157.
354. Ibid., p. 166.
355. Wald, *Hearings,* p. 132.
356. Dr. Murray Grant, *Hearings,* p. 421.
357. Chriss Nicholas, *Nation.*
358. Michael Meltsner, *Southern Justice* (New York: Pantheon, 1965).
359. 4 *Houston Law Review* 448-452 (Winter 1966).
360. Morris J. Bloomstein, *Verdict* (New York: Dodd, Mead, 1968), p. 53.
361. Ibid., p. 54.
362. *Time,* Mar. 29, 1968, pp. 78-79.
363. U.S. Commission on Civil Rights, *1961 Report,* 1:108.
364. Allan Lichtman, *Journal of Negro History* (Oct. 1969), p. 365.
365. Ibid.
366. Bloomstein, *Verdict,* p. 52.
367. Abraham Blumberg, *Crime and Justice in American Society* (New York: Bobbs-Merrill, 1971), p. 78.
368. 232 U.S. 383.
369. *Wolf* v. *Colorado,* 338 U.S. 25 (1949).
370. *Mapp* v. *Ohio,* 367 U.S. 643 (1961).
371. Lichtman, op. cit., p. 360.
372. Frank McGurr, *Political Power and Individual Freedom* (Chicago: Aldine, 1962), p. 101.
373. Ibid.
374. *Challenge,* p. 115.
375. 373 U.S. 335 (1963).
376. 377 U.S. 201.
377. 381 U.S. 356.
378. 378 U.S. 478 (1964).
379. 79 *Harvard Law Review* 1000 (Mar. 1966).
380. 384 U.S. 436 (1966).
381. Judge Nathan Sobel, 79 *Harvard Law Review* 942.
382. John Rogge, *Villanova Law Review* (Fall 1966).
383. Sobel, op. cit., p. 942.
384. 76 *Yale Law Journal* 1589 (July 1967).
385. Ibid., p. 1613.
386. 29 *University of Pittsburgh Law Review* 23 (Oct. 1967).
387. Ibid., p. 22.
388. 91 S.C. 643 (1971). To some extent, *Harris* undermines the deterrent effect of the *Miranda* rule. If a statement obtained from a defendant may be used to impeach him should he elect to testify at trial, even if *Miranda* warnings were not given, the police have some incentive to interrogate without warnings that they would not otherwise have. This effect should not be exaggerated, however. The primary purpose of in-custody interrogation is to obtain a confession that can be used to prove the defendant's guilt. If warnings are not given, any statement obtained cannot be used for that purpose, and since there may be insufficient independent evidence to make out a case against the accused, the inability to use a confession may mean that prosecution is imposible. If the prosecution cannot

prove a prima facie case against the defendant, he will not be required to put on any defense at all, and therefore will not have occasion to testify so that his credibility as a witness becomes an issue. Therefore, from the standpoint of the police, the small chance that a confession obtained without warnings may become usable against a defendant who elects to testify is considerd by some to be outweighed by the very substantial risk that the prosecution will have to be foregone entirely because the confession cannot be used in the case in chief and there is insufficient evidence. This interpretation assumes, however that the exclusionary rule serves as an effective deterrent, an assumption which remains an open question.

389. Yale Kamisar, *Michigan Law Review* (Nov. 1966) p. 67.

390. President's Commission on Law Enforcement and the Administration of Justice, *Task Force Report on the Police* (1967), p. 184.

391. Ibid., p. 185.

392. Ibid., p. 183.

393. Ibid., p. 184.

394. 392 U.S. 1.

395. 384 U.S. 457

396. 384 U.S. 449.

397. 384 U.S. 445.

398. 384 U.S. 451.

399. 384 U.S. 446.

400. 319 U.S. 624 (1942).

401. 89 S.C. 733 (1969).

402. *Dixon v. Alabama State Board of Education,* 294 F 2nd 150 (1961).

403. 4 *San Francisco Law Review* 54 (Oct. 1969).

404. 387 U.S. 523 (1967).

405. Smuggling Act, 314 Stat. 178 (1866).

406. 53 *Cornell Law Review* 871 (Mar. 1968).

407. 267 U.S. 132.

408. Ibid. at 153-154.

409. 287 F 2nd 389.

410. 362 F. 2nd 379 (1966).

411. 362 F 2nd 870.

412. 53 *Cornell Law Review* 880 (May 1968).

413. Ibid., p. 878.

414. *Challenge,* p. 217.

415. Ibid.

416. Ibid.

417. 277 U.S. 438.

418. 347 U.S. 128.

419. 367 U.S. 643.

420. Ibid. at 655.

421. 388 U.S. 41.

422. Ibid., at 56.

423. 388 U.S. 347 (1967).

424. Ibid., at 353.

425. 17 *Buffalo Law Review* 464-465 (Winter 1968).

426. Stephen Linzer, *Journal of Criminal Law, Criminology and Police Science* (June 1968), p. 207.

427. Walter Reckless, *The Crime Problem* (New York: Appleton-Century-Crofts, 1964).

428. Thornstein Sellin, *Annals of the American Academy* (May 1963), p. 18.

429. *Popular Science,* Jan. 1966.

430. Herman Schwartz, *Congressional Record* (Feb. 3, 1965), p. 1916.

431. Samuel Dash, *The Eavesdroppers* (1959).

432. Aryeh Neier, *Brooklyn Law Review* (Winter 1967), p. 273.

433. Ibid.

434. *New York Times,* Mar. 13, 1969, p. 1.

6 Military Justice

435. Ralph C. Deans, "Military Justice," *Editorial Research Reports,* 2 (Oct.7, 1970), 733.

436. Robert Sherrill, *Military Justice Is to Justice as Military Music Is to Music,* p. 93.

437. Ralph Deans, op. cit., p. 740.

438. John Adams, *Works* (1850), 3:68, 82.

439. Henry Knox, cited in Sherrill, op. cit., p. 72.

440. Frederick B. Wiener, "Courts-Martial and the Bill of Rights: The Original Practice: II," 72 *Harvard Law Review* 290 (1958).

441. Frederick B. Wiener, "Courts-Martial and the Bill of Rights: The Original Practice: I," 72 *Harvard Law Review* 8-9 (1959).

442. Ibid., pp. 10-11.

443. Ibid., p. 44.

444. Sherrill, op. cit., p. 72.

445. *Ex parte Milligan,* 71 U.S. 2 at 138 (1866).

446. Sherrill, op. cit., p. 72.

447. Deans, op. cit., p. 740.

448. The author of the article, S. T. Ansell, was a former Army Judge Advocate General who had been demoted for his persistent pleas for reform.

449. Deans, loc. cit.

450. Ibid.

451. D. Karlan, "Personal Factor in Military Justice," *Wisconsin Law Review* (1946), p. 364.

452. Sherrill, op. cit., p. 76.

453. Field-grade officers hold the rank of major or higher in the army and the air force and lieutenant commander in the navy.

454. Deans, op. cit., p. 745.

455. Ibid.

456. James A. Mounts and Myron G. Sugarman, "The Military Justice Act of 1968," 55 *American Bar Association Journal* 472 (May 1969).

457. Edward F. Sherman, "The Right to Competent Counsel in Special Courts-Martial," 54 *American Bar Association Journal* 866 (Sept. 1968).

458. Mounts and Sugarman, op. cit., p. 472.

459. Ibid.

460. Sherrill, op. cit., p. 89.

461. Mounts and Sugarman, op. cit., p. 471.

462. Sherman, op. cit., p. 867.

463. Mounts and Sugarman, op. cit., p. 472.

464. Ibid., p. 471.

465. Ibid., p. 472.

466. Ibid.

467. Sherman, op. cit., p. 867.

468. Sherrill, op. cit., p. 89.

469. Mounts and Sugarman, op. cit., p. 471.

470. Ibid.

471. Sherrill, op. cit., p. 89.

472. Edward J. Bellen, "The Revolution in Military Law," 54 *American Bar Association Journal* 1197 (Dec. 1968).

473. Deans, op. cit., p. 747.

474. Mounts and Sugarman, op. cit., pp. 470-471.

475. Sherrill, op. cit., p. 89.

476. Ibid.

477. Bellen, op. cit., p. 1195.

478. Ibid.

479. Ibid. p. 1196.

480. Uniform Code of Military Justice, art. 37, cited in Deans, op. cit., p. 742.

481. Bellen, op. cit., p. 1198.

482. Ibid.

483. Deans, op. cit., p. 743.
484. Joseph Bishop, "The Quality of Military Justice," *New York Times Magazine,* Feb. 22, 1970, p. 36.
485. Bellen, op. cit., p. 1198.
486. Deans, op. cit., p. 743.
487. Ibid.
488. Ibid.
489. Sherrill, op. cit., p. 93.
490. Sam Ervin, "Military Justice," *Hearings before the Subcommittee on Constitutional Rights of the Senate Judiciary Committee and a Special Subcommittee of the Senate Armed Services Committee,* Jan. 18-Mar. 3, 1966, pt. 1, p. 4 (hereafter cited as *Hearings 2*).
491. Wiener, op. cit., 2:294-296.
492. Ibid., p. 290.
493. Charles Morgan, quoted in Bishop, op. cit., p. 33.
494. Sherrill, op. cit., p. 79.
495. Robert E. Quinn, cited in *Hearings 2,* p. 733.
496. Emile Zola Berman, quoted in *Newsweek,* Aug. 31, 1970, p. 22.
497. Sherrill, op. cit., p. 79.
498. *Newsweek,* Aug. 31, 1970, p. 22.
499. Morgan, cited in *Newsweek,* Aug. 31, 1970, p. 18.
500. Sherrill, op. cit., pp. 43, 168. Peterson's conviction was overturned thirteen months later on a technicality.
501. For a lengthy account of the Presidio events see Fred Gardner, *The Unlawful Concert* (1970).
502. William C. Mott, *Hearings 2,* p. 721.
503. Bishop, op. cit., p. 38.
504. Ibid., pp. 33-34.
505. Ervin, *Hearings 2,* p. 452.
506. Fred B. Smith, *Hearings 2,* p. 517.
507. Ervin, *Hearings 2,* p. 3.
508. Bishop, op. cit., p. 38.
509. Sherrill, op. cit., p. 223.
510. Mounts and Sugarman, op. cit., p. 471.
511. Mott, *Hearings 2,* p. 722.
512. Bishop, op. cit., p. 38.
513. *Sheppard* v. *Maxwell,* 384 U.S. 352 (1966).
514. Sherrill, op. cit., p. 93.
515. Ervin, *Hearings 2,* p. 4.
516. Ibid., p. 452.
517. Cited by Ervin, *Hearings 2,* p. 4.
518. Sherrill, op. cit., pp. 98-99.
519. Ervin, *Hearings 2,* p. 4.
520. Leonard Hippchen, "Employer Attitudes toward Hiring Dishonorably Discharged Servicemen," in Stanley Brodsky and Norman Eggleston, eds., *The Military Prison,* p. 172.
521. Ibid., p. 173.
522. Sherrill, op. cit., p. 220.
523. *Burns* v. *Wilson,* 346 U.S. 133 at 142 (1953).
524. Ervin, *Hearings 2,* p. 2
525. Earl Warren, cited in Sherrill, op. cit., p. 192.
526. Bishop, op. cit., p. 37.
527. Ibid., p. 36.
528. Bellen, op. cit., p. 1196.
529. Quinn, *Hearings 2,* p. 737.
530. *Newsweek,* Aug. 31, 1970, p. 23.
531. Sherrill, op. cit., p. 228.
532. Ibid., p. 227.
533. New York State Bar Association letter to the editor, *New York Times,* Mar. 1, 1949, p. 24.
534. Sherrill, op. cit., p. 227.

7 Capital Punishment

535. *Boston Globe,* May 4, 1971, p. 6.
536. U.S. Bureau of Prisons, *National Prisoner Statistics: Executions 1930-66* (Apr. 1967), p. 9.
537. Gerald Gottlieb, *Crime and Delinquency* (Jan. 1969), p. 12.
538. Clarence H. Patrick, *Journal of Criminal Law, Criminology, and Police Science* (Dec. 1965), pp. 397-411.
539. 99 U.S. 130 (1878).
540. 217 U.S. 349 (1910).
541. Ibid. at 366.
542. 356 U.S. 86 (1958).
543. 356 U.S. 86. "The death penalty does not violate the constitutional prohibition of cruel punishment, but the existence of the death penalty is not a license to the government to devise any punishment short of death within the limit of its imagination."
544. 54 *Kentucky Law Journal* 744 (Summer 1966).
545. F.B.I., U.S. Department of Justice, *Uniform Crime Reports, 1967* (Washington 1968), pp. 62-79.
546. Walter Reckless, *Crime and Delinquency* (Jan. 1969), p. 55.
547. Ibid.
548. F.B.I., U.S. Department of Justice, *Uniform Crime Reports, 1963, 1964, 1965.*
549. Ibid., 1964, 1965, 1966.
550. Ibid.
551. Exodus, 21:12 (King James version).
552. Sol Rubin, *Crime and Delinquency* (Jan. 1969), p. 128.
553. Ibid., p. 129.
554. Reckless, *Crime and Delinquency,* p. 56.
555. Ibid., p. 60.
556. Ibid.
557. Ibid.
558. Ibid.
559. *Kentucky Law Journal,* op. cit., p. 742.
560. Bureau of Prisons, *National Prisoner Statistics: Executions 1930-67,* no. 42 (June 1968), pp. 10-11.
561. Ibid., no. 41 (June 1967), p. 9.
562. Ibid.
563. Jack Greenberg and Jack Himmelstein, *Crime and Delinquency* (Jan. 1969), p. 113.
564. Ibid., pp. 113-114.
565. 363 U.S. 852 (1960).
566. Greenberg and Himmelstein, op. cit., p. 117.
567. *Boston Globe,* May 4, 1971, p. 6.
568. Ibid.
569. Ibid.
570. Ibid.
571. Arthur Goldberg and Alan Dershowitz, 183 *Harvard Law Review* 1723, 1814-1815.
572. 384 U.S. 641 (1966).
573. Nos. 5049, 5059, 5133, 5135, 39 L.W. 3566-67.
574. Lawrence H. Tribe, *Constitutional Regulation of the Death Penalty* (testimony before the Massachusetts legislature, Mar. 10, 1971), p. 5.

III Alternatives to the Jury System

Notes

8 Plea Bargaining

1. Donald Newman, *Conviction: The Process of Determining Guilt or Innocence without Trial,* p. 3.
2. Jonas A. Myhre, "Conviction without Trial in the U.S. and Norway: A Comparison,'" 5 1 *Houston Law Review* 652 (Mar. 1968).
3. Harry Kalven and Hans Zeisel, *The American Jury,* p. 19.
4. Ibid., pp. 19-20.
5. *Boykin* v. *Alabama,* 395 U.S. 238-244 (1969).
6. Newman, op. cit., p. 4.
7. Ibid.
8. Arnold Enker, "Prosecutions in Plea Bargaining," in *Task Force Report: The Courts,* app. A, p. 108.
9. 83 *Harvard Law Review* 1389 (1970).
10. Myhre, op. cit., p. 657.
11. Steinberg, "The Responsibility of the Defense Lawyer in Criminal Cases," 12 *Syracuse Law Review* 447 (1961).
12. Myhre, op. cit., p. 657.
13. Ibid.
14. Newman, op. cit., p. 4.
15. Abraham Blumberg, "Criminal Justice in America," in Jack Douglas, ed., *Crime and Justice in America,* p. 62.
16. Ibid., p. 65.
17. Ibid.
18. Enker, op. cit., p. 113.
19. Blumberg, op. cit., p. 75.
20. 83 *Harvard Law Review* 1389 (1970).
21. Newman, op. cit., p. 18.
22. Ibid., pp. 15-16.
23. Myhre, op. cit., p. 655.
24. Newman, op. cit., p. 79.
25. Ibid., p. 19.
26. Enker, op. cit., p. 114.
27. Blumberg, op. cit., p. 62.
28. Newman, op. cit., p. 204.
29. Ibid., p. 203.
30. Blumberg, op. cit., p. 66.
31. 83 *Harvard Law Review* 1390 (1970).
32. Newman, op. cit., p. 228.
33. Ibid., p. 242.
34. Ibid., p. 101.
35. 83 *Harvard Law Review* 1391 (1970).
36. Newman, op. cit., p. 227.
37. Ibid., p. 227.
38. Enker, op. cit., p. 115.
39. Newman, op. cit., p. 227.
40. Ibid., p. 215.
41. Enker, op. cit., p. 116.
42. *Garrity* v. *New Jersey,* 385 U.S. 493 (1967).
43. *Spevak* v. *Klein,* 385 U.S. 511 (1967).
44. *U.S.* v. *Jackson,* 390 U.S. 570 (1968).
45. "Trial by Jury in Criminal Cases," 69 *Columbia Law Review* 418 (1969).
46. *North Carolina* v. *Pearce,* 395 U.S. 711 (1969).
47. Enker, op. cit., p. 112.
48. *Brady* v. *U.S.,* 397 U.S. 742 (1970).
49. *Machibroda* v. *U.S.,* 368 U.S. 487 (1962).
50. *People* v. *Vester,* 309 Mich. 409, 15 NW 2nd 687 (1944).
51. Newman, op. cit., p. 27.
52. Ibid., p. 20.
53. Ibid., p. 19.
54. 83 *Harvard Law Review* 1406 (1970).

9 Juvenile Courts

55. Joel F. Handler, "The Juvenile Court and the Adversary System: Problems of Function and Form," *Wisconsin Law Review* (1965), p. 7.

56. Sol Rubin, "The Juvenile Court System in Evolution," 2 *Valparaiso Law Review* 1 (1967).

57. Handler, op. cit., p. 7.

58. "Statutory Vagueness in Juvenile Law: The Supreme Court and *Mattielo* v. *Connecticut*," 118 *Pennsylvania Law Review* 143 (1969).

59. J. Edgar Hoover, cited in *Crime in the United States* (1968), p. 121.

60. Lloyd E. Ohlin, in *Boston Sunday Globe*, Apr. 11, 1971, p. 25.

61. Hoover, op. cit., p. 121.

62. "Statutory Vagueness in Juvenile Law," p. 151.

63. *In re Gault*, 387 U.S. 541 (1966).

64. President's Commission on Law Enforcement and the Administration of Justice, *The Challenge of Crime in a Free Society*.

65. Elyce Ferster and Thomas Courtless, "The Beginning of Juvenile Justice: Police Practices and the Juvenile Offender," 22 *Vanderbilt Law Review* 574 (1969).

66. Ibid., p. 572.

67. Richard Fazzone, "Juvenile Court Procedures beyond Gault," 32 *Albany Law Review* 131 (1967).

68. Ibid., p. 129.

69. *Miranda* v. *Arizona*, 384 U.S. 436 (1966).

70. Fazzone, op. cit., p. 126.

71. *Gallegos* v. *Colorado*, 370 U.S. 49 (1962).

72. Handler, op. cit., p. 12.

73. *A. B. Small Co.* v. *American Sugar Refining Co.*, 267 U.S. 233 (1925).

74. *Conally* v. *General Construction Co.*, 269 U.S. 385 at 391 (1926).

75. *In re Gault* at 23.

76. "Statutory Vagueness in Juvenile Law," p. 146.

77. *In re Gault*, p. 14.

78. Howard James, *Crisis in the Courts* (1967), p. 62.

79. Ibid.

80. *Kent* v. *U.S.*, 383 U.S. 541 (1966).

81. *Gallegos* v. *U.S.* at 54.

82. James, op. cit., pp. 74-75.

83. *In re Winship*, 397 U.S. 358 (1970).

84. "A Due Process Dilemma: Juries for Juveniles," 45 *Notre Dame Law Review* 278 (1969).

85. *McKeiver* v. *Pennsylvania*, 39 L.W. 4777 (June 21, 1971).

86. "Trial by Jury in Criminal Cases," p. 428.

87. "Right to Jury Trial: Indiana's Misapplication of Due Process Standards in Delinquency Hearings," 45 *Indiana Law Journal* 578 (1970).

88. James, op. cit., p. 65.

89. Rubin, op. cit., p. 16.

90. Dr. Seymour Hallett, *Psychiatry and the Dilemmas of Crime* (1967).

91. John F. X. Irving, in James, op. cit., p. 72.

92. "Right to Jury Trial: Indiana's Misapplication of Due Process Standards in Delinquency Hearings," p. 592.

93. President's Commission on Law Enforcement and the Administration of Justice, *Challenge of Crime in a Free Society*, p. 85.

94. James, op. cit., p. 77.

10 First Amendment Rights

95. For a list of works relating to civil liberties see Thomas I. Emerson, *Toward a General Theory of the First Amendment* (1966), pp. 3-4; pp. 4-15 set forth a similar defense of First Amendment freedoms.

96. See Erich Fromm, *Escape from Freedom* (1965), *passim,* and pp. 123-156.

97. Ibid., pp. 157-230.

98. Ibid., p. 287.

99. John Stuart Mill, *On Liberty,* p. 21.

100. Ibid., pp. 28-38.

101. Martin Buber, *Tales of the Hasadim* (1957), p. 71.

102. Mill, op. cit., p. 64.

103. Herbert Marcuse, "Repressive Tolerance," in Robert Paul Wolff et al., eds., *A Critique of Pure Tolerance* (1965), pp. 100-101.

104. Ibid., p. 109.

105. Ibid., p. 100.

106. Leonard Levy, *Legacy of Suppression* (1960), pp. 176-309.

107. William Spinrad, *Civil Liberties* (1970), pp. 31-32.

108. David Brian Davis, *The Slave Power Conspiracy and the Paranoid Style* (1969), pp. 3-61; T. Harry Williams et al., *A History of the United States to 1877* (1969), pp. 447-452, 493-500.

109. Leon Litwack, *North of Slavery* (1961).

110. J. G. Randall and David Donald, *The Civil War and Reconstruction* (1966), pp. 293-309.

111. Spinrad, op. cit., pp. 36-37; Henry Pelling, *American Labor* (1960), pp. 48-103.

112. Spinrad, op. cit., pp. 35-37.

113. J. Morris Clark, "Guidelines for the Free Exercise Clause," 83 *Harvard Law Review* 327 (1969).

114. Ibid., pp. 328-329.

115. Milton R. Konvitz, *Fundamental Liberties of a Free People* (1957), pp. 163-169.

116. *Roth* v. *U.S.,* 354 U.S. 476 (1957).

117. Henry P. Monaghan, "First Amendment Due Process," 83 *Harvard Law Review* 520-524 (1969).

118. Lucius J. Barker and Twiley W. Barker, *Civil Liberties and the Constitution* (1970), pp. 94-110.

119. Ibid., pp. 104-108.

120. Ibid., pp. 190-191.

121. "Civil Disabilities and the First Amendment," 78 *Yale Law Journal* 843-848 (1969).

122. Ibid., pp. 857-858.

123. Barker and Barker, op. cit., p. 195.

124. Ibid., p. 189.

125. Ibid., pp. 198-200.

126. See Walter Goodman, *The Committee* (1968).

127. Barker and Barker, op. cit., p. 198.

128. Konvitz, op. cit., p. 136.

129. William O. Bertelsman, "The First Amendment and Protection of Reputation and Privacy—*New York Times Co.* v. *Sullivan* and How It Grew," 56 *Kentucky Law Journal* 720-723 (1968).

130. Konvitz, op. cit., pp. 141-142.

131. Ibid., and Bertelsman, op. cit., pp. 722-724.

132. Harry Kalven Jr., "The Reasonable Man and the First Amendment: Hill, Butts, and Walker," *Supreme Court Review* (1967), pp. 379-390.

133. Ibid.

134. Ibid., pp. 282-285.

135. Arthur R. Miller, "Personal Privacy in the Computer Age: The Challenge

of a New Technology in an Information-Oriented Society," 67 *Michigan Law Review* 1119-1124 (1969).

136. Zechariah Chafee, *Free Speech in the United States* (1941), pp. 36-80.

137. Robert G. McCloskey, *The American Supreme Court* (1960), pp. 172, 178.

138. Samuel Krislov, *The Supreme Court and Political Freedom* (1968), pp. 120-121.

139. The following arguments on the clear-and-present-danger test draw heavily on Emerson, op. cit., pp. 51-56.

140. "Less Drastic Means and the First Amendment," 78 *Yale Law Journal* 462-472 (1969).

141. Emerson, op. cit., pp. 56-62.

142. Ibid., p. 83.

143. S. J. Micchiche, "Army Spying on Top Politicians," *Boston Globe*, Dec. 17, 1970, pp. 1, 13.

144. Ibid., p. 13.

145. *New York Times*, Dec. 18, 1970, p. 1.

146. See, for example, "Mr. Laird's Flawed Reply," *New York Times*, Dec. 27, 1970, p. 16.

147. *Boston Globe*, Mar. 10, 1971, p. 2.

148. *Baltimore Sun*, Apr. 15, 1971; *Boston Globe*, Apr. 12, 1971; *Boston Globe*, Apr. 6, 1971, p. 2.

149. *Congressional Record*, Feb. 10, 1971, p. H-612.

150. *New York Daily News*, May 10, 1971.

151. *Time*, Mar. 8, 1971, p. 9.

152. See National Commission on the Causes and Prevention of Violence, *Rights in Conflict: The Chicago Police Riot* (1968).

153. *New York Times*, May 4, 1971, p. 32, and May 5, 1971, p. 1.

154. Cited in Krislov, op. cit., p. 47.

155. "Conspiracy and the First Amendment," 79 *Yale Law Journal* 875-877 (1970).

156. Nathaniel L. Nathanson, "Freedom of Association and the Quest for Internal Security: Conspiracy from Dennis to Dr. Spock," 65 *Northwestern University Law Review* 190-193 (1970).

157. "Conspiracy and the First Amendment," pp. 876-877.

158. Ibid., pp. 881-884.

159. *Von Moltke* v. *Gilles*, 332 U.S. 708 at 728 (1948).

160. Jason Epstein, *The Great Conspiracy Trial* (1971), pp. 91-93.

161. Ibid., see also "Conspiracy and the First Amendment," p. 894.

162. "Conspiracy and the First Amendment," p. 894.

163. Jefferson Fordham, "Hearings on the Anti-Riot Bill," Senate Judiciary Committee, 90th Cong., 1st sess. (1967).

164. Ibid.

165. "The Riot Act of 1968," 4 *Georgia Law Review* 374-379 (1969/1970).

166. American Friends' Service Committee, *The Draft* (1968), p. 24.

167. Barker and Barker, op. cit., pp. 28-29.

168. J. Morris Clark, op. cit., p. 340-344.

169. *Estep* v. *U.S.*, 327 U.S. 114 (1946).

170. James B. White, "Processing Conscientious Objector Claims: Constitutional Inquiry," 56 *California Law Review* 668-672. (1968).

171. Ibid., p. 653.

172. Ibid., p. 673.

173. American Friends' Service Committee, op. cit., pp. 30-31.

174. Jeff Greenfield, "The Selective C.O.," in Harry Girvetz and Elsie Leach, eds., *Moral Issues Today* (1969), pp. 73-74.

175. Ibid., p. 76.

176. Ibid.

177. "Counseling Draft Resistance: The Case for a Good Faith Belief Defense," 78 *Yale Law Journal* 1011 (1969).

178. Ibid., pp. 1022-1027.

179. Ibid., pp. 1027-1037.

180. Eugene V. Rostow, *The Sovereign Prerogative* (1962), pp. 193-213.

181. Studs Terkel, *Hard Times: An Oral History of the Great Depresion* (1967), pp. 233-234.

182. Rostow, op. cit., pp. 193-194.
183. *Hirabayashi* v. *U.S.,* 320 U.S. 81 (1943): *Korematsu* v. *U.S.,* 323 U.S. 214 (1944); *ex parte Mitsoye Endo,* 323 U.S. 283 (1944).
184. *Ex parte Milligan,* 71 U.S. 2 (1866).
185. Monaghan, op. cit., pp. 531-532.
186. Ibid., pp. 529-531.
187. Clyde E. Jacobs, "Trial by Jury, Petty Offenses, and the First Amendment," 46 *Notre Dame Lawyer* 307 (1971).
188. Monaghan, op. cit., pp. 531-532.
189. Jacobs, op. cit., pp. 298-300.
190. Ibid., p. 304.

11 No-Fault Insurance

191. Robert Keeton and Jeffrey O'Connell, *Basic Protection for the Traffic Victim,* (1965), p. 14 (hereafter cited as *Basic Protection*).
192. Alfred F. Conard et al., *Automobile Accident Costs and Payments: Studies in the Economics of Injury Reparation* (1963), p. 255.
193. *Basic Protection,* p. 11.
194. William L. Prosser and Young B. Smith, *Cases and Materials on Torts* (1967), p. 718.
195. National Safety Council, *Accident Facts* (1964), p. 5.
196. Prosser and Smith, op. cit., p. 721.
197. Robert E. Keeton, *Venturing to Do Justice* (1969), p. 126.
198. For a discussion of the principles and development of this law, see ibid., pp. 147-166.
199. Jeffrey O'Connell, "Taming the Automobile," 58 *Northwestern Law Review* 323 (1963).
200. This does not mean that a plaintiff with a preexisting complaint may not recover for its aggravation, but he must prove that the accident caused the aggravation, which is often difficult.
201. Prosser and Smith, op. cit., p. 721.
202. *Basic Protection,* p. 25.
203. Ibid., p. 26.
204. Ibid.
205. Prosser and Smith, loc. cit.
206. See Keeton, *Venturing to Do Justice,* p. 127.
207. Abraham Markhoff, "Compensation without Fault and the Keeton-O'Connell Plan: A Critique," 43 *St. John's Law Review* 178 (Oct. 1969).
208. Keeton, *Venturing to Do Justice,* p. 128.
209. Harold S. Baile, cited in Markhoff, op. cit., p. 179.
210. Prosser and Smith, op. cit., p. 719.
211. Ibid.
212. Ibid., p. 725.
213. Ibid., p. 726.
214. Ibid.
215. See ibid., pp. 592-599, for a description of the damages one may recover.
216. *Basic Protection,* p. 30.
217. Jacob D. Fuchsberg, "Lawyer's View of Proposed Changes," *University of Illinois Law Forum* (1967), p. 479.
218. Prosser and Smith, op. cit., p. 722.
219. Conard, op. cit., pp. 190-191.
220. Walter Blum and Harry Kalven, cited in Markhoff, op. cit., p. 184.
221. Conard, op. cit., p. 8.
222. Prosser and Smith, op. cit., p. 731.
223. Markhoff, op. cit., p. 176.

224. See *Boston College Industrial and Commercial Law Review* (Summer 1967) for a discussion of the labyrinthian depths of insurance accounting.

225. Markhoff, op. cit., p. 188.

226. Edward W. Kuhn, "The Keeton-O'Connell Basic Protection Plan for Automobile Insurance: A Practicing Lawyer's View," 22 *Alabama Law Review* 7 (1969).

227. James Kemper, *Trial* (Oct.-Nov. 1967), pp. 21-22.

228. "Don't By-Pass the Courts," *Judicature,* 51 (Dec. 1967), 151.

229. *Basic Protection,* p. 15; see also Conard, op. cit., p. 4.

230. Prosser and Smith., op. cit., pp. 722-723.

231. Conard, op. cit., p. 196.

232. *Basic Protection,* p. 32.

233. Conard, op. cit., p. 172.

234. Ibid., pp. 139, 149.

235. Ibid., p. 250.

236. *Basic Protection,* p. 17.

12 Arbitration, Mediation,
and No-Fault Alternatives

237. Robert Leiter, *Labor Economics and Industrial Relations* (1960), p. 259.

238. Howard James, *Crisis in the Courts,* p. 193.

239. 68 *Columbia Law Review* 1316 (1968).

240. Wiehl, op. cit., p. 4.

241. Sykes and Isbell, op. cit., p. 44.

242. Wiehl, op. cit., pp. 37-38.

243. *Basic Protection,* pp. 299-339.

244. Ibid., pp. 5-10.

245. Ibid., pp. 295-296.

246. Frank Harwayne, "Insurance Costs of the Basic Protection Plan in Michigan," *University of Illinois Law Forum* (1967), p. 479.

247. M. G. McDonald, cited in Kemper, op. cit., p. 21.

248. Kemper, op. cit., p. 21.

249. Prosser and Smith, op. cit., p. 731.

250. Markhoff, op. cit., p. 192.

251. Milton Green, "Basic Protection and Court Congestion," 52 *American Bar Association Journal* 928 (1966).

252. Kemper, op. cit., p. 22.

253. *Cardillo v. Liberty Mutual Insurance Co.,* 330 U.S. 469 at 479.

254. *Boston Globe,* May 7, 1971, p. 42.

255. See, for example, Markhoff, op. cit.. p. 190.